IMAGES
of America

GOVERNORS ISLAND

On the cover: Liggett Hall, building 100 and later 400, was designed by McKim, Meade and White. (Courtesy of John T. Lowe, National Park Service/Historic American Building Survey.)

IMAGES *of America*
GOVERNORS ISLAND

Susan L. Glen
Foreword by Michael Shaver

ARCADIA
PUBLISHING

ISBN 978-0-7385-3895-2

Published by Arcadia Publishing
Charleston, South Carolina

Printed in the United States of America

Library of Congress Catalog Card Number: 2005928465

For all general information contact Arcadia Publishing at:
Telephone 843-853-2070
Fax 843-853-0044
E-mail sales@arcadiapublishing.com
For customer service and orders:
Toll-Free 1-888-313-2665

Visit us on the Internet at www.arcadiapublishing.com

To Ella May Snyder, longtime library aide on Governors Island, and to Chris Leone, who spent over 40 years on the island as a soldier, ferryman, and security guard.

Contents

ACKNOWLEDGMENTS

This book would not have been possible without the cooperation and assistance of Mike Shaver of the National Park Service, the U.S. Coast Guard Archives, the Cartophilians, and the numerous libraries who allowed me access to their archives during my research. I would also like to express my appreciation to the many people who lived on the island over the years who have also granted permission to use pictures from their own collections. Many photographs came from negatives presented to the Governors Island National Monument by the U.S. Coast Guard Public Affairs Office at Fort Wadsworth. Many of these give credit to the National Archives and the U.S. Army Signal Corps.

FOREWORD

Governors Island is a curious place. A 172-acre island just 800 yards off the south end of Manhattan Island, it sits within a mile of Wall Street, the Statue of Liberty, and Ellis Island. Only a half-mile more includes the Brooklyn Bridge and the site of the World Trade Center. Perched at the convergence of the East River and the Hudson River, the island occupies a commanding position in New York Harbor and played an important role in the military history of this country. Its location should have afforded it great public recognition, but as an island only accessible by ferry and as a military post from 1794 to 1996, it remained apart from the city and from the public conscience.

The island began its military career in 1776 during the American Revolution, when Gen. George Washington fortified it with several large cannon, one of several factors in discouraging the British navy from moving into the East River. When the young American army was routed in the Battle of Long Island, Washington and his troops were ferried across the East River under the cover of darkness to go on to fight another day. The American Revolution might have stopped dead in its tracks, but it did not, even though New York City was occupied by the British army for the next seven years.

After the Revolutionary War, the new United States Government decided the protection of New York City and its harbor was a matter of national importance, so a system of harbor fortifications was constructed in the first decade of the 1800s. Governors Island became home to three fortifications: Fort Jay (alternately named Fort Columbus during the 19th century), a star-shaped fort placed on high ground on the center of the island was first built in 1794 and improved in 1811; Castle Williams, also finished in 1811, a three-story circular fortress constructed on a rocky shoal at a corner of the island; and South Battery, a small wedge-shaped fort, completed in 1812. For the next three decades, these forts, along with others in the harbor, ensured no enemy power would try to invade the city again.

By the 1830s, technology began to render the forts obsolete, so Governors Island was assigned additional missions. The Army Ordinance Department took advantage of the island's location to house the New York Arsenal, which remained until 1920. Four Greek Revival brick barracks, to increase and improved military housing, were constructed inside Fort Jay. The South Battery became an army music school, where young teenage boys learned drum rolls and bugle calls that moved armies in combat before the days of walkie-talkies and satellites. Castle Williams was then alternately maintained and neglected but was almost always ready for war, and it became an occasional recruit barracks and a prisoner of war holding pen during the Civil War.

In the 1870s, the army made Governors Island a headquarters post for most of the eastern United States. In 1878, the army named a hero of Gettysburg, Winfield Scott Hancock, as

Governors Island's commander. Hancock, a respected military professional, brought much improvement to the languishing urban garrison. From that time until its closure in 1996, the regional commands, both U.S. Army and Coast Guard, based at Governors Island were coveted posting for senior commanders ending distinguished careers or for individuals advancing to posts such as commanding general of the army, army chief of staff, or coast guard commandant in Washington, D.C.

In both World War I and World War II, the island played an important role as command headquarters, staging area, and supply depot. In 1917, Gen. John Pershing departed from the island for France to command the largest overseas assemblage of American troops to that time. One of the first units to leave with Pershing for France, the 16th Infantry Regiment, was stationed on the island. That regiment suffered the first American casualties of the war, and many of the street names on Governors Island honor the sacrifices of those doughboys. In 1933, Governors Island became the home of the U.S. First Army, an organization that commanded even larger military combat forces as the United States assumed a greater role in international affairs and a future world war. Within a decade, First Army decamped to Bristol, England, and, with Gen. Omar Bradley commanding, led the American portion of the D-Day invasion, on June 6, 1944.

After the war, Headquarters First Army returned to Governors Island and resumed the role of peacetime military training and administration of the army reserves. On November 20, 1964, Secretary of Defense Robert McNamara announced, as a cost-savings measure, the departure of the army and the closure of Governors Island. On June 30, 1966, the army departed and the post took on a new life as the newest and largest U.S. Coast Guard base in the world. The army traditions that governed life on the island for decades continued: from the bugle calls marking the end of the day to the shore duty patrolling the golf course for trespassing teenagers in the moonlight, as their military police predecessors had done years earlier.

Some 30 years later, the same issue of costs for an island military installation in New York City were cited as the Coast Guard announced the closure of its Governors Island base in 1995. It was a quiet admission that in this modern world, island fortresses and urban military garrisons were no longer important in defending against this nation's threats. But for many who were stationed here with the U.S. Army or the Coast Guard, and to the dependents who followed their servicemen and servicewomen, Governors Island has an important place in their memories. It was as close to a hometown as a military family—moving from place to place over a military career—might ever expect to encounter, and the postcards and personal photographs appearing in *Governors Island* attest to that.

In 2003, the federal government transferred Governors Island to the City and State of New York to be redeveloped for public purposes. A national historic landmark district assures that over 60 buildings and the landscapes that reflect the long military heritage of the island will remain, along with the preservation of Fort Jay and Castle Williams by the National Park Service, as part of the Governors Island National Monument. With its heritage secure as a foundation for its future, the island holds great promise to become one of the great urban spaces of New York City.

—Michael Shaver, Historian
Governors Island, New York

INTRODUCTION

This pictorial history is the result of a curiosity as to why Governors Island has only a brief description in encyclopedias and why news cameras panning Manhattan always exclude the tiny island in the harbor.

The following chronology offers a brief overview of the island's history.

1524: Explorer Giovanni da Verrazano reaches New York Harbor.
1609: The Dutch come to the area.
1614: The first Dutch settlement is established on Manhattan.
1625: The Dutch attempt a settlement on Governors Island (then called Nuttin Island); their ships *Orange Tree*, *Love*, and *Eagle* arrive.
1637: Wouter van Twiller buys the island (then called Pagganack Island) from the Manahatas.
1638: Van Twiller leaves on the island the frame of a house, a sawmill, and 42 goats.
1639: Van Twiller leases the island to Evert Bishop, Sibout Clausen, and Herman Bastiense.
1648: Dutch administrator Peter Stuyvesant orders the removal of the sawmill.
1652: The island purchase is annulled; the island opens for public recreation (through 1664).
1664: Stuyvesant surrenders to the English; New Amsterdam becomes New York.
1673: The Dutch retake New York for one year.
1691: The island is transferred to "the Count of New York as His Majesty's Fort and Garrison."
1692: The house is rebuilt.
1698: The island is renamed Governor's Island, reserved for the king's governors and councilors.
1703: Lord Cornbury is instructed to make a local map.
1708: Queen Anne pays for 40 refugees to come to the colony.
1710: The island becomes a quarantine station for some 10,000 Palatines; a court of judicature is established.
1738: The English pass an act for the breeding of pheasants on the island.
1745: A lottery is proposed to raise funds for fortifications.
1755: The British encamp on the island and construct an earthen works battery.
1759: A regimental hospital is built.
1775: Women and children of British troops arrive; the British withdraw from the island.
1776: Benjamin Franklin inspects the island; Gen. George Washington orders the building of fortifications; the submersible *Turtle* is seen from the island; loyalists row from Manhattan to remove all fortifications; the British return and garrison and fortify the island.
1783: The British leave Governors, Staten, and Long Islands; the Royal Navy surrenders.

1786: Buttermilk Channel is widened.
1790: Columbia College acquires the island; Gov. De Witt Clinton leases land for a resort; a horse race is advertised.
1793: Yellow fever patients are quarantined on the island.
1794: A ferry service to the island is established; Clinton retakes the island; Fort Jay is begun.
1798: The Blockhouse, barracks, and hospital are built.
1800: New York cedes the island to the United States; Fort Jay is completed.
1806: Fort Jay is partially demolished.
1807: Inventor Robert Fulton meets on the island to discuss his torpedo experiment.
1809: Fort Jay is rebuilt as Fort Columbus.
1811: Castle Williams, dubbed "Cheesebox," is completed.
1812: The South Battery is built.
1838: Quarters 1 is begun (completed in 1840, south wing added in 1887, restored in the 1930s).
1842: Samuel B. Morse tests his telegraph invention between the island and Battery Park.
1846: St. Cornelius chapel is built of wood (rebuilt in stone in 1906).
1852: The artillery leaves; the island becomes an army-recruiting depot (through 1878).
1861: Castle Williams is used as a prison for up to 1,500 rebel prisoners of war.
1865: Capt. John Beall is hanged; Capt. William Webb escapes, swims 3,200 feet to the Battery.
1873: Fog bell erected; Grand Duke Alexis of Russia visits.
1878: The cemetery closes; the artillery returns.
1880: New York City cedes 103 underwater acres to the island; city water service arrives.
1886: Gen. Winfield Scott Hancock dies on the island.
1887: Buttermilk Channel is deepened.
1888: A winter storm takes the fog bell.
1895: Squirrels come to the island.
1900: The island's original 170-acre size is reduced by erosion to 70 acres.
1901: Underwater acreage is filled (ongoing to 1912).
1904: Fort Columbus is renamed Fort Jay; electricity comes to the island.
1909: Pioneer aviators Orville and Wilbur Wright take off from the island.
1910: The lighthouse is built on the island; other aviators land.
1916: A flying center and civilian flying school are established; more aviators land.
1917: A railroad and 70 structures are built for World War I; the 22nd Infantry arrives.
1927: Fiorello LaGuardia introduces a bill to turn the island into an airport; the War Department offers to sell the island for $40 million.
1934: LaGuardia campaigns to have the island become an airport.
1936: The Committee on Military Affairs discusses the island as an airfield.
1947: Castle Williams is repaired and modernized.
1957: Queen Elizabeth II visits the island.
1958: Condemnation proceedings give clear title to the United States.
1962: The U.S. Coast Guard holds an open house.
1966: The U.S. Coast Guard assumes possession of the island; the U.S. Army departs.
1986: Operation Sail honors Liberty; Francois Mitterand and Ronald Reagan relight the statue.
1988: Secret talks to end the war in Angola are held; the Reagan-Gorbachev Summit takes place on the island.
1993: The Governors Island Accord (talks on Haiti) is held.
1994: Human remains (likely Colonial) are discovered (reinterred in 1995).
1995: Norway's King Harold and Queen Sonja visit the island.
1996: The U.S. Coast Guard leaves the island.
1997: Congress sets a 2002 deadline for disposal of the island; the island is turned over to the Government Services Administration.
2002: Governors Island is returned to New York; a portion of the island becomes a national park.

One

The Early Years

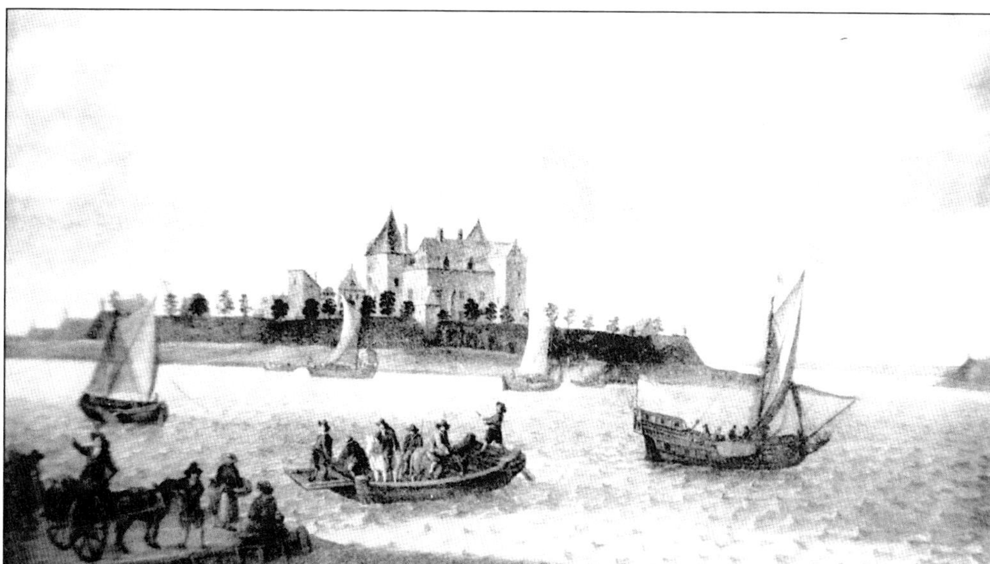

Governors Island, in 1750, is portrayed in an oil painting by F. Willa. The painting is now in the U.S. Coast Guard Archives.

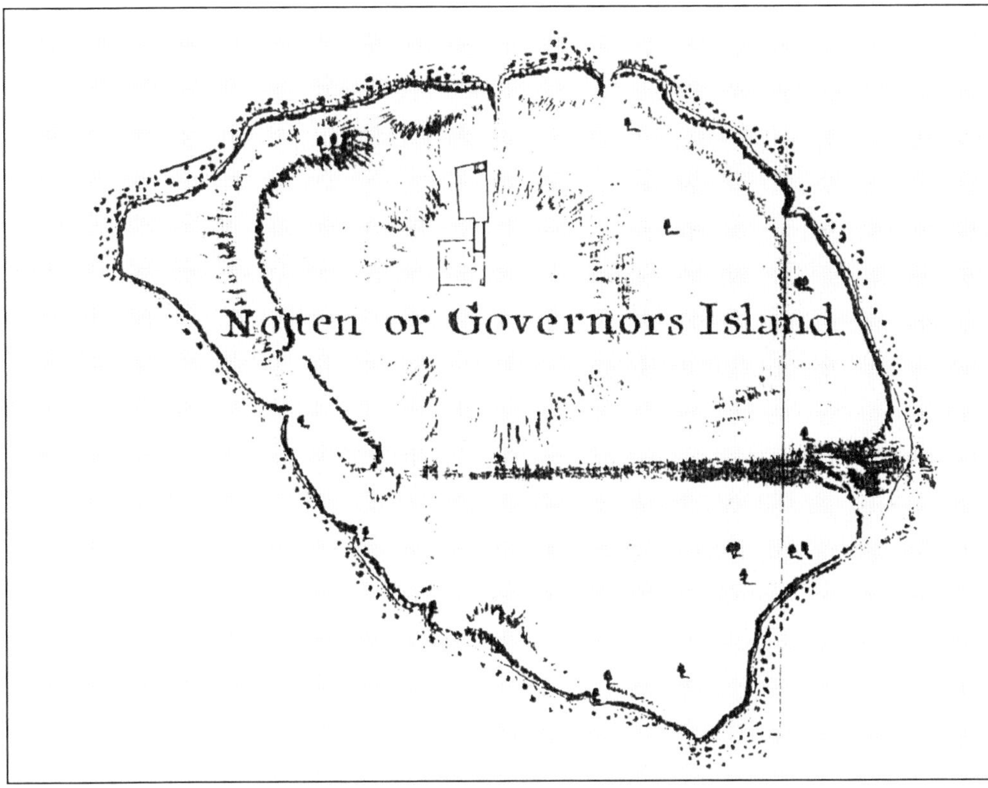

This c. 1776 map of Governors Island shows the British encampment.

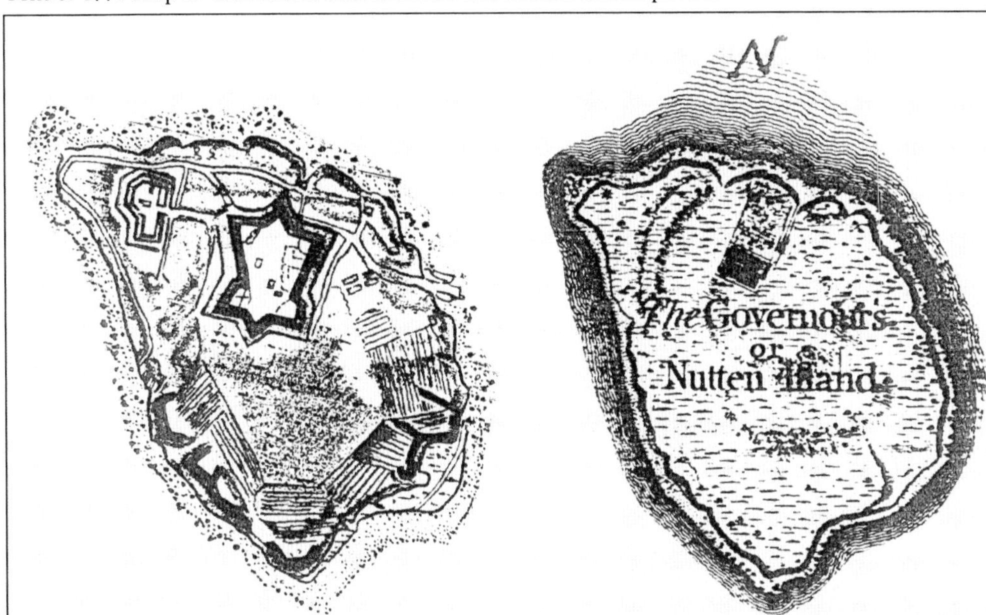

The map on the left depicts Governors Island in 1782. It is from a facsimile of the unpublished British Headquarters colored manuscript of New York and environs. The map on the right represents Governors Island as it appeared in 1789.

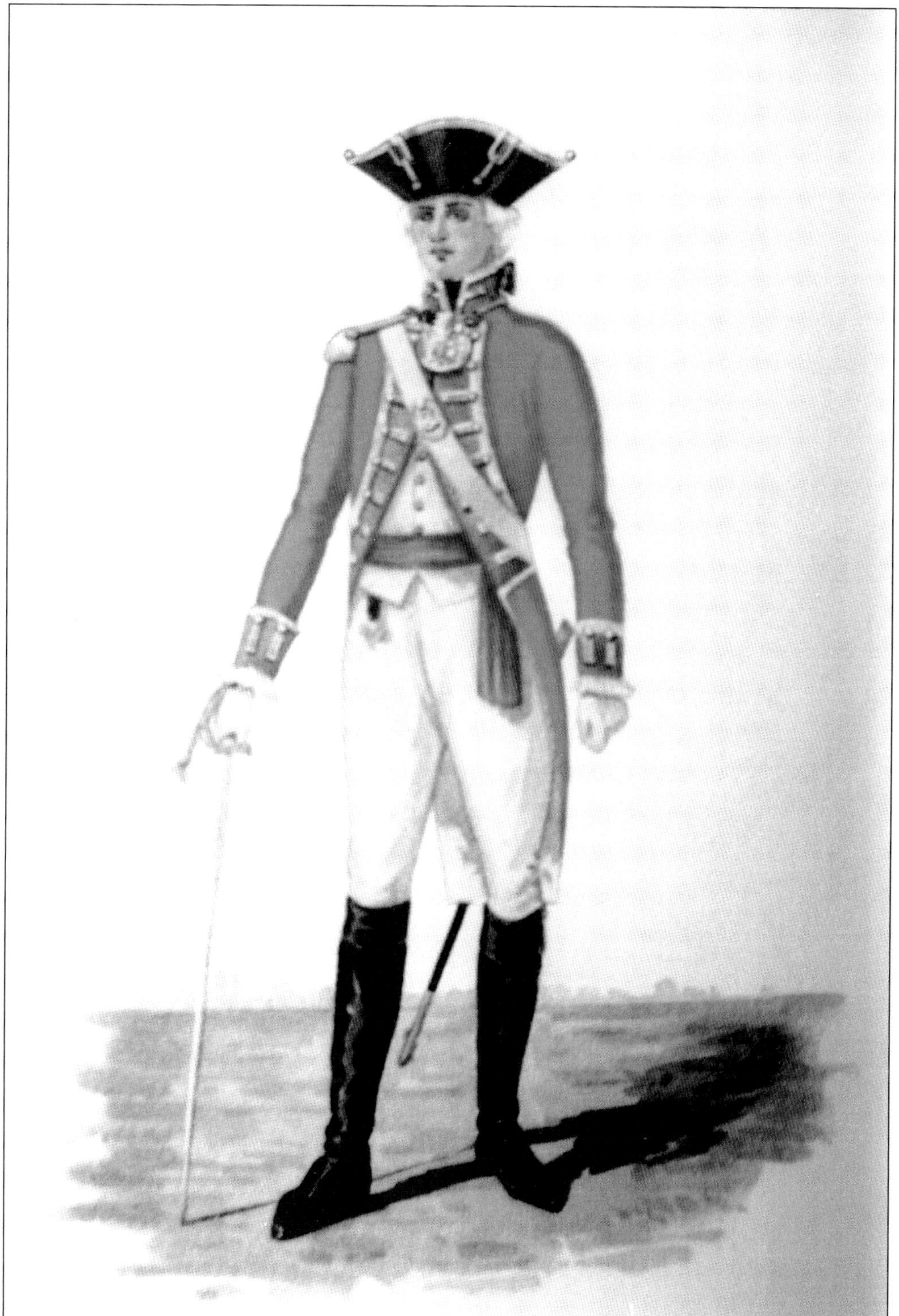

Depicted on Governors Island in 1755 is a captain of the Royal American Regiment, 60th Foot, also called the 62nd Loyal American Provincials.

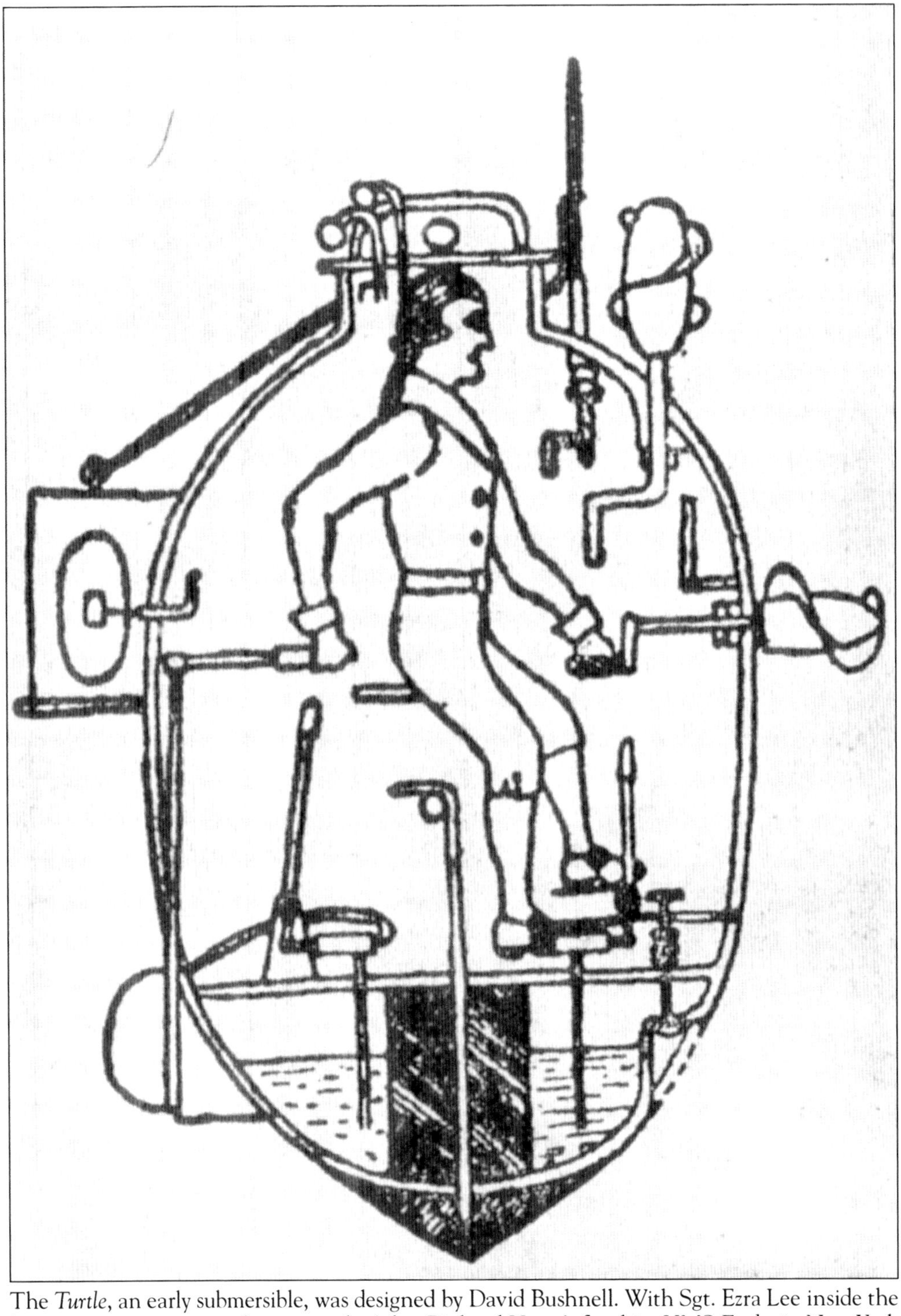

The *Turtle*, an early submersible, was designed by David Bushnell. With Sgt. Ezra Lee inside the boat, an attempt was made to torpedo Adm. Richard Howe's flagship, HMS *Eagle*, in New York Harbor during the Revolutionary War. After two unsuccessful attempts, the idea was abandoned. This view of the *Turtle* is from Governors Island.

Two

The U.S. Army

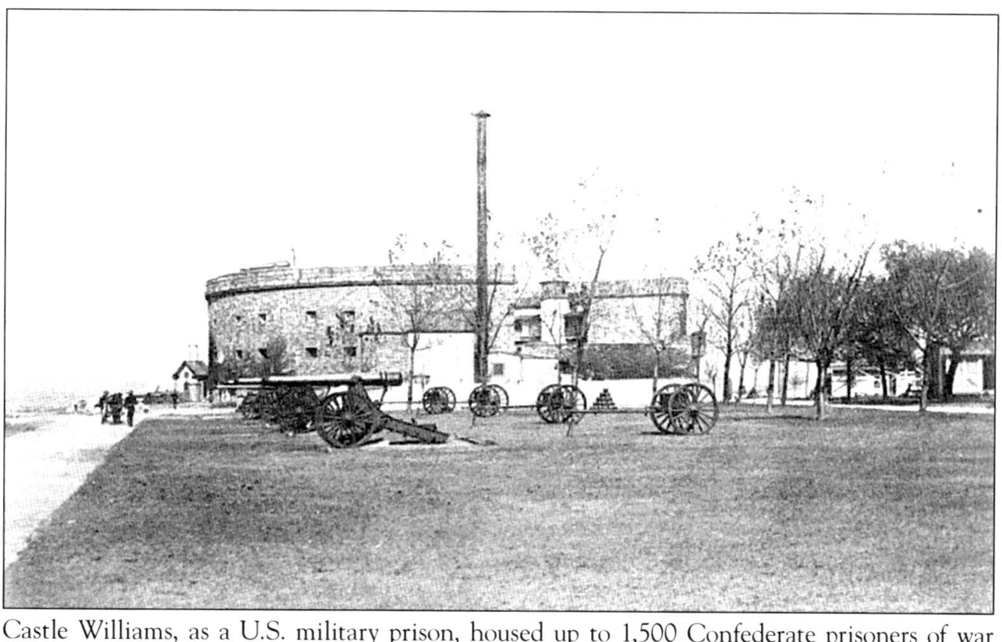

Castle Williams, as a U.S. military prison, housed up to 1,500 Confederate prisoners of war during the Civil War.

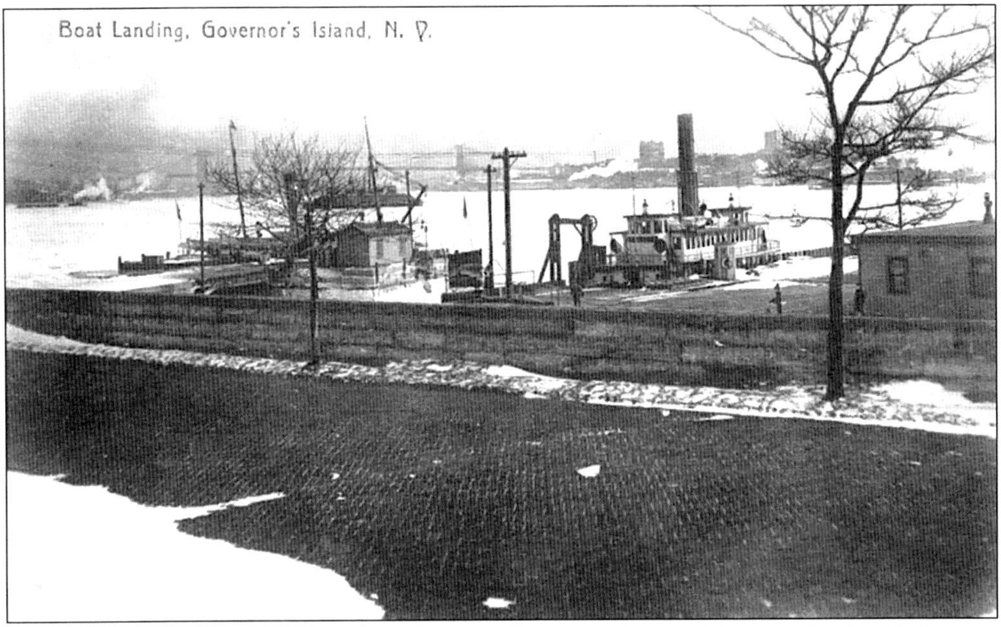

The boat and ferry landing was on the Buttermilk Channel side of the island. John Hillger ran the first ferry to the island for three pence per ride in 1794. The following year the fee was raised to six pence.

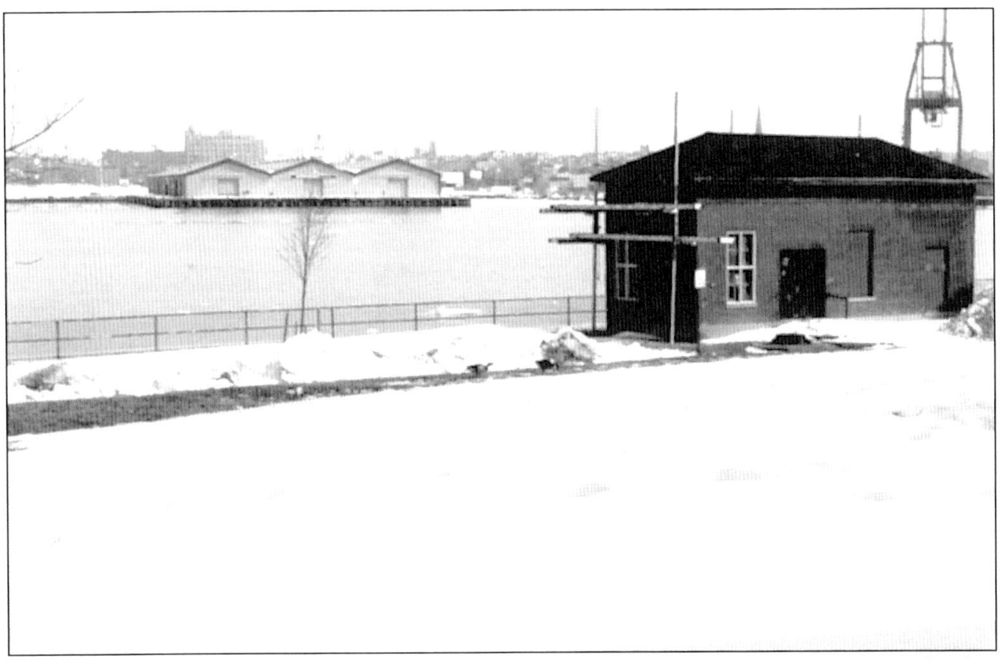

The steps leading to the old ferry landing can be seen below the water level and sea wall. This brick building remains from that period of the island's history.

TIME TABLE of the Steamer "ATLANTIC."

WEEK DAYS.

Leaves Governor's Island for New York, 6 15, 7 30, 8 30, 9 30, 10 15, 10 45, 11 30, A. M., 12 15, 1 30, 2 30, 3 30, 4 30, 5 30, 6 30, 7 30, 10 00, P. M.

Leaves the Battery, New York, for Governor's Island, 7 00, 8 00, 9 00, 10 00, 10 30, 11 00, A. M., 12 Noon, 1 15, 2 00, 3 00, 4 00, 5 00, 6 15, 7 00, 8 00, 10 30, P. M.

In addition to the regular trips prescribed above, the Captain of the "*Atlantic*," when notified on any week day before 10 30 P. M., by a commissioned officer stationed at Governor's Island, that an additional trip is desired that night, said additional trip shall be made as follows:—

Leave Governor's Island for New York, at 11 30 P. M.
Leave New York for Governor's Island. at 12 M.

If notice for this additional trip is not received as above directed, the boat will lay up for the night as soon as she has completed the 10 30 P. M. trip from New York.

SUNDAYS.

Leaves Governor's Island, for New York, 7 30, 8 45, 9 30, 10 15, 10 45, 11 30, A. M., 12 15, 1 30, 2 30, 3 30, 4 30, 5 30, 6 30, 7 30, P. M.

Leaves the Battery, New York, for Governor's Island, 8 30, 9 00, 10 00, 10 30, 11 00, A. M., 12 00, Noon, 1 15, 2 00, 3 00, 4 00, 5 00, 6 15, 7 00, 8 00, P. M.

Operating in 1890, the government steamer *Atlantic* provided a seven-minute ride to the island from the Battery. Shown is a printed timetable for the steamer.

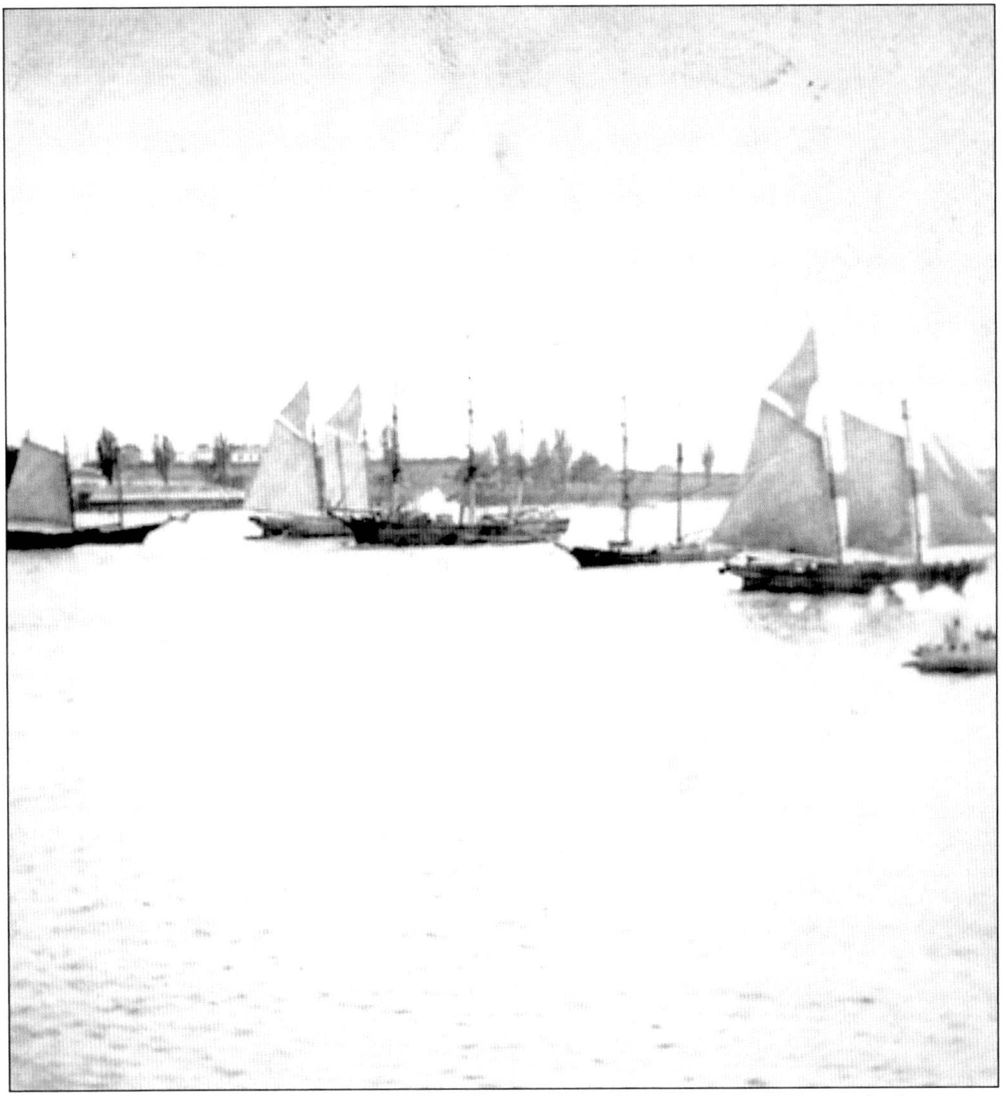

This early stereopticon slide, produced by John P. Soule, shows New York Bay with Governors Island in the background.

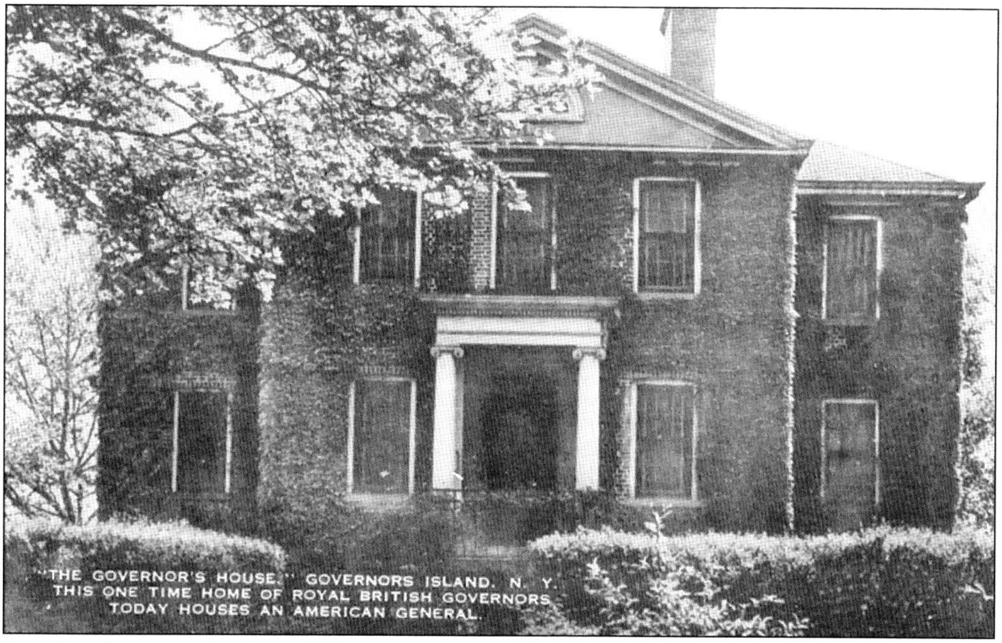

Post Headquarters, built in 1798, was later mistakenly labeled "the Governor's House." This building has served as a guardhouse, courtroom, and home to many officers and their families. When first built, the first floor held the offices for the commanding officer and his adjutant, the second floor was the court martial room, and the basement held a dungeon, or "black hole."

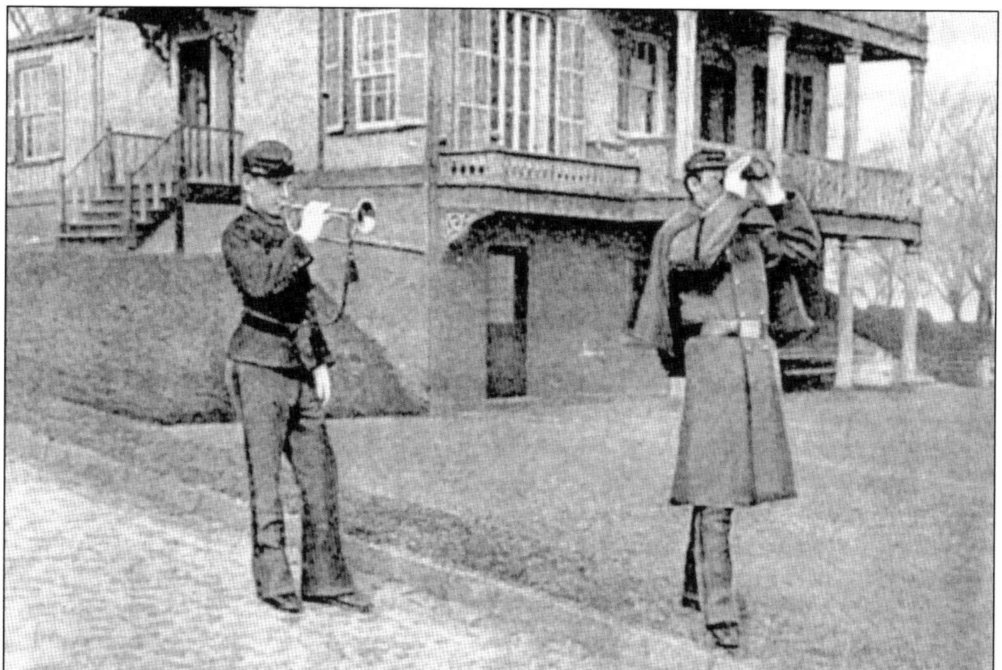

At the back of the Post Headquarters building, a sergeant watches the time ball on the Western Union Telegraph building on Broadway. When the ball falls, the bugler will blow the 12:00 p.m. call. (Courtesy of the *Illustrated American*, March 15, 1890.)

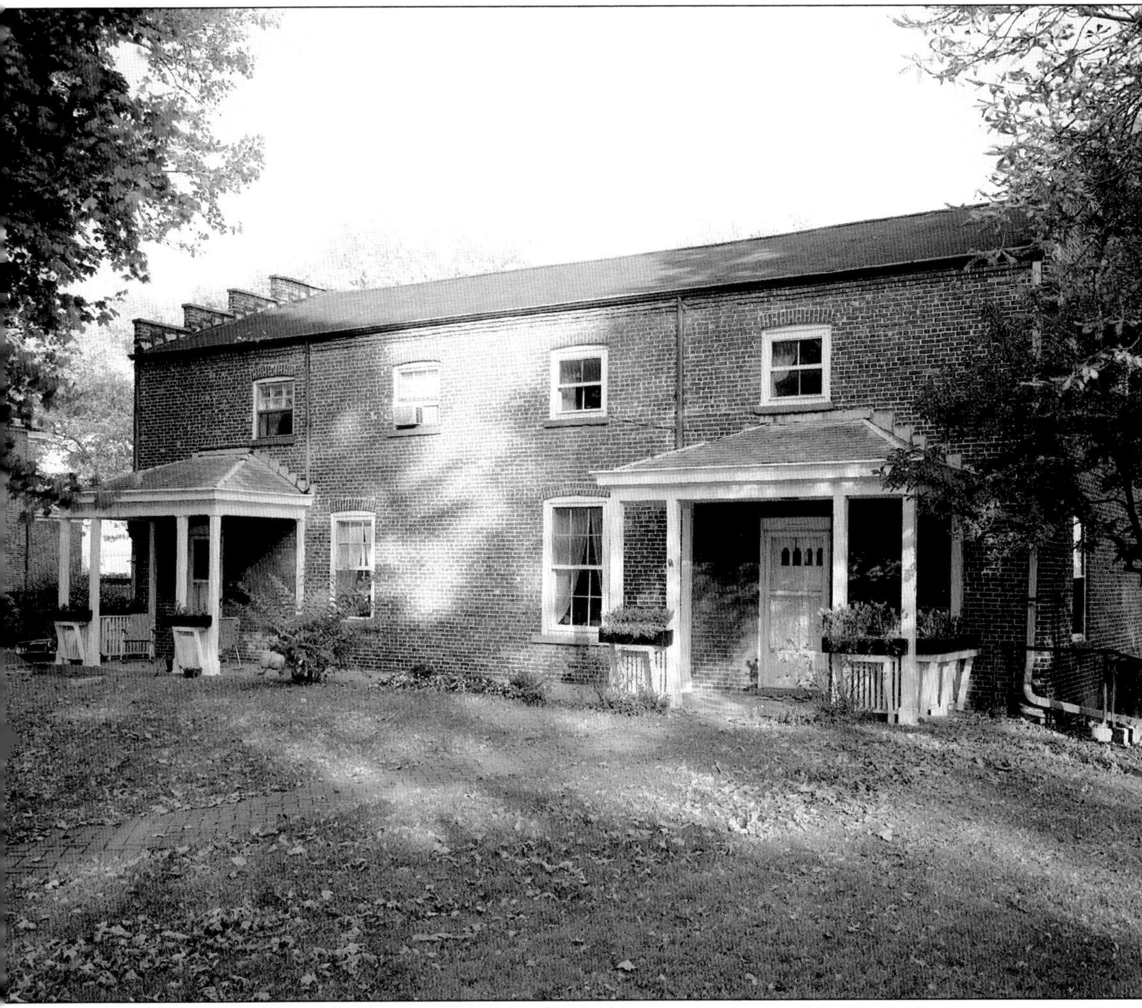

The Dutch House was built in 1845 and used to hold commissary supplies. In 1920, it was converted to officers' housing. The architecture is said to be an authentic copy of an early Dutch settler's home. (Courtesy of John T. Lowe, National Park Service/Historic American Building Survey.)

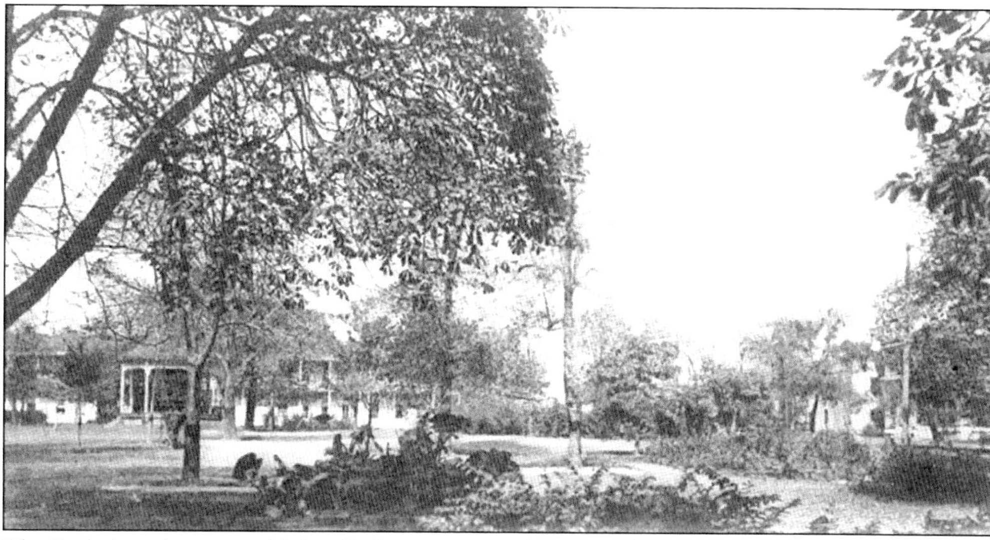

The Park, later known as Nolan Park, was an area between the two rows of officers' houses built between 1840 and 1904.

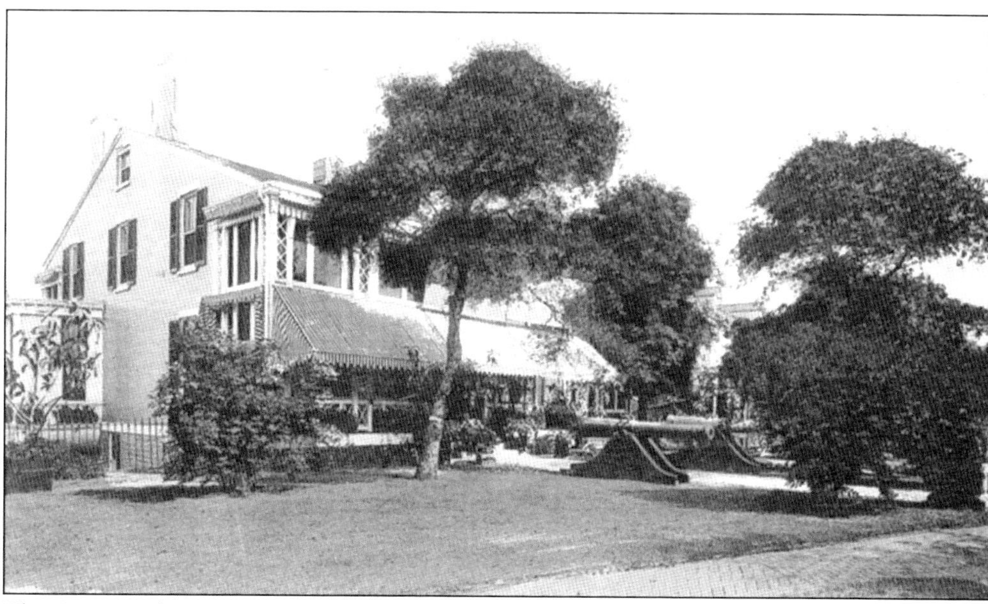

The Commanding Officer's Quarters, built in 1840, has had many additions and renovations.

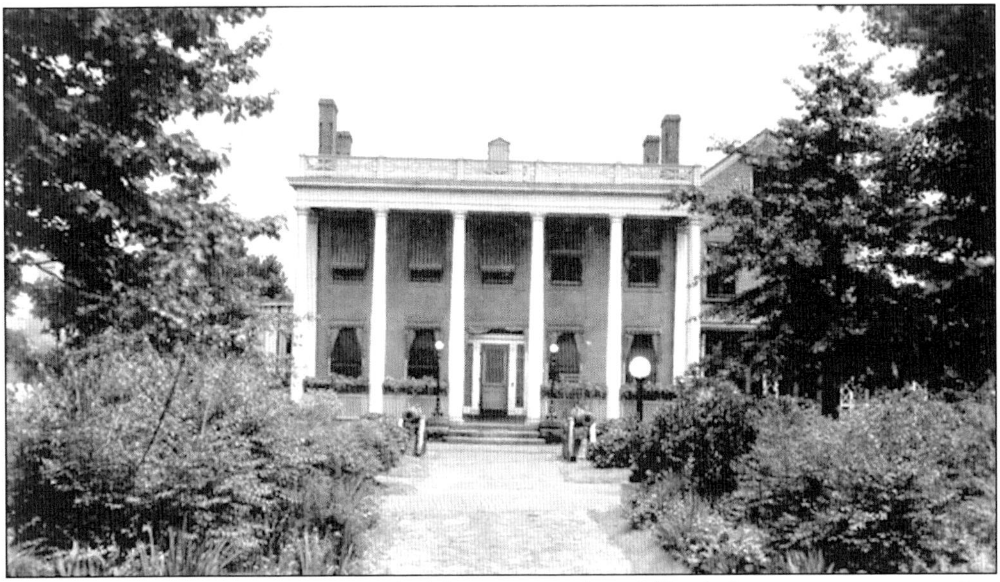

The bronze cannon in the foreground of the Commanding Officer's Quarters were captured in the Spanish-American War. Theodorico (left) is a 6,600-pound, 6.4-caliber gun made in Sevilla, Spain, on January 3, 1786. It was later converted into a muzzle-loading rifle cannon. El Alejandro (right) was made in Barcelona, Spain, in October 1769.

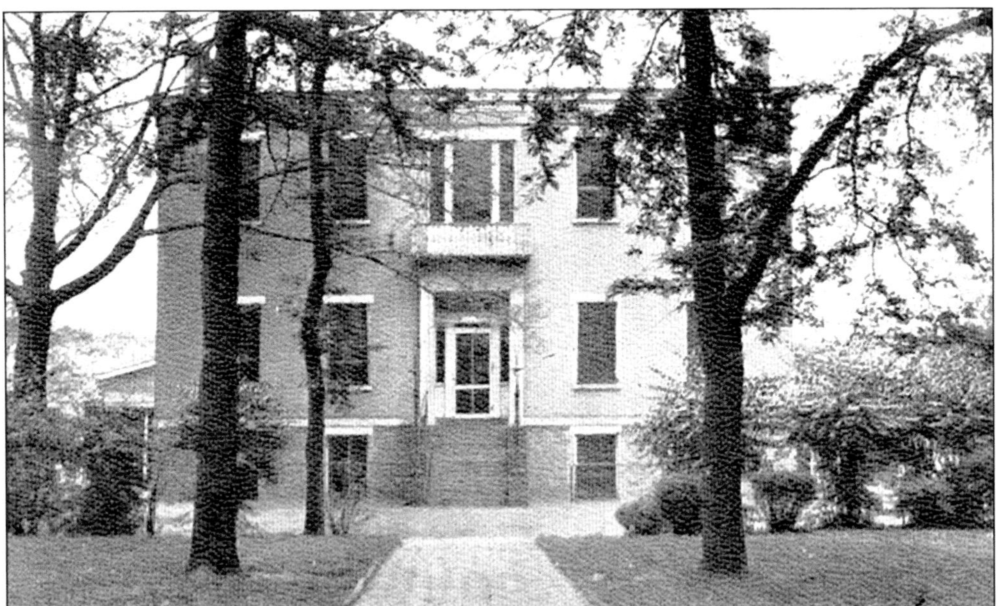

The Blockhouse, used as a headquarters building, hospital, and officer's quarters, was built in 1838–1839.

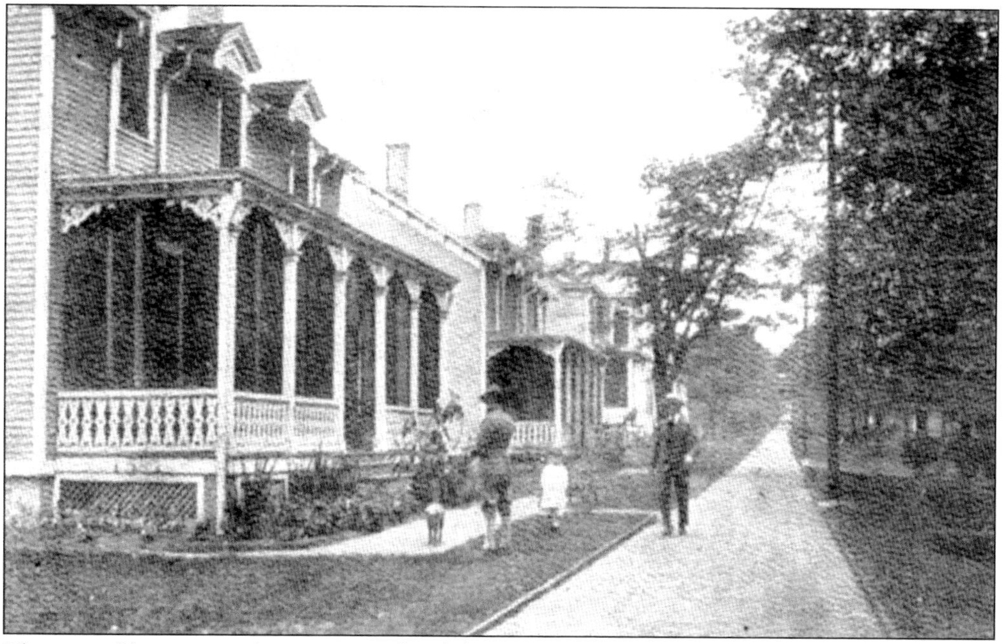

The row of houses on the western side of the park was known as General's Row and later as Colonel's Row.

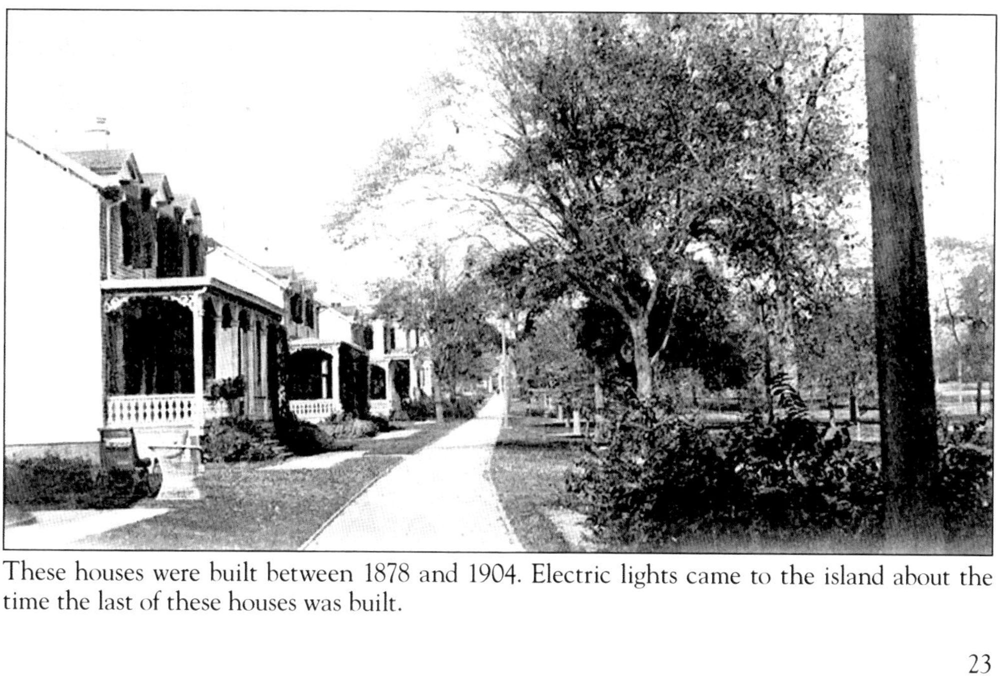

These houses were built between 1878 and 1904. Electric lights came to the island about the time the last of these houses was built.

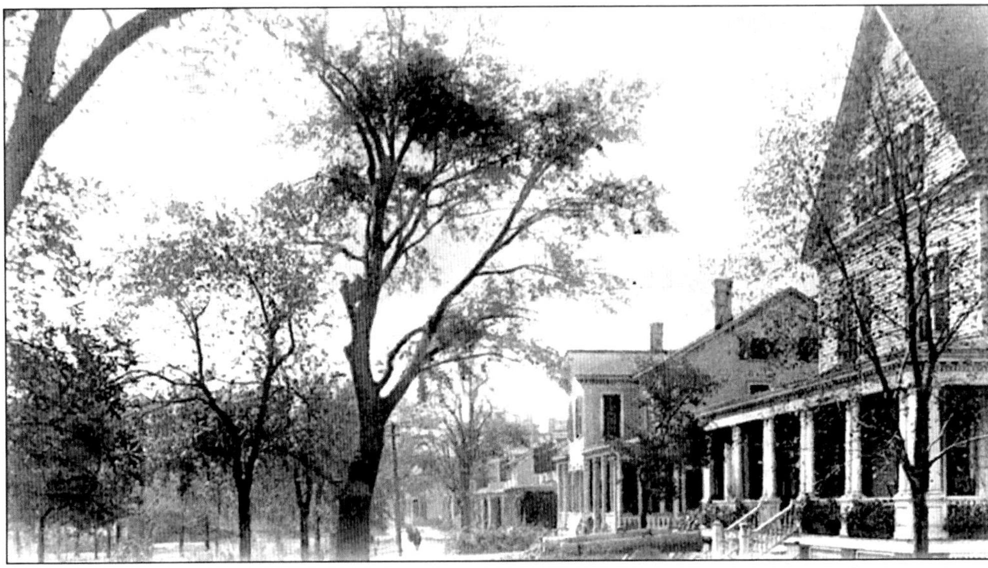

Several houses were built as duplexes and were occupied by two officers' families at a time. Shown is the same row of houses in a view that looks toward the southern end of Nolan Park.

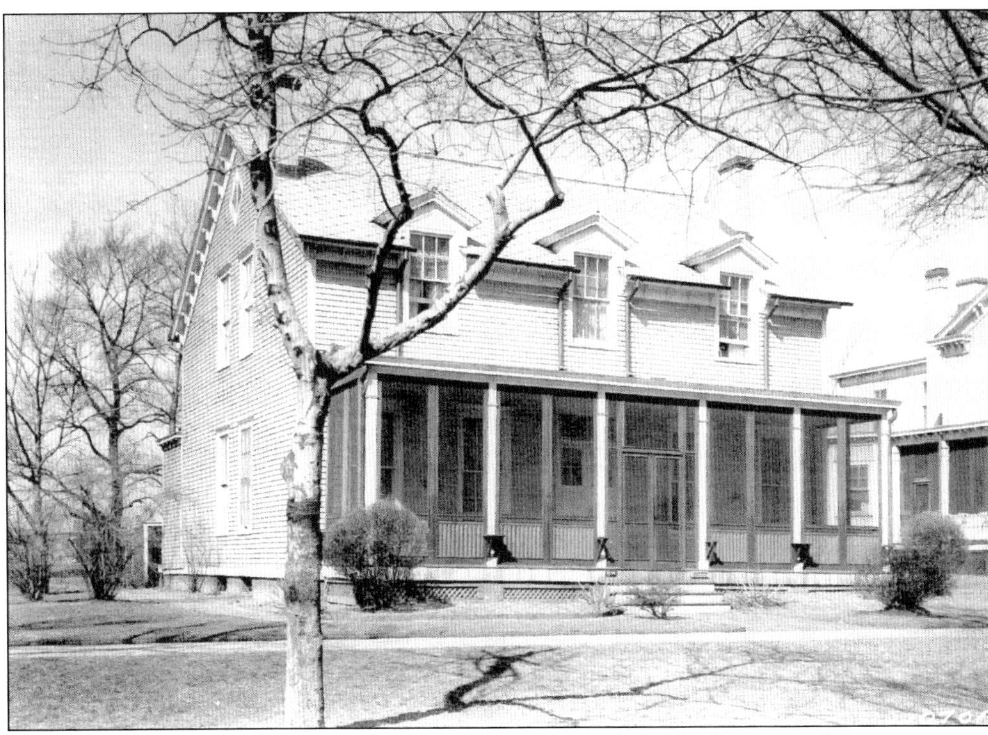

Screens were added to enclose the expansive porches. (U.S. Army photograph.)

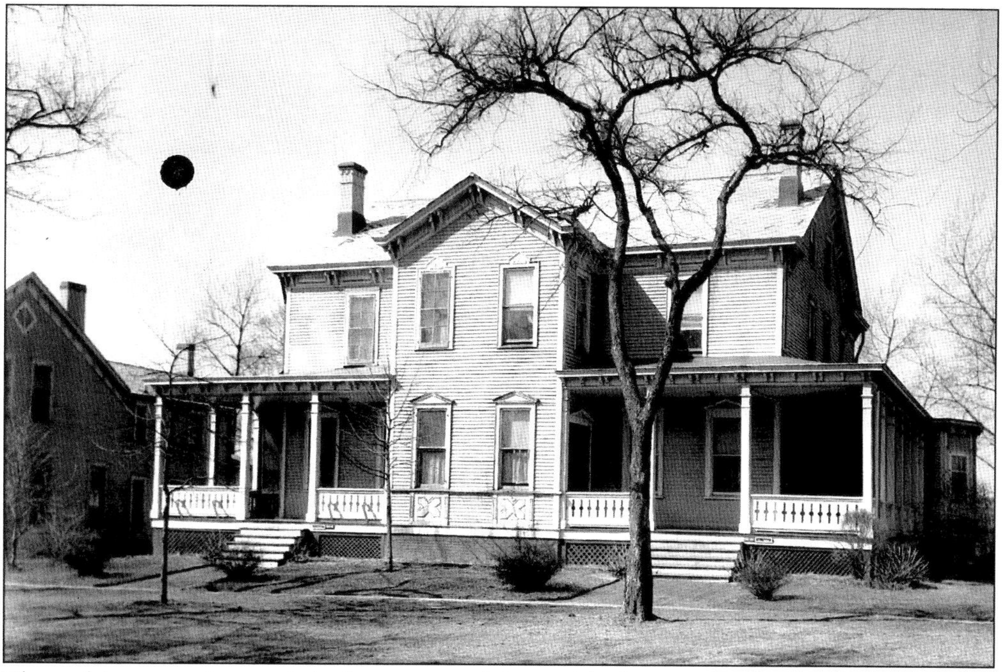

The architecture of most of the houses varied. Several had wraparound verandas, and all had one or more fireplaces to provide heat. Steam radiators and furnaces were added later. This two-family house, also in the park, was built several years later with less detail in the woodwork. (U.S. Army photograph.)

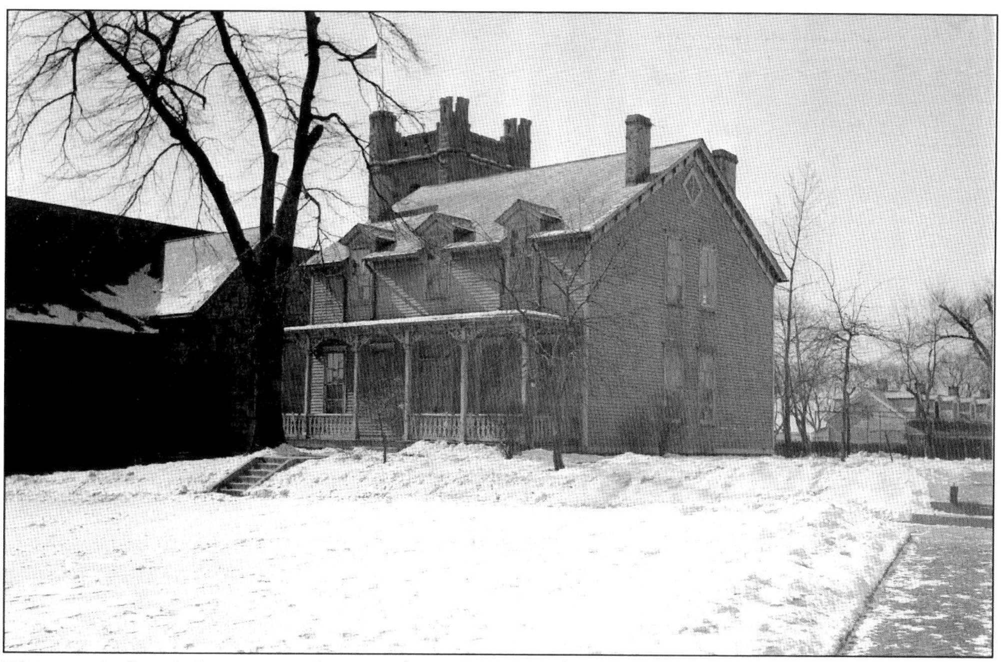

This single-family house stood across from St. Cornelius chapel. It was typical of many houses built by the U.S. Army during the late 1800s. Note the dormers above the upstairs windows and the ornate woodwork on the porch. (U.S. Army photograph.)

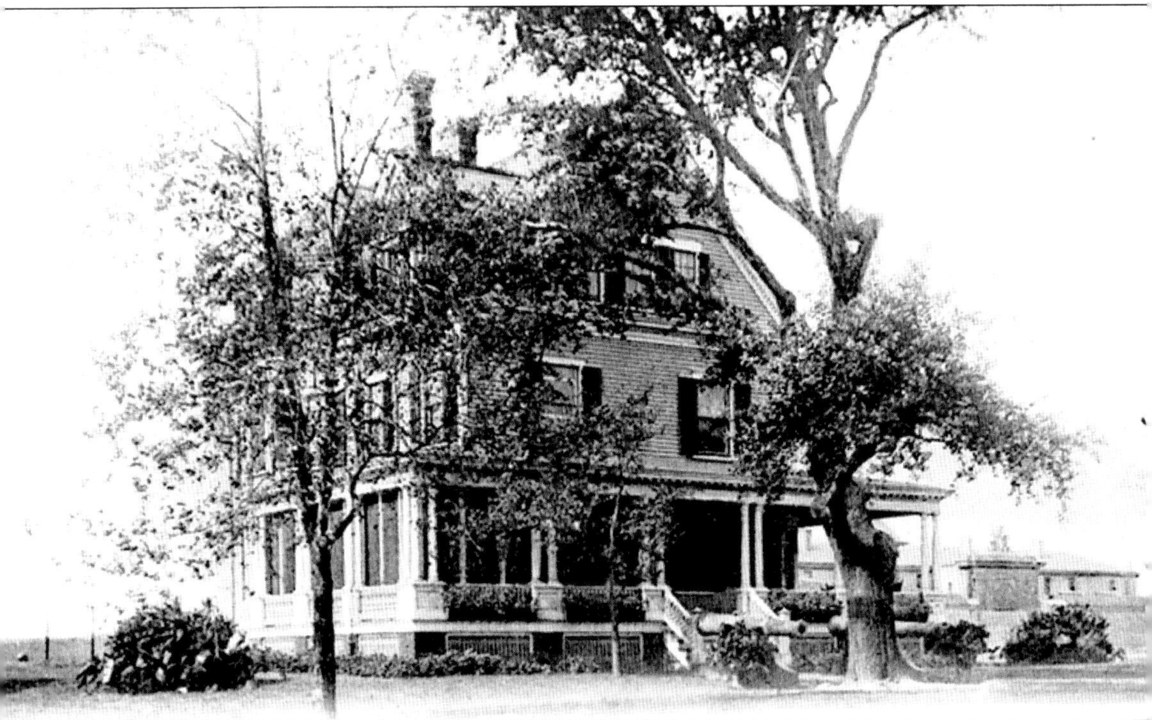

In 1904, the last house was built. Gen. Frederick Grant, son of Ulysses S. Grant, lived there while on the island. Ulysses S. Grant was stationed on the island as a captain, and his grandson Col. Ulysses S. Grant II was the chief of staff in 1937. Fort Jay can be seen in the background.

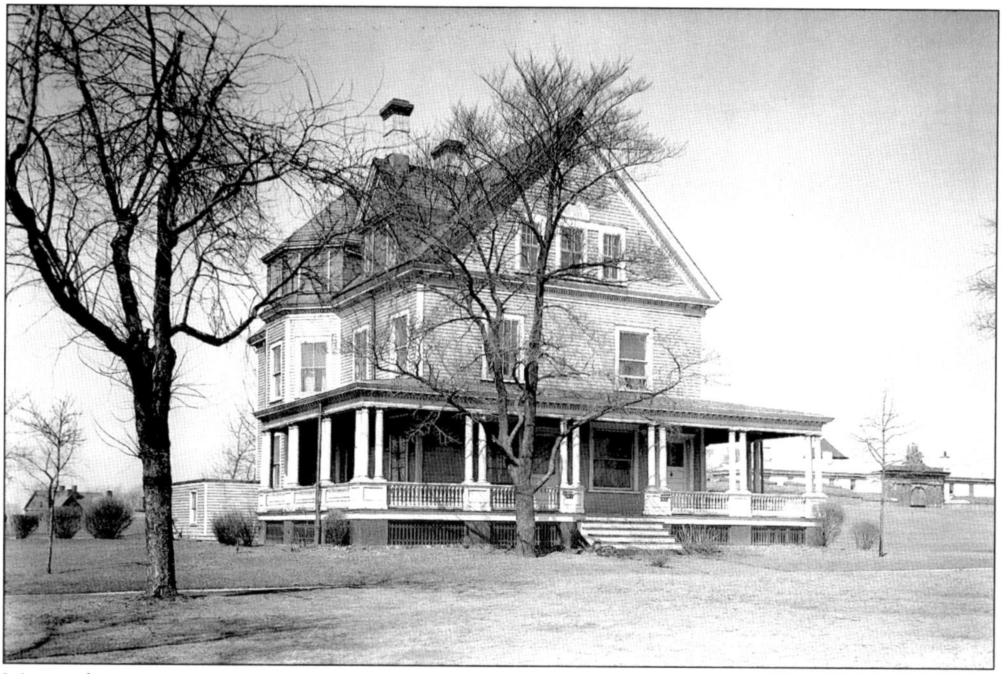

Minor changes were made to the house along with the addition of electric lighting. Some of the changes can be seen by comparing this picture with the previous one. (U.S. Army photograph.)

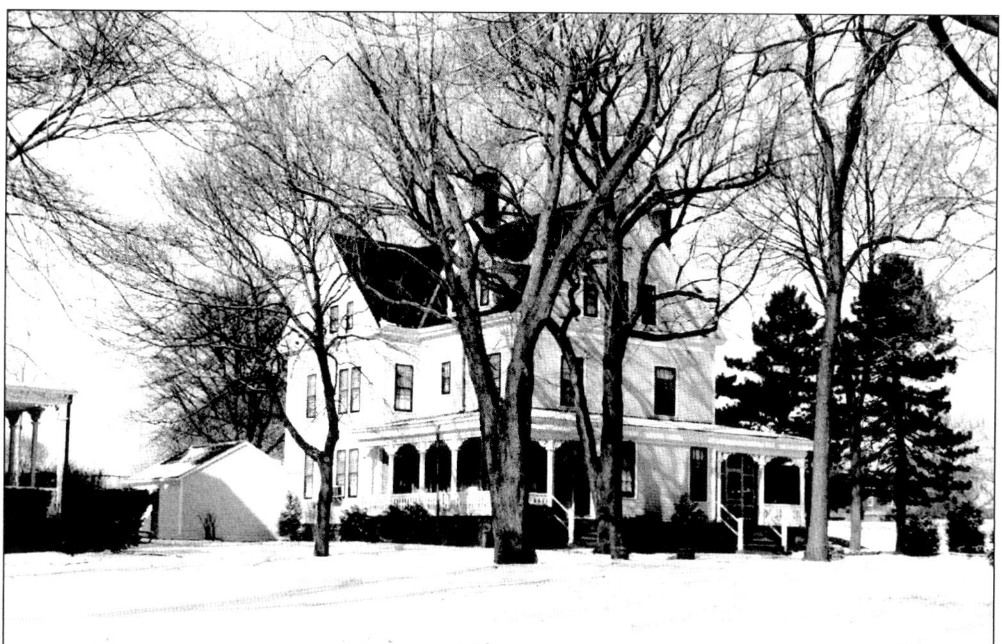

Here is the same house as it appeared in 1993, after it was returned to its original form.

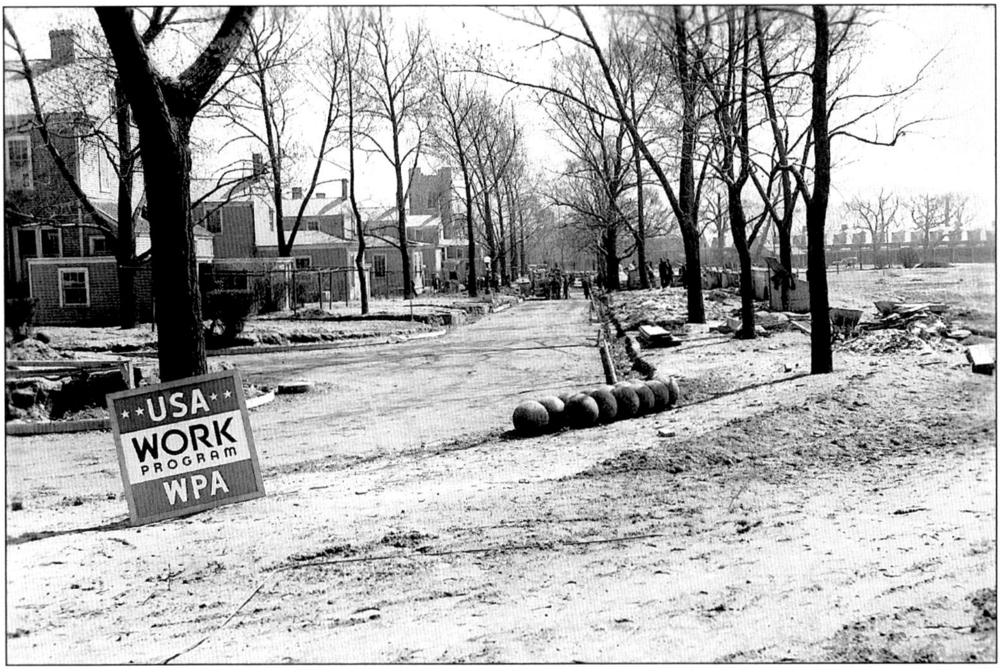

This view, taken from the southern end of Nolan Park, offers a glimpse of St. Cornelius chapel. It shows work being done in that area in the 1940s by the Works Progress Administration.

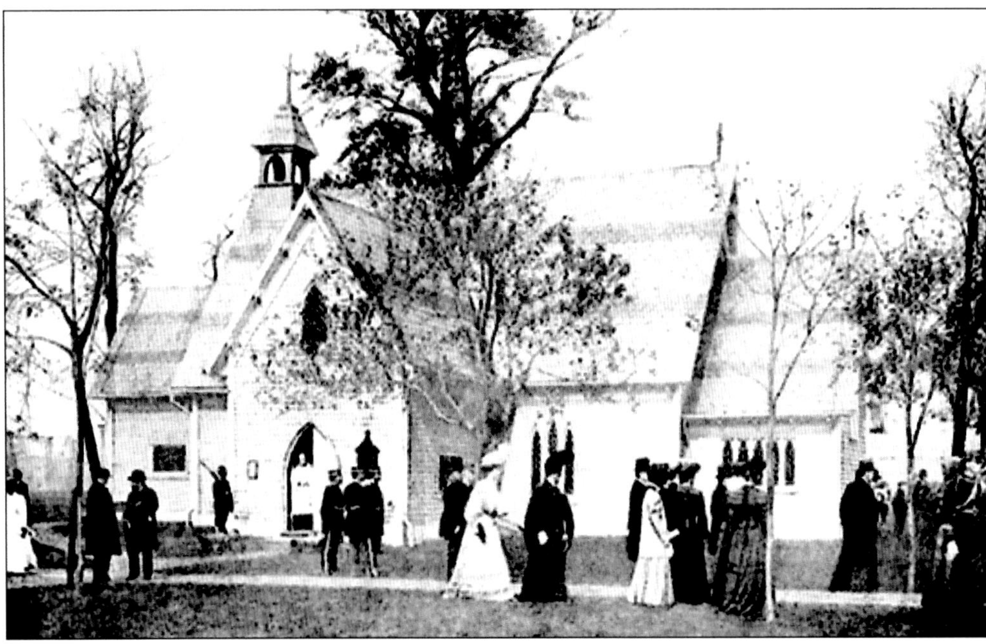

Rev. John McVickar, D.D., was the first chaplain at Fort Columbus (Fort Jay). It was due to his concern for the soldiers that the Chapel of Cornelius the Centurion was built in 1846. This photograph was taken shortly after the chapel's completion.

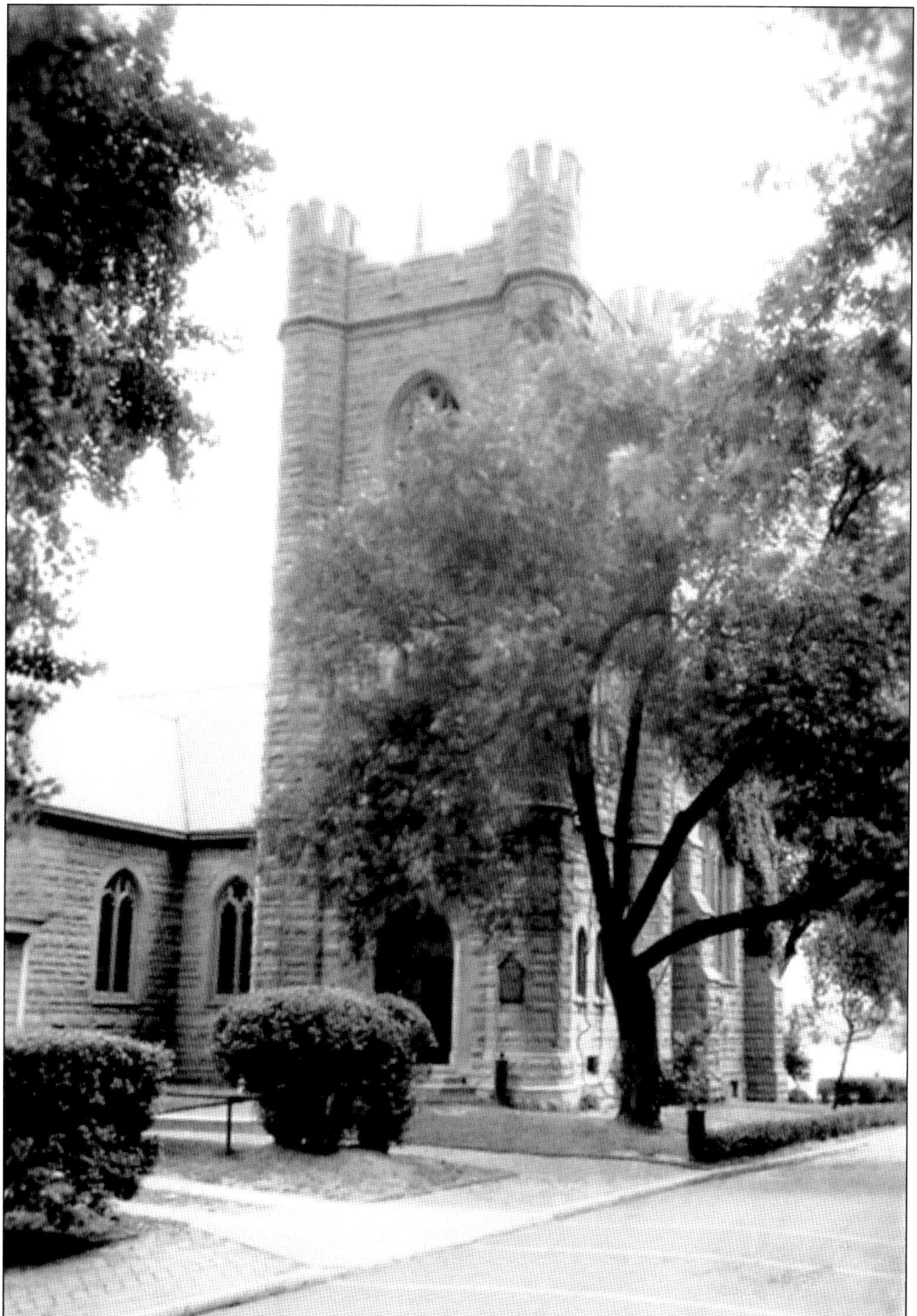

Rebuilt in 1905–1906, St. Cornelius chapel was under the auspices of Trinity Church in Manhattan. It is built of granite in 14th century English Gothic style. The stained-glass window above the high altar is in memory of Gen. and Mrs. Winfield Scott Hancock.

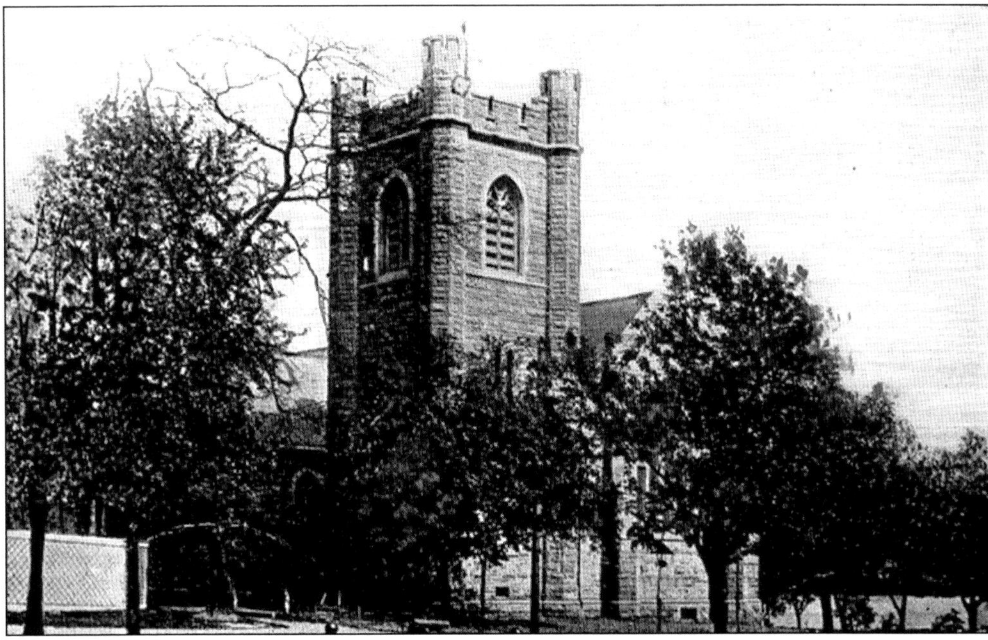

Charles C. Haight was the architect selected to build the new chapel. His wife was the granddaughter of Rev. Dr. John McVickar.

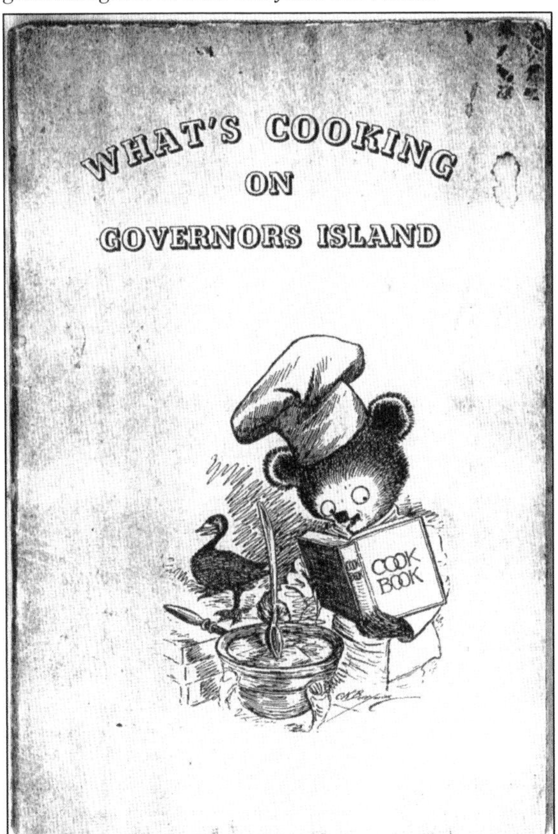

The members of the St. Cornelius Altar Guild were very active in the church activities. In 1949, they published a cookbook, which in addition to recipes provided a brief history of the island. Shown here is the cover of the third edition of that cookbook. It was dedicated to Chaplain Julian S. Ellenberg, a major in the U.S. Army, and compiled and edited by Isabel Mayer, Vinita Schall, and Ethel Wyman.

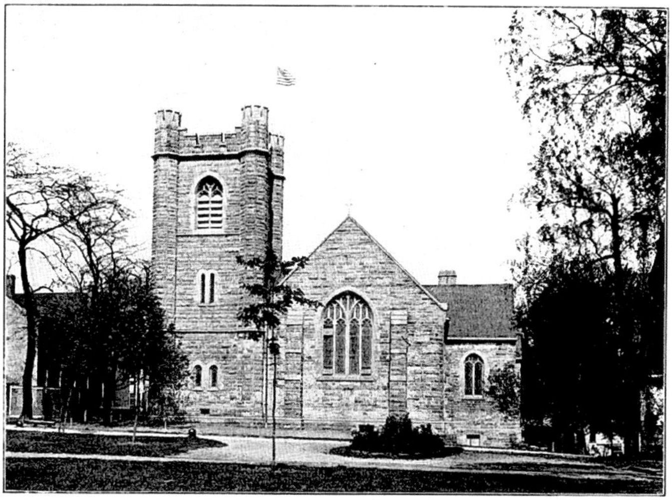

The Battle Flags, Paintings and Memorials

in the

Chapel of Saint Cornelius the Centurion

Trinity Parish

Governors Island, New York Harbour

Published by the Mary Washington Colonial Chapter
of the City of New York

Daughters of the American Revolution

in commemoration of the

Blessing and Installation of the

Regimental Colour of the King's Royal Rifle Corps 60th Foot

formerly

The Royal American Regiment
60th Foot

January 9th, 1921

This brochure was published in 1921 by the Mary Washington Colonial Chapter of the Daughters of the American Revolution.

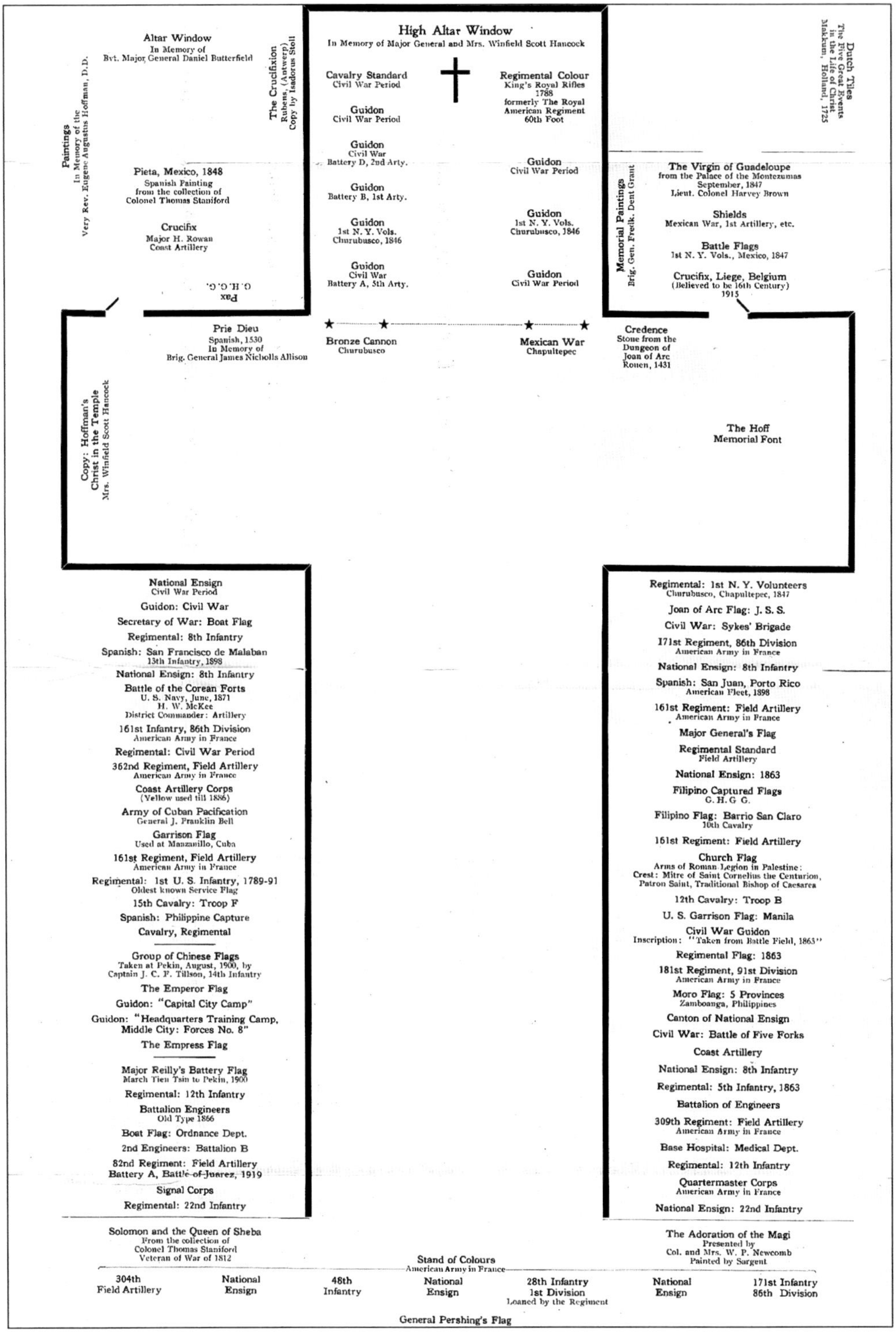

The brochure depicts and describes the battle flags, paintings, and memorials in St. Cornelius chapel.

Memorials in the Chapel

✝

Requiescant in Pace

Sanctuary Sedilia
Chaplain John McVickar, 1787-1868
Chaplain John Armour Moore La Tourette
Chaplain Alexander Davidson

Stone Tablets
Surgeon Joseph Pynchon Russell, 1790-1840
Katherine Kirby Russell
Lieut. Colonel Edmund K. Russell
1st Artillery
Josephine Martha Pynchon

Credence and Piscina
Sumter Loring Edmunds

Altar Cross
Captain Charles Morrison, Ordnance Dept.

Processional Cross
The Rev. John McVickar, D.D., Chaplain

Altar Vases
Major Clifford Comly, Ordnance Dept.

Font
Brevet Colonel Alexander Hoff
Medical Department
Colonel John Van Rensselaer Hoff
Medical Department
Anne Van Rensselaer Hoff
Harriet Louise Hoff

Ancient Mexican Pax
Colonel George Henry Goodwin Gale

Altar Vases
Sylvester Day, Surgeon
Russell Day, Lieutenant, U. S. A.
Murray Day, Lieutenant, U. S. N.
Maria Houghton Day
Hannibal Day, Brevet Brigadier General

Pall
James Jacob Roth

Lecturn Bible
Brigadier General John Walter Clous

Altar Window
Major General Winfield Scott Hancock
Almira Russell Hancock

Painting
From Mexico, 1848
Colonel Thomas Staniford

Painting
Pieta from Mexico, 1848
Jennie Jarvis

Paintings
Major General Frederick Dent Grant
The Very Rev. Eugene Augustus Hoffman, D. D.

Porch Windows
Saint Michael and Saint Gabriel
Margaret Lybrand Smith Dennison

Altar Books
General Daniel Butterfield
Sarah Garrod

Altar Desks
A Thanksgiving . . . Abby Arnold
E. K. S. . . . . E. B. S.

Prie Dieu
Brigadier General James Nicholls Allison

Crucifix
Major Hamilton Rowan, C. A. C.

Civil War Flag
Captain Luis Emilio

Corean Battle Flag
Lieutenant Hugh W. McKee, U. S. N.

Joan of Arc Flag
John Sanford Saltus

Other Objects not Memorials
Stones from the Dungeon of Joan of Arc
Nieux Chateau, Rouen

Crucifix from Liege, Belgium
Believed to be 16th Century

Dutch Tiles, setting forth the Five Great Events
in the Life of Christ
Makkum, Holland, 1725

Credence, commemorating the marriage of
Henry Fairfield Osborn
and
Lucretia Thatcher Perry
September 29, 1881

Painting
Adoration of the Magi, by Sargent

This is the back of chapel brochure, published in 1921.

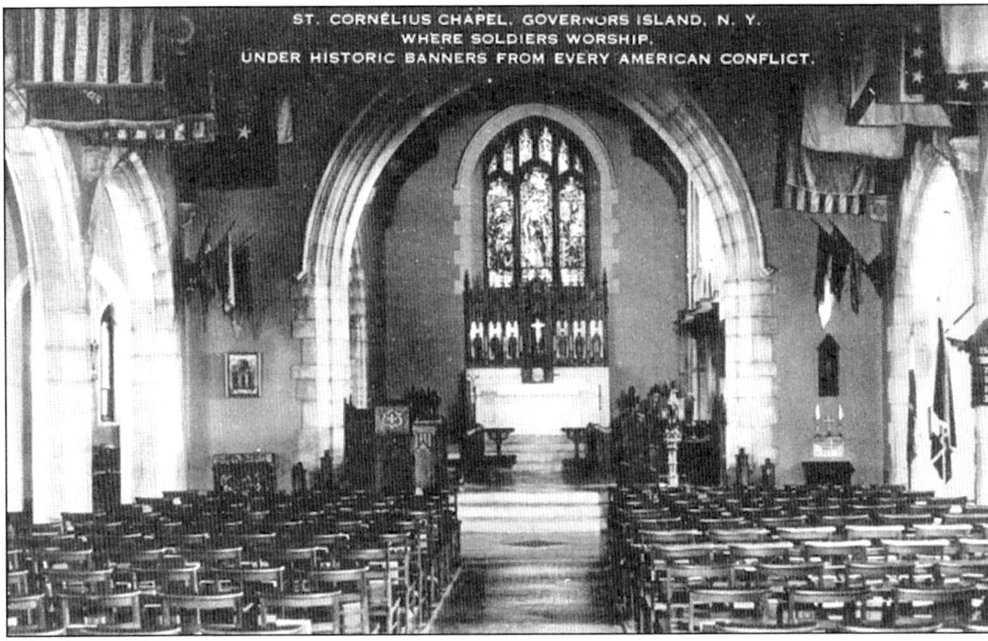

Soldiers worshiped beneath banners from every American conflict.

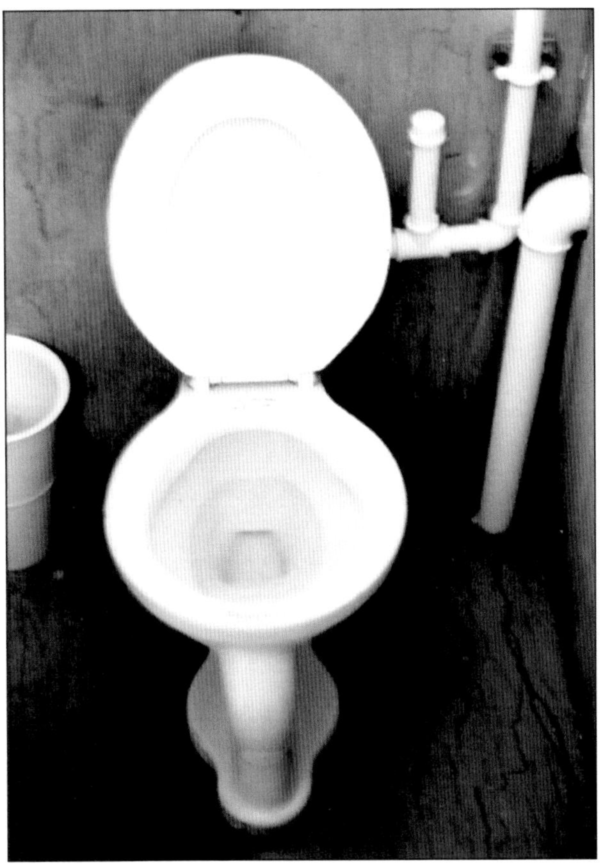

Among the many historic relics on the island is an original J. L. Mott commode, patent pending December 21, 1897. It is located in the men's room of St. Cornelius and is one of two commodes on the island.

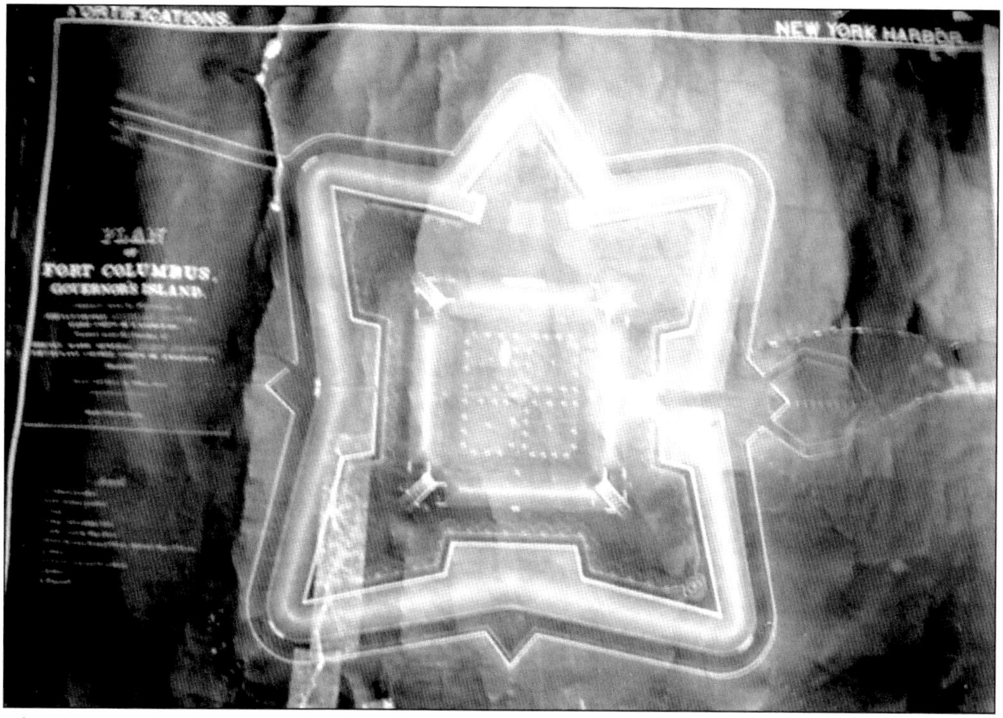

The construction of star-shaped Fort Jay was begun in 1794 and completed in 1800. The fort was partially demolished in 1806 and reconstructed and renamed Fort Columbus in 1809. Although the fort was rebuilt many times over the years, the original counterscarp, decorated gate, sally port, and magazine built in the 1800s have been preserved.

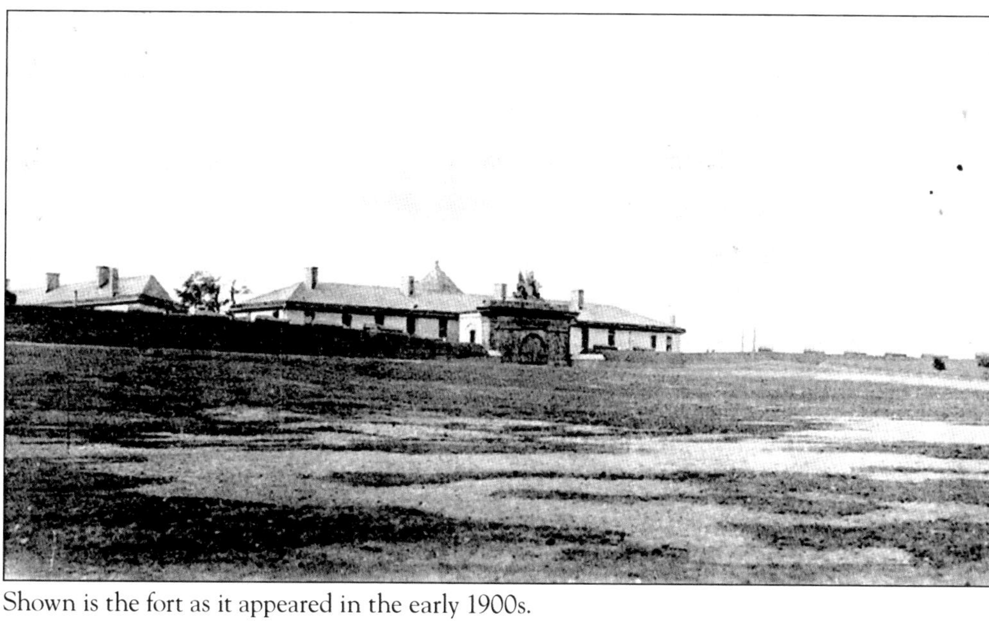

Shown is the fort as it appeared in the early 1900s.

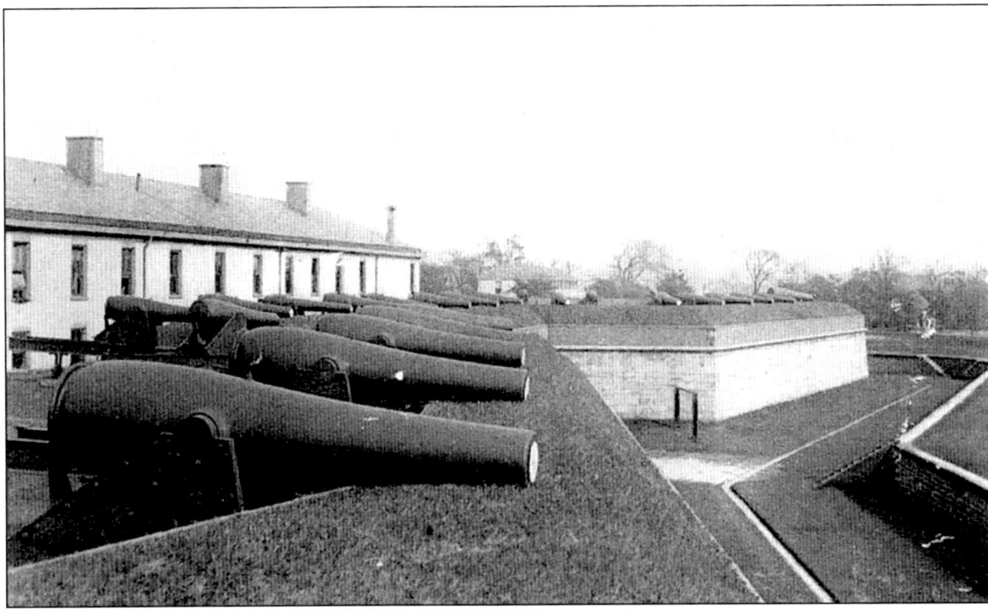

Cannon were mounted on the fort to protect New York Harbor.

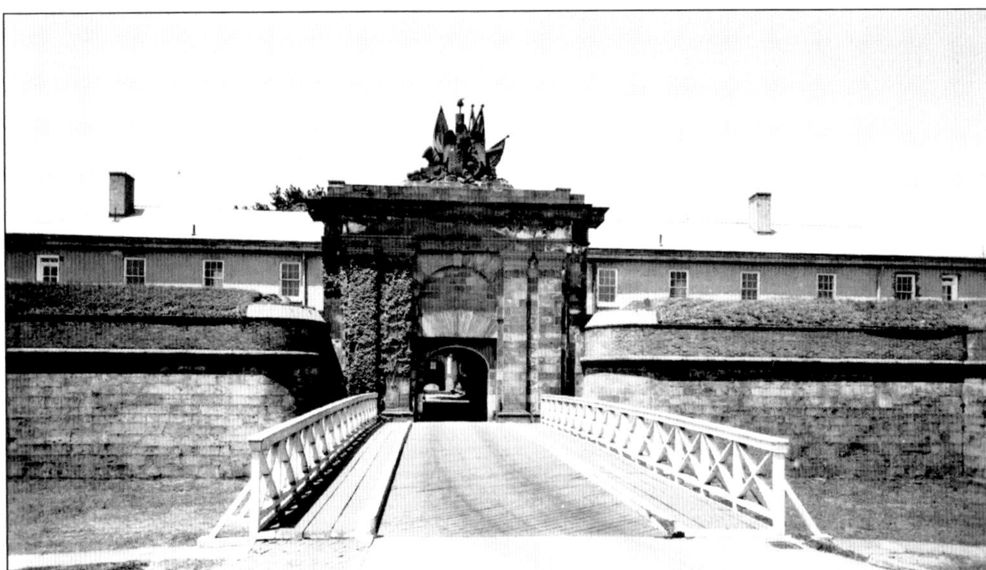

Shown here is the crossing of the sally port to the entrance of Fort Jay. Named for Secretary of Foreign Affairs John Jay, the fort consisted of four bastions of masonry, 100 guns, and a drawbridge over a dry moat to a sally port. The name Fort Jay was restored in 1904.

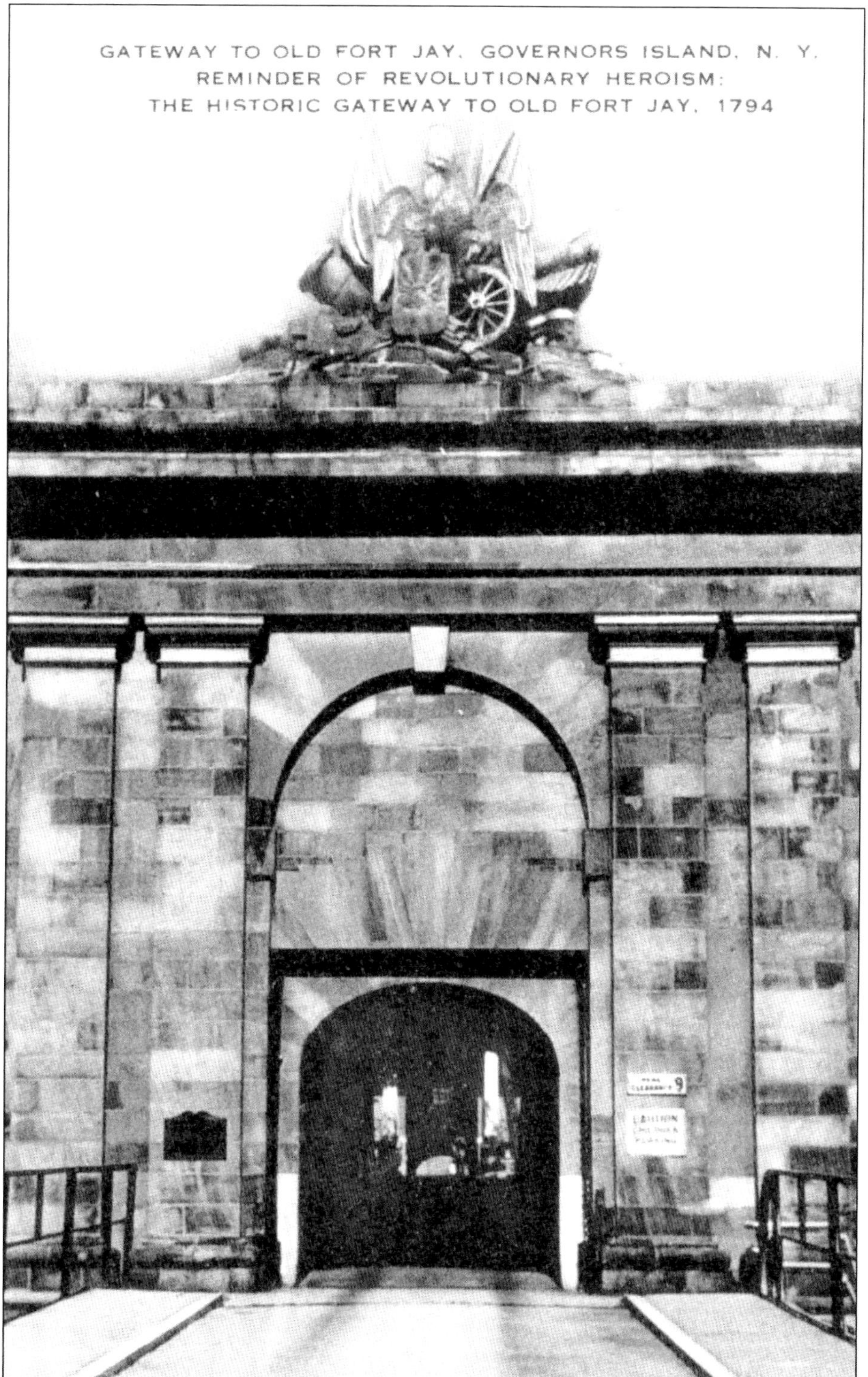

The stonework over the entrance to Fort Jay was done by a young Tory spy held prisoner on the island. One wing of the eagle had broken away and had to be replaced several years ago.

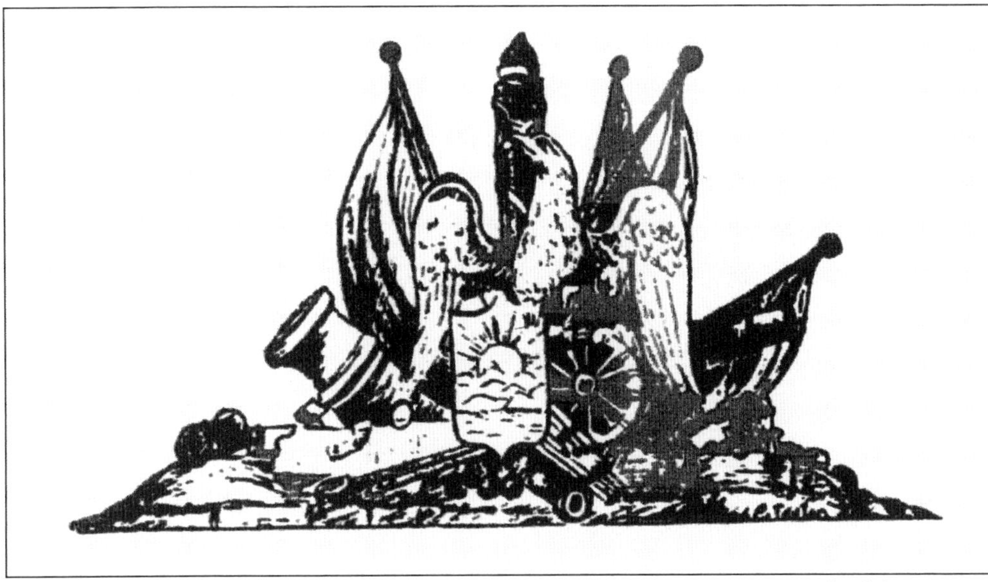

This close-up sketch of the stonework over the entrance shows the intricate work of the carving. Several romantic tales relate to the carving. One tells that a piece of stone fell and the carver kept it from hitting the Commanding Officer's daughter. The prisoner's sentence was reduced and he married the daughter.

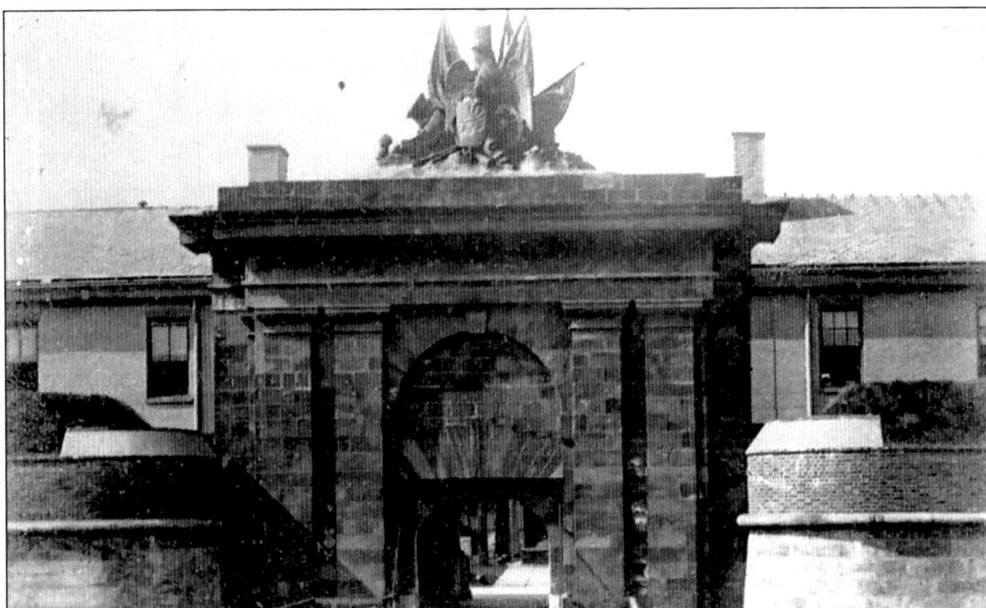

Inside the fort were barracks for 1,000 men, kitchens, one of the islands five wells, a hospital, and a powder magazine.

John Beall, Confederate spy, was executed by hanging February 24, 1865, on the southern side of the fort. He had been lodged in a dungeon cell in the cellar under the barracks to the right of the sally port. For many years, persons living in the fort have told of seeing his ghost walk the parapets of the fort. (Courtesy of Cameron Moseley.)

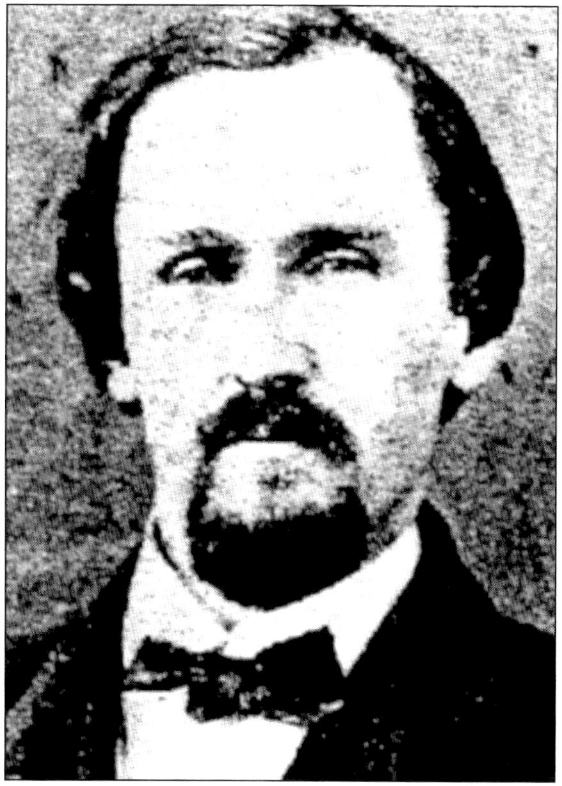

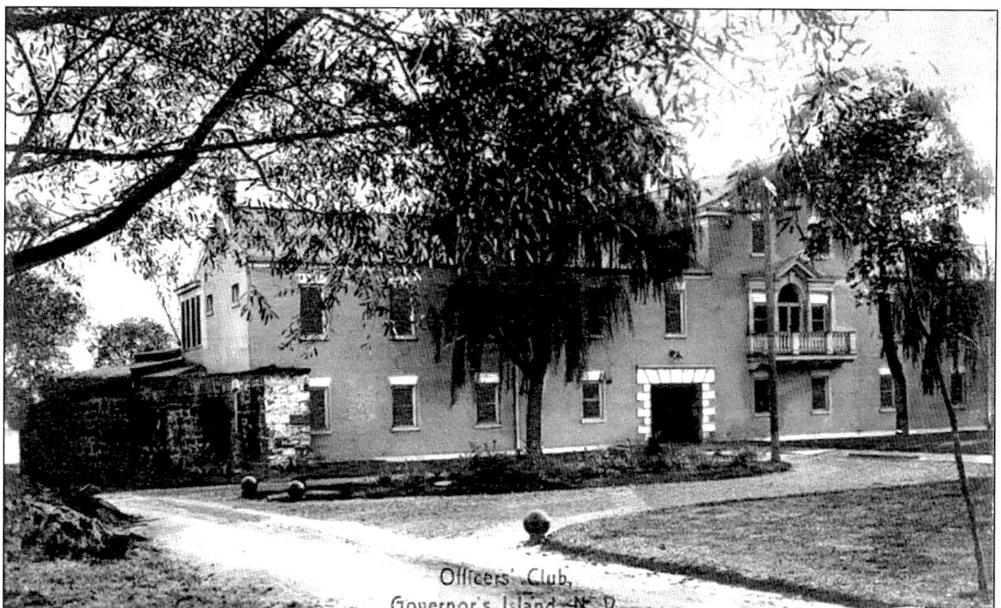

South Battery was built in 1812 to defend the southern part of the island. It was used as the officer's mess beginning in 1879 and then became the Officer's Club. A second story of red brick was added in 1834 with further additions in 1904. Beginning in 1834, the band, or "Music Boys," was quartered here.

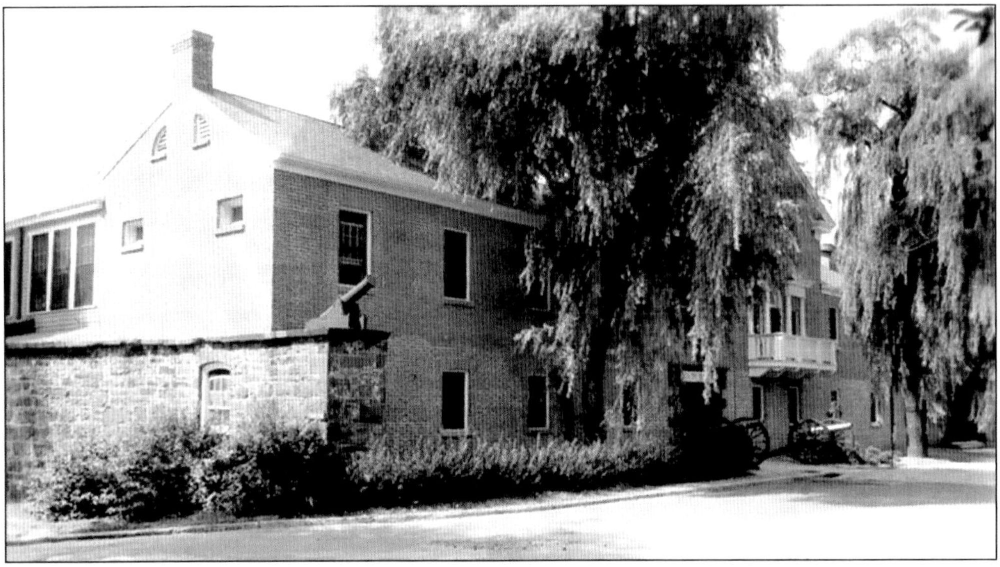

Two small Moro guns from the Philippine Insurrection guard the entrance.

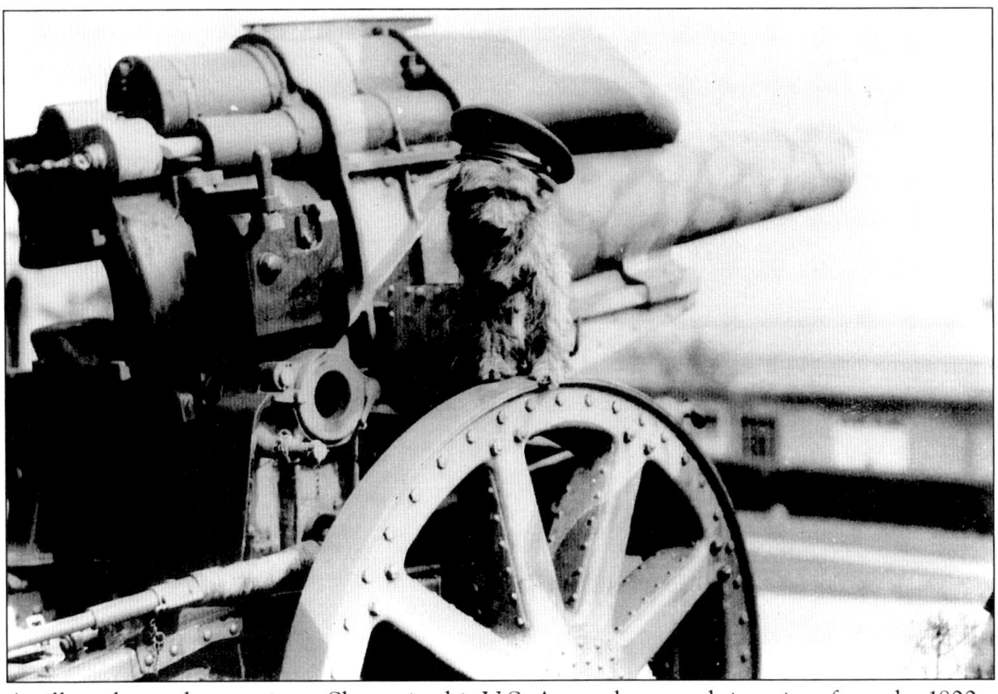

Artillery changed many times. Shown in this U.S. Army photograph is a piece from the 1800s.

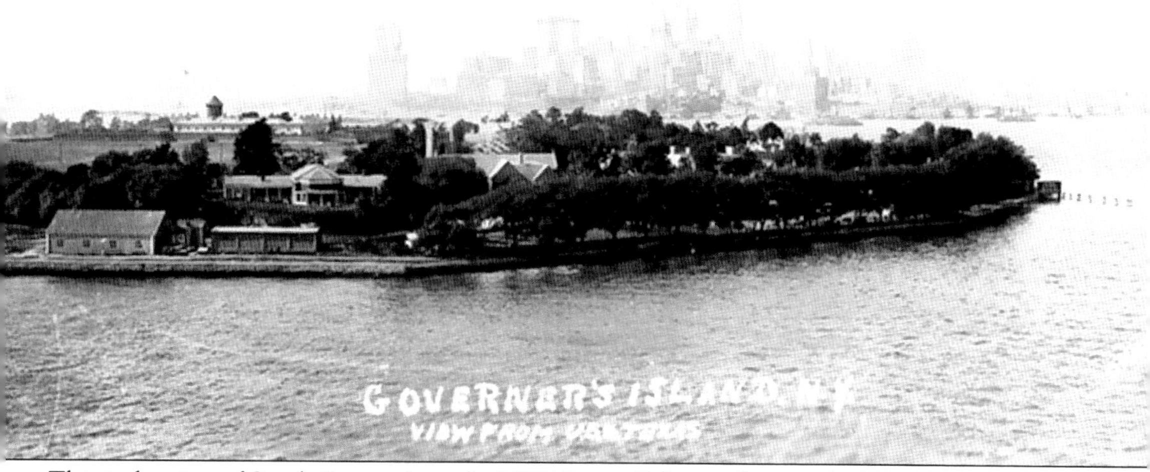

This is the view of South Battery from the USS *Texas* off the southern end of the island before the addition of land.

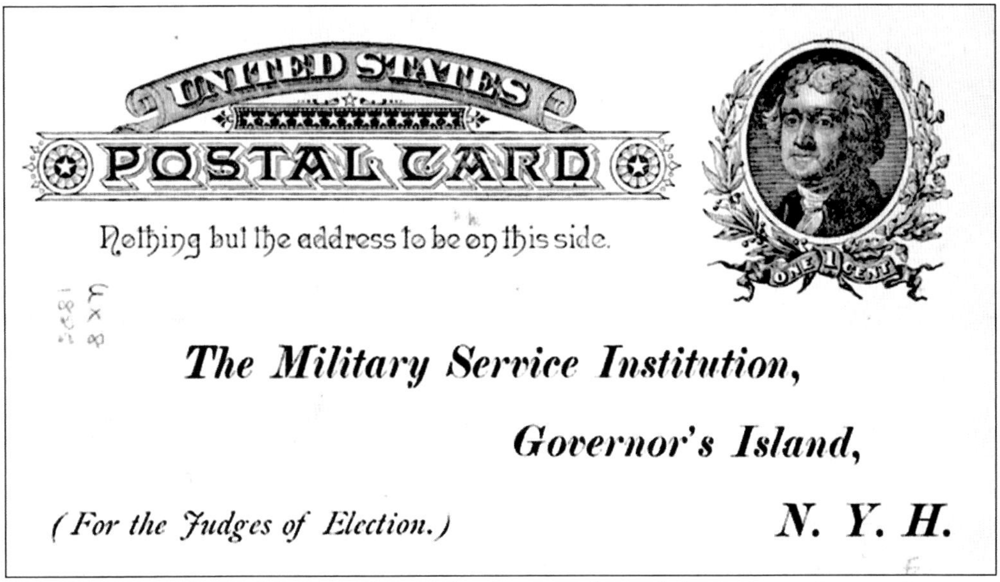

UNITED STATES

POSTAL CARD

Nothing but the address to be on this side.

The Military Service Institution,

Governor's Island,

(For the Judges of Election.)

N. Y. H.

Maj. Gen. Winfield Scott Hancock was the first president of the Military Service Institute, established in June 1884. This is a ballot for an election at the Military Service Institute, 1887.

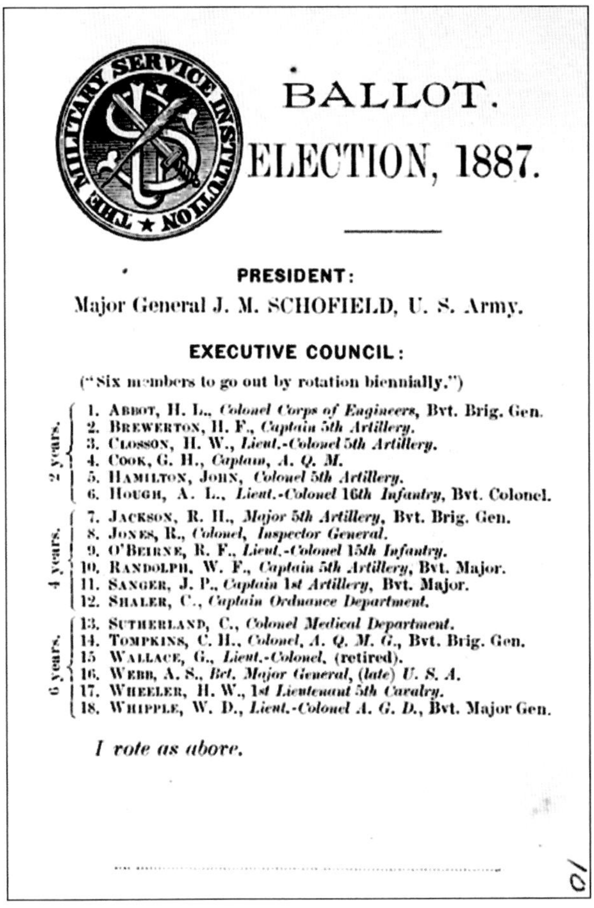

BALLOT.

ELECTION, 1887.

PRESIDENT:

Major General J. M. SCHOFIELD, U. S. Army.

EXECUTIVE COUNCIL:

("Six members to go out by rotation biennially.")

2 years.
1. ABBOT, H. L., *Colonel Corps of Engineers*, Bvt. Brig. Gen.
2. BREWERTON, H. F., *Captain 5th Artillery.*
3. CLOSSON, H. W., *Lieut.-Colonel 5th Artillery.*
4. COOK, G. H., *Captain, A. Q. M.*
5. HAMILTON, JOHN, *Colonel 5th Artillery.*
6. HOUGH, A. L., *Lieut.-Colonel 16th Infantry*, Bvt. Colonel.

4 years.
7. JACKSON, R. H., *Major 5th Artillery*, Bvt. Brig. Gen.
8. JONES, R., *Colonel, Inspector General.*
9. O'BEIRNE, R. F., *Lieut.-Colonel 15th Infantry.*
10. RANDOLPH, W. F., *Captain 5th Artillery*, Bvt. Major.
11. SANGER, J. P., *Captain 1st Artillery*, Bvt. Major.
12. SHALER, C., *Captain Ordnance Department.*

6 years.
13. SUTHERLAND, C., *Colonel Medical Department.*
14. TOMPKINS, C. H., *Colonel, A. Q. M. G.*, Bvt. Brig. Gen.
15. WALLACE, G., *Lieut.-Colonel*, (retired).
16. WEBB, A. S., *Bvt. Major General*, (late) *U. S. A.*
17. WHEELER, H. W., 1st *Lieutenant 5th Cavalry.*
18. WHIPPLE, W. D., *Lieut.-Colonel A. G. D.*, Bvt. Major Gen.

I vote as above.

In addition to helping organize the Military Service Institute, Hancock brought street lamps to the island. The institute published a journal on military subjects, maintained a museum of military memorabilia, and assembled a library of historical interest. Much of the museum's collection is now housed at the Smithsonian.

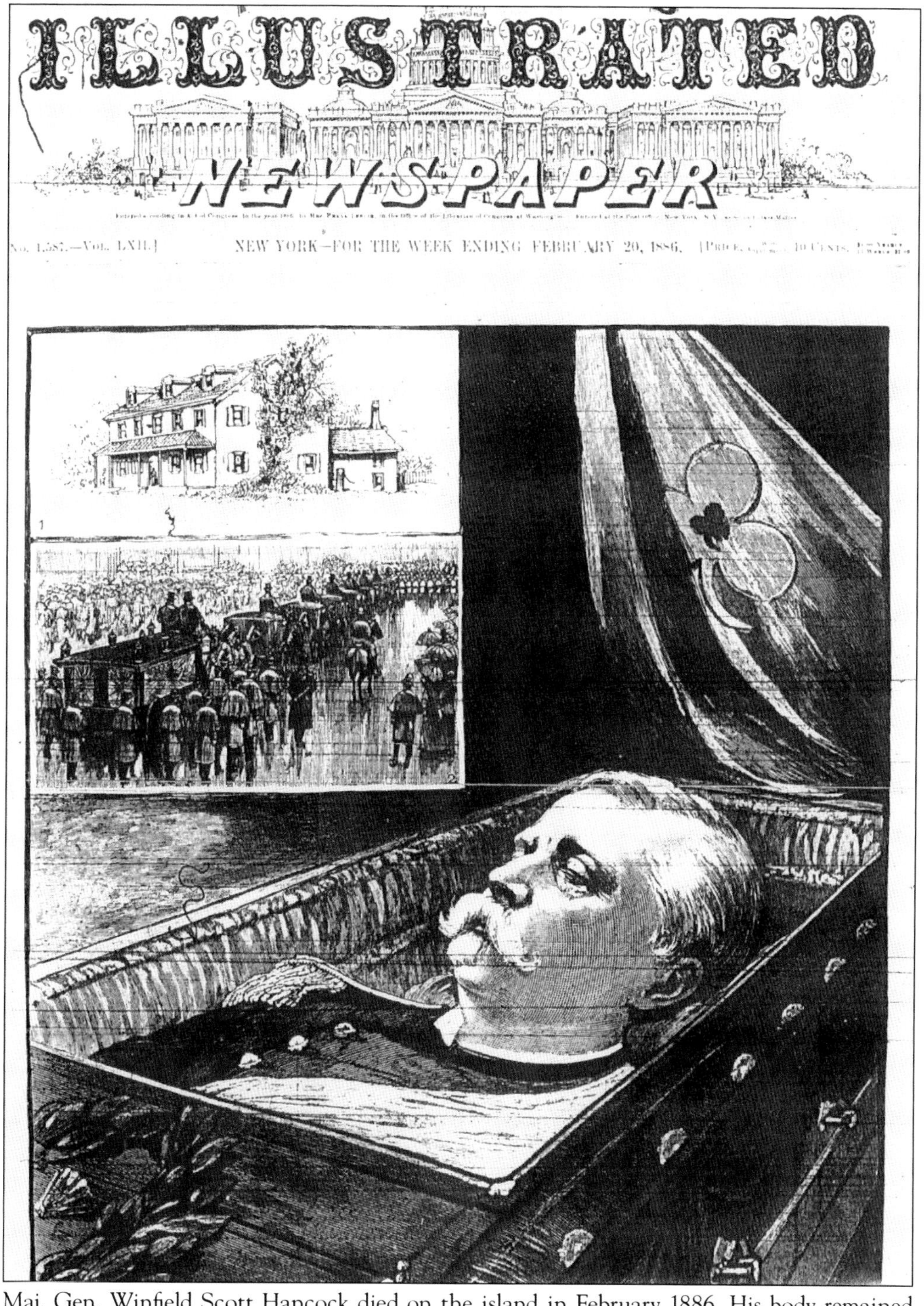

Maj. Gen. Winfield Scott Hancock died on the island in February 1886. His body remained in the Commanding Officer's Quarters until his funeral at Trinity Church. (Courtesy of *Frank Leslie's Illustrated Newspaper.*)

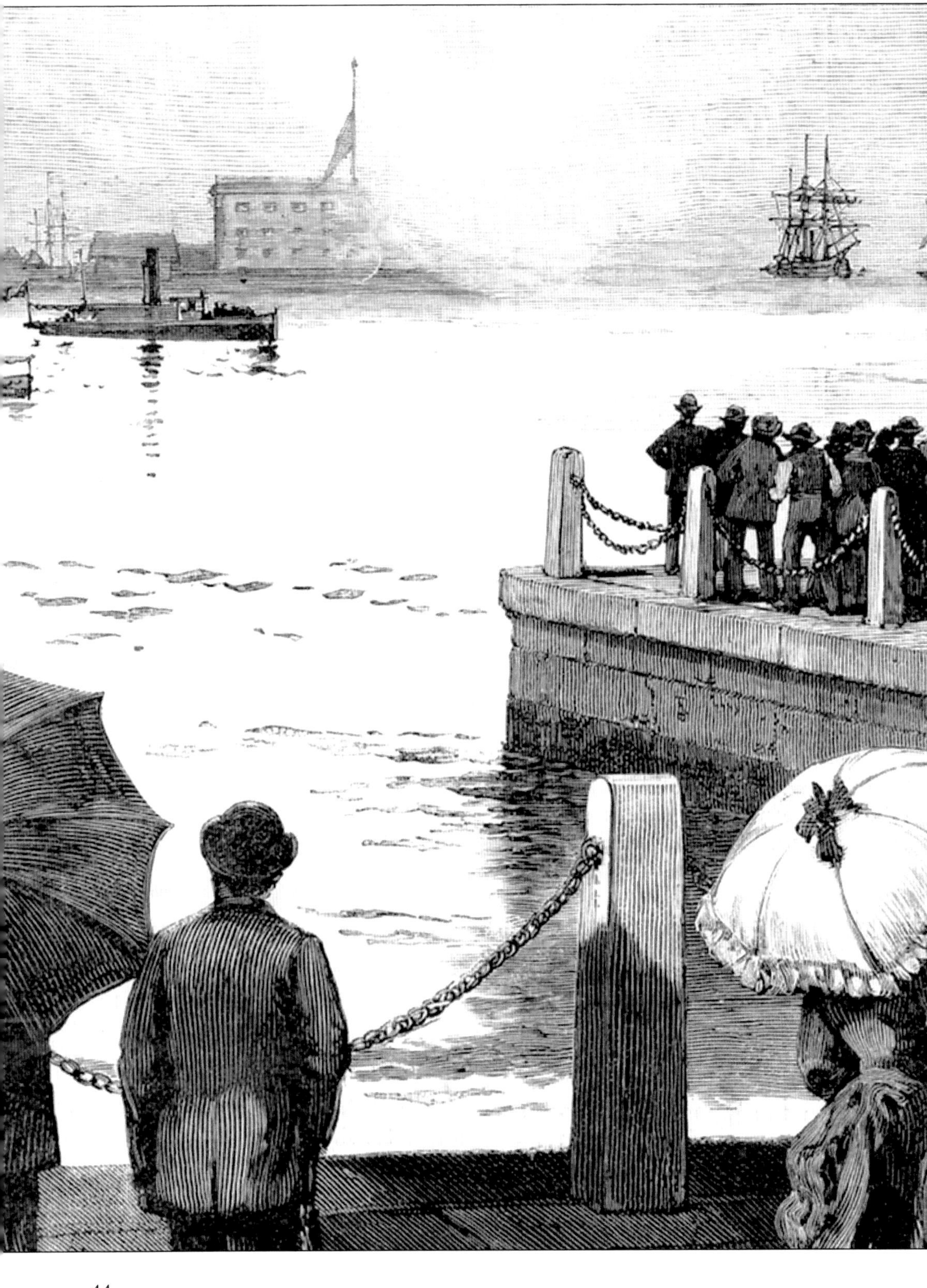

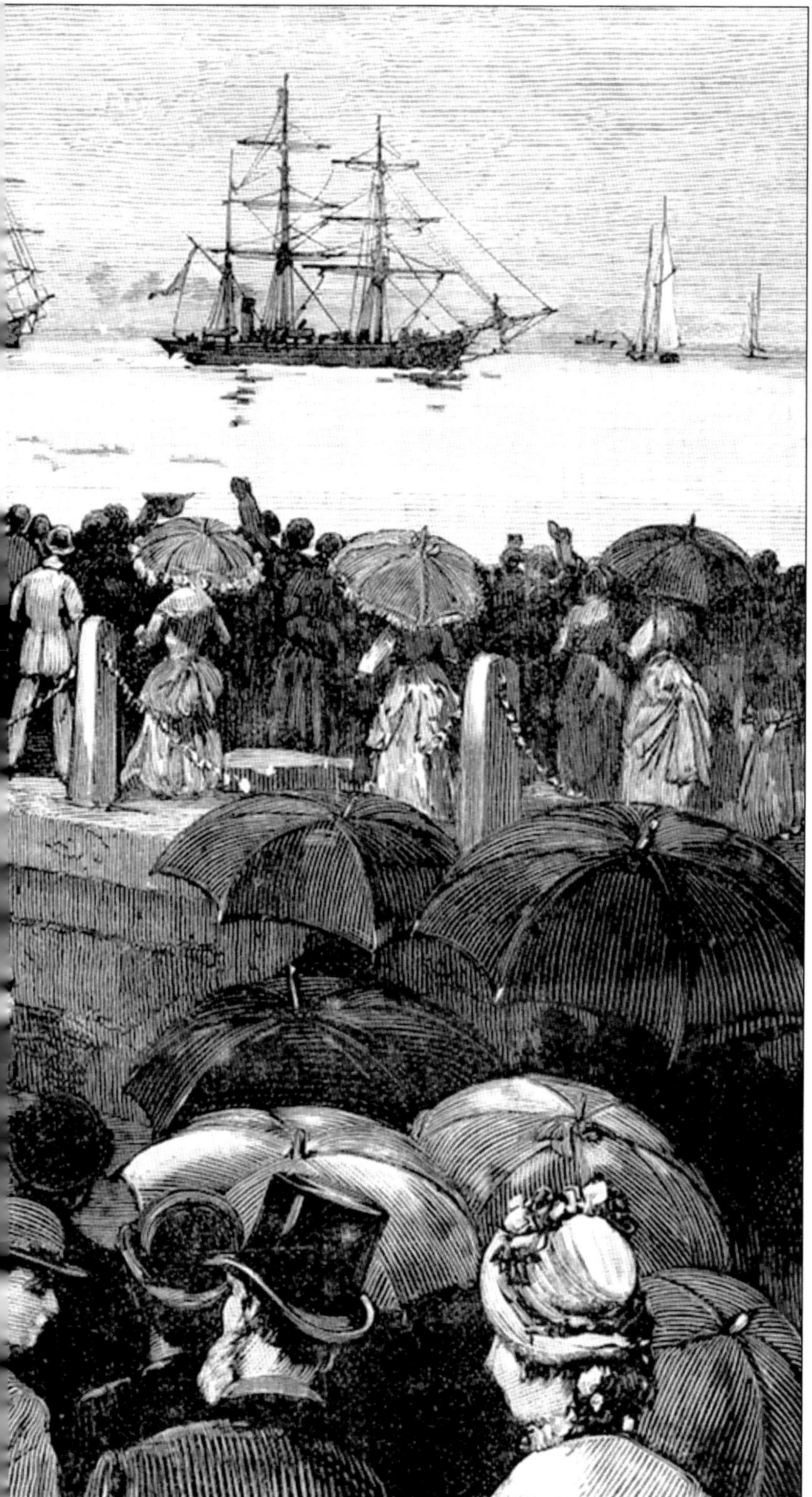

This *Harper's Weekly* drawing, by Charles Graham, shows the arrival of the Greely Relief Expedition ships carrying the Arctic dead to Governors Island in August 1884.

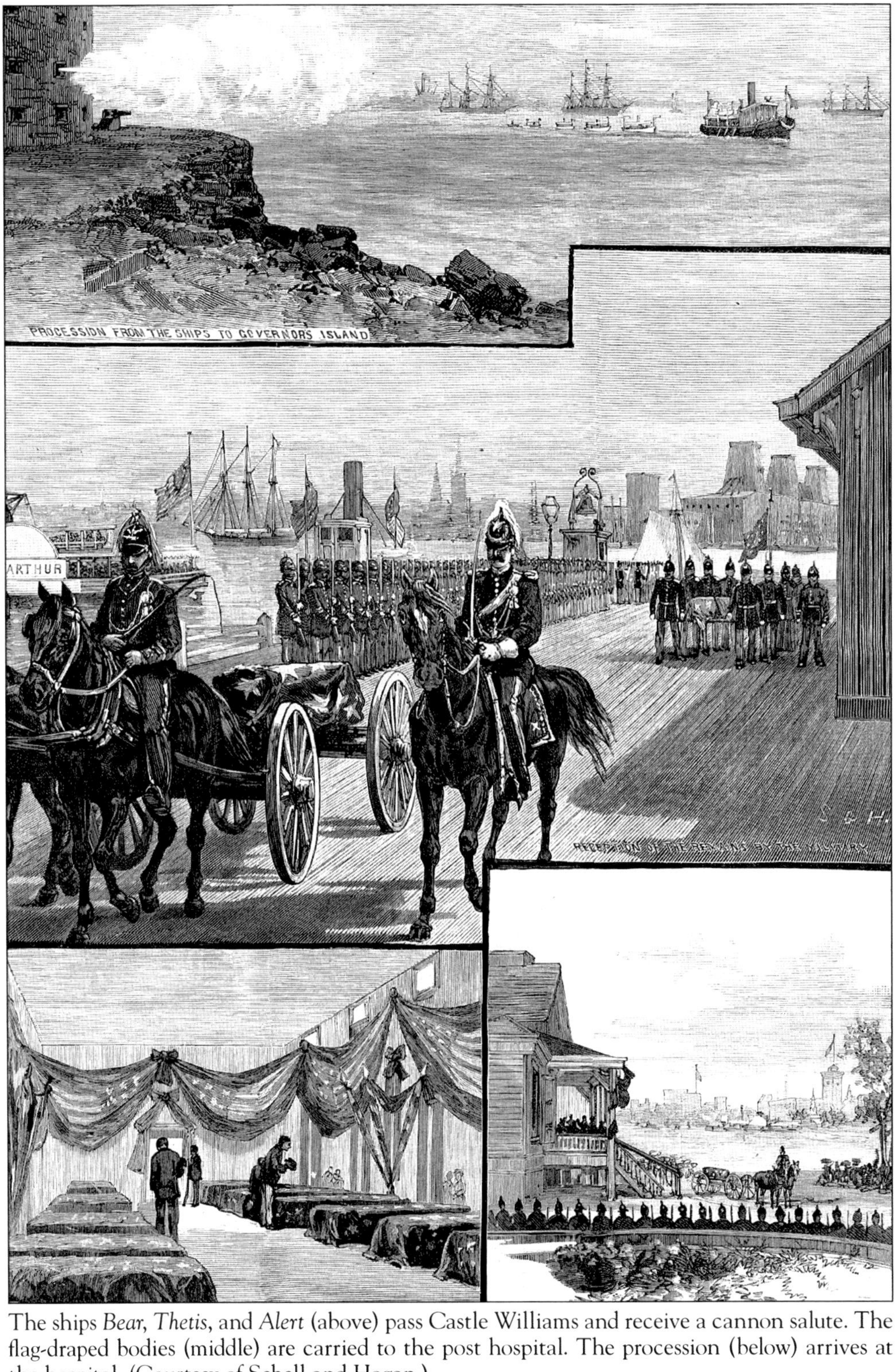

The ships *Bear*, *Thetis*, and *Alert* (above) pass Castle Williams and receive a cannon salute. The flag-draped bodies (middle) are carried to the post hospital. The procession (below) arrives at the hospital. (Courtesy of Schell and Hogan.)

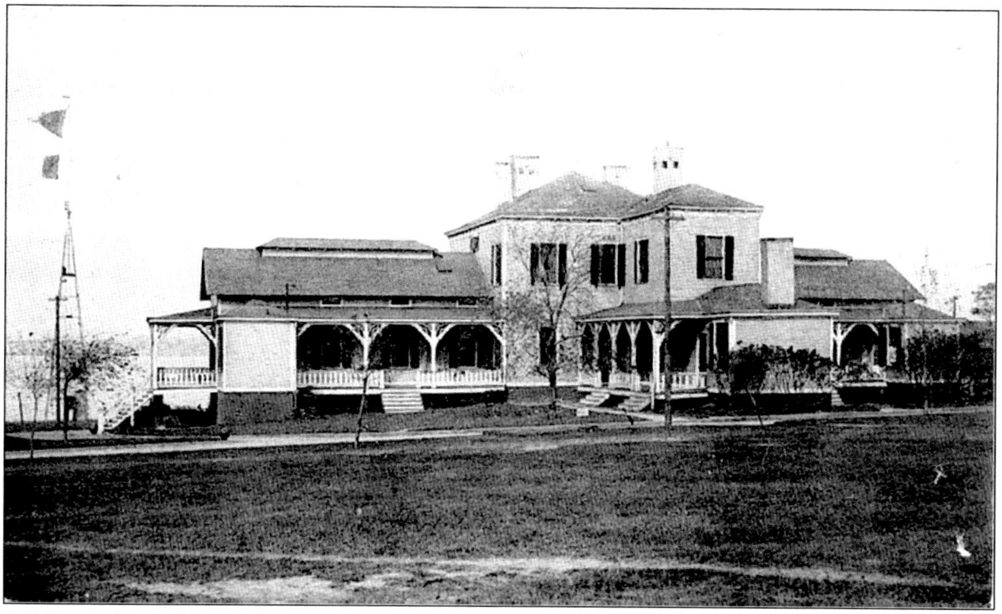

A U.S. Military hospital was built in 1798 on the eastern side of the island along Buttermilk Channel. It was here that the bodies of the Arctic dead lay in state.

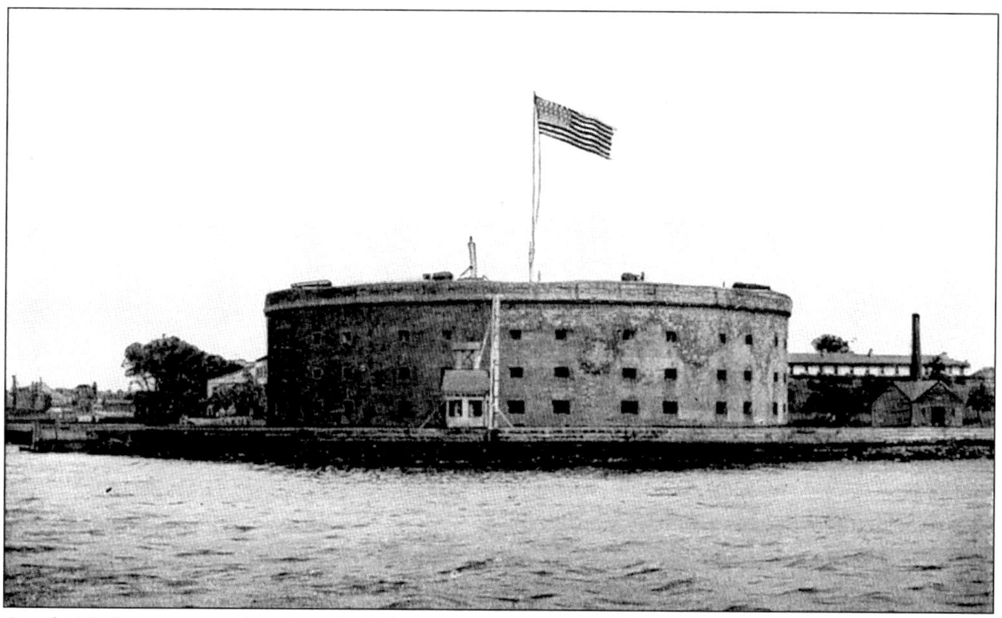

Castle Williams, completed in 1811, has undergone many changes during its long history. It is 200 feet in diameter with red sandstone walls 40 feet high and 8 feet thick. Governors Island was designated a "saluting station" and foreign ships of war were required to raise the flag of the United States upon entering the harbor and salute it by firing 21 guns. Castle Williams would return a salute—gun for gun—within 24 hours.

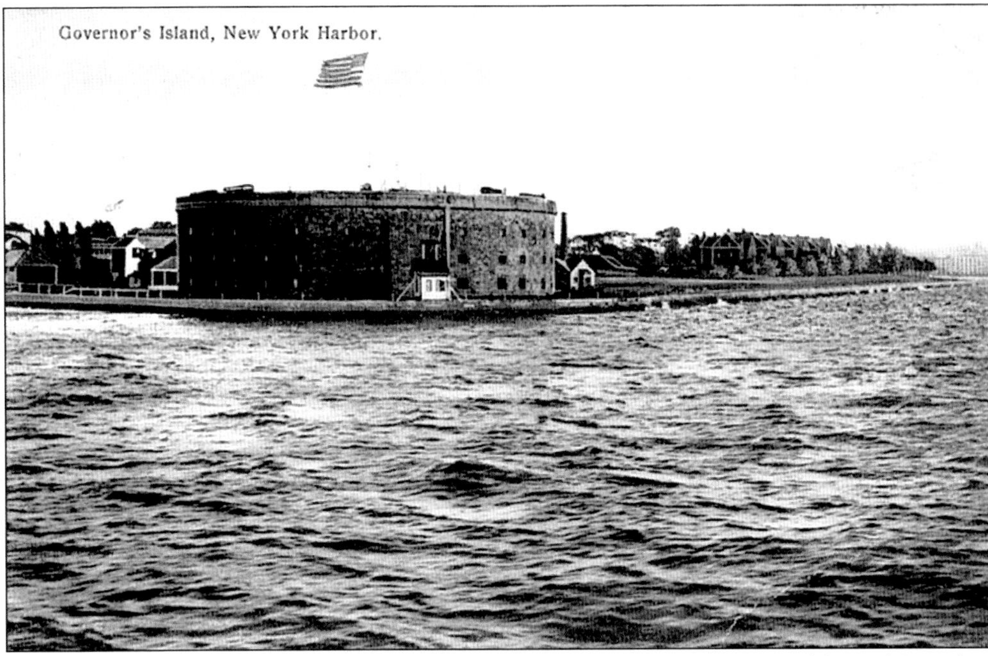

A crematorium was built alongside Castle Williams. Castle Williams was named for Col. Jonathan Williams of the Corps of Engineers. He was a nephew of Benjamin Franklin and the first superintendent of West Point.

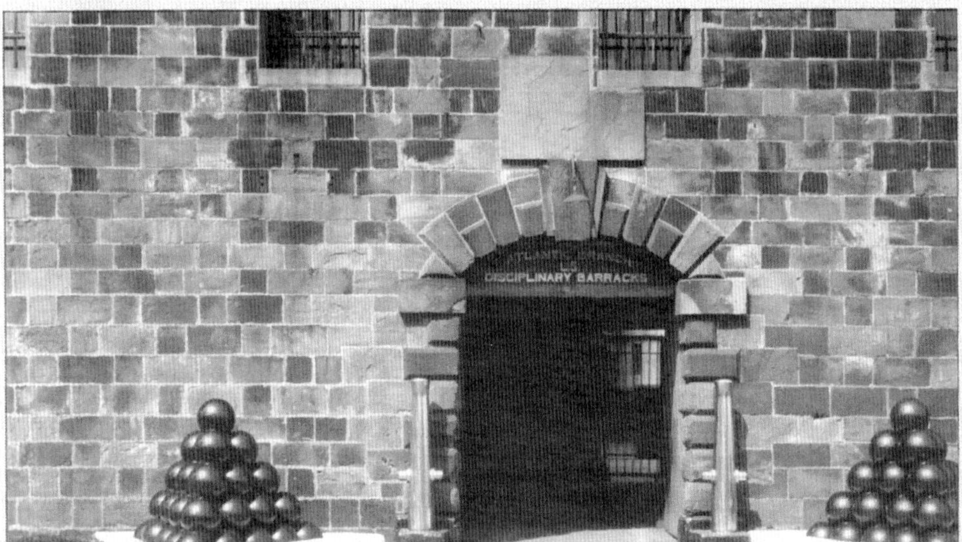

Castle Williams in princely condition

The castle has served as a military prison periodically since its completion in 1811. It became the Atlantic Branch Disciplinary Barracks in 1922. The cannons in the photo now adorn the entrance to the officer's club _(Courtesy of Governors Island Gazette Historical File)_

Castle Williams served as a Confederate prison and later as a disciplinary barracks. Up to 1,500 prisoners were detained at a time with only one successful escape. During this time, a stockade was built around the castle where Confederate prisoners awaiting exchange were kept.

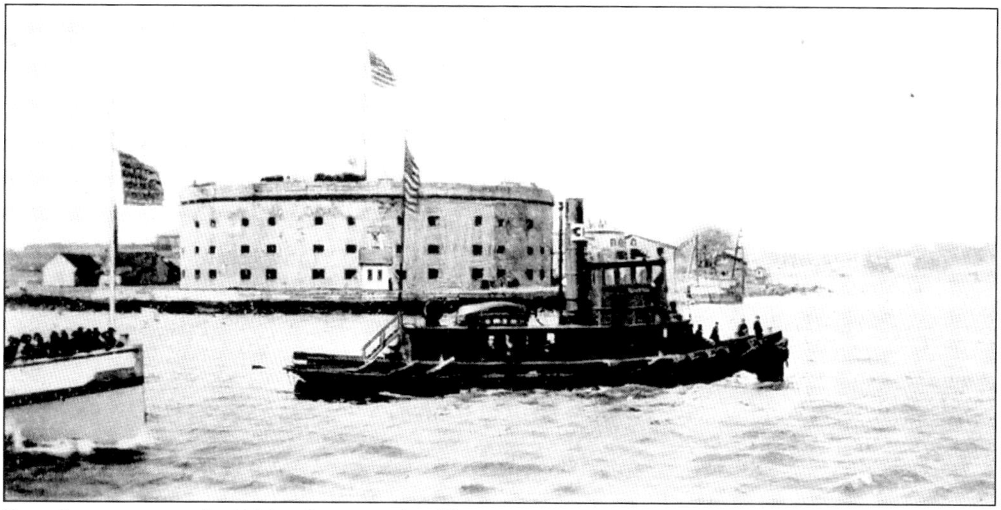

Seen here is an early 1900s photograph of boats passing Castle Williams before the addition of the land extension.

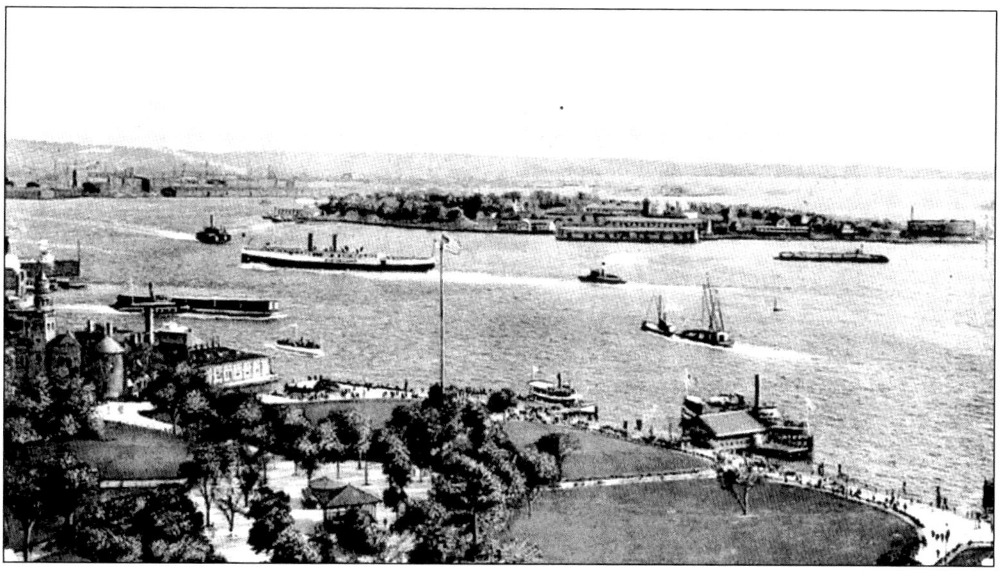

This aerial view is of Battery Park looking toward Governors Island before the extension. In the foreground of the island are Castle Williams and the harbor.

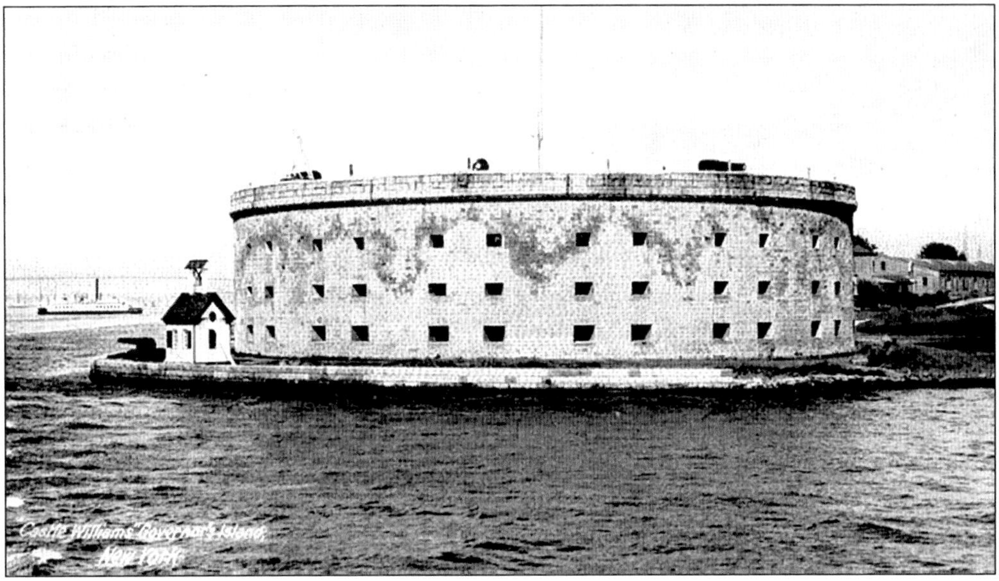

The Lighthouse Service established a fog bell and cannon on the western side of Castle Williams in March 1873. The bell was struck by machinery twice in quick succession at intervals of 20 seconds during foggy weather. The "sunset gun" was fired every morning at sunrise and in the evening at sunset. The evening firing signaled the ships in the harbor to turn on their lights.

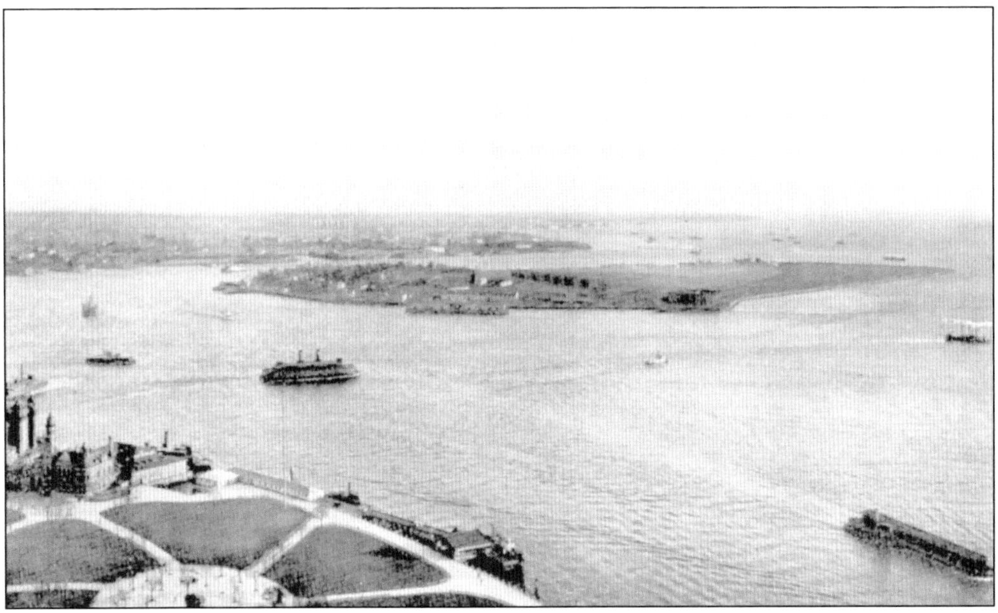

Governors Island and other smaller islands in the area were ceded to the United States Government by an act of the legislature on February 15, 1800. The Sundry Civil Act of 1901 made an appropriation to begin the extension of the island to include an addition of approximately 82 acres. This is an aerial view from Manhattan showing the flat expanse created when the island was increased to 173 acres.

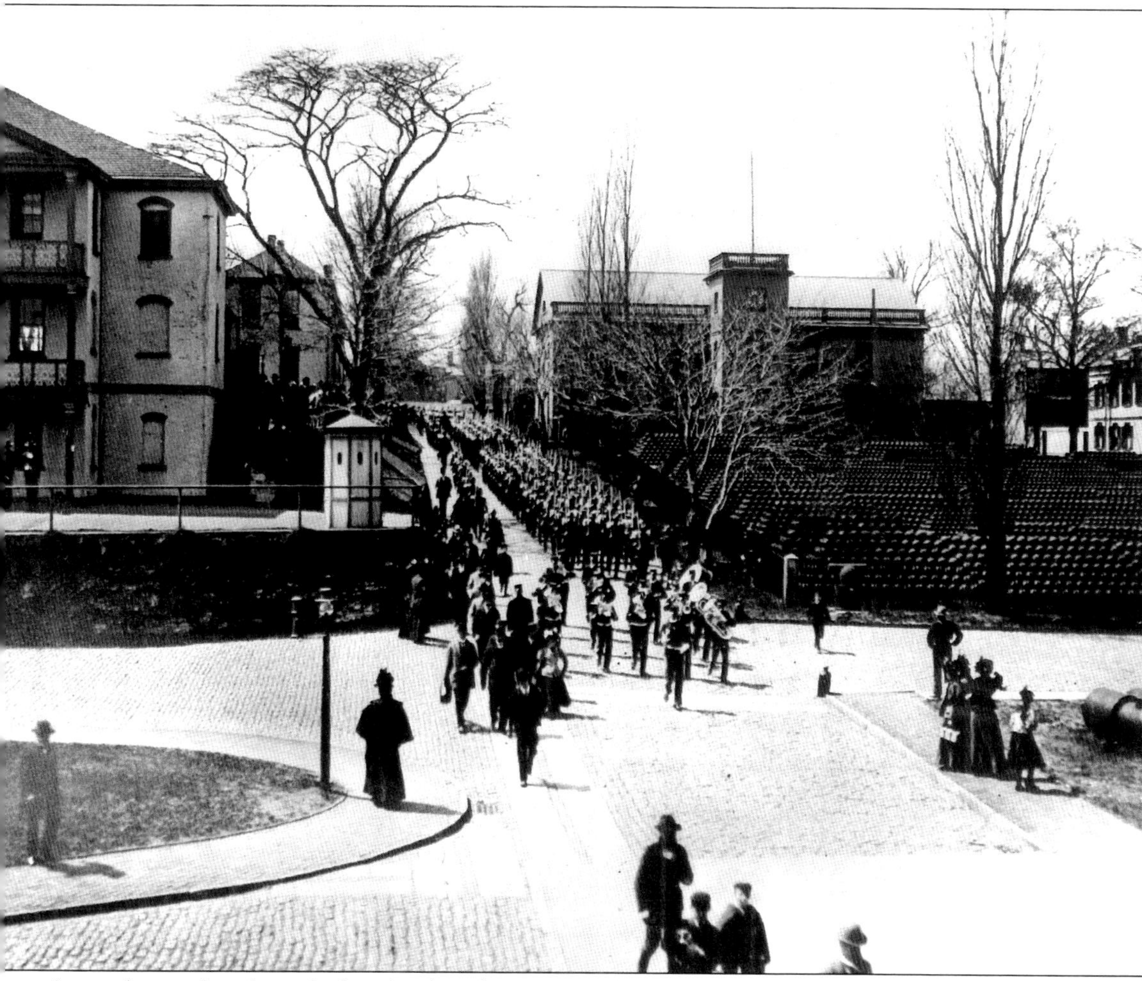

A parade marches through the island in the 1890s. Cobblestone streets lined with cannon balls were the precursor to later paved roads, sidewalks, and curbs.

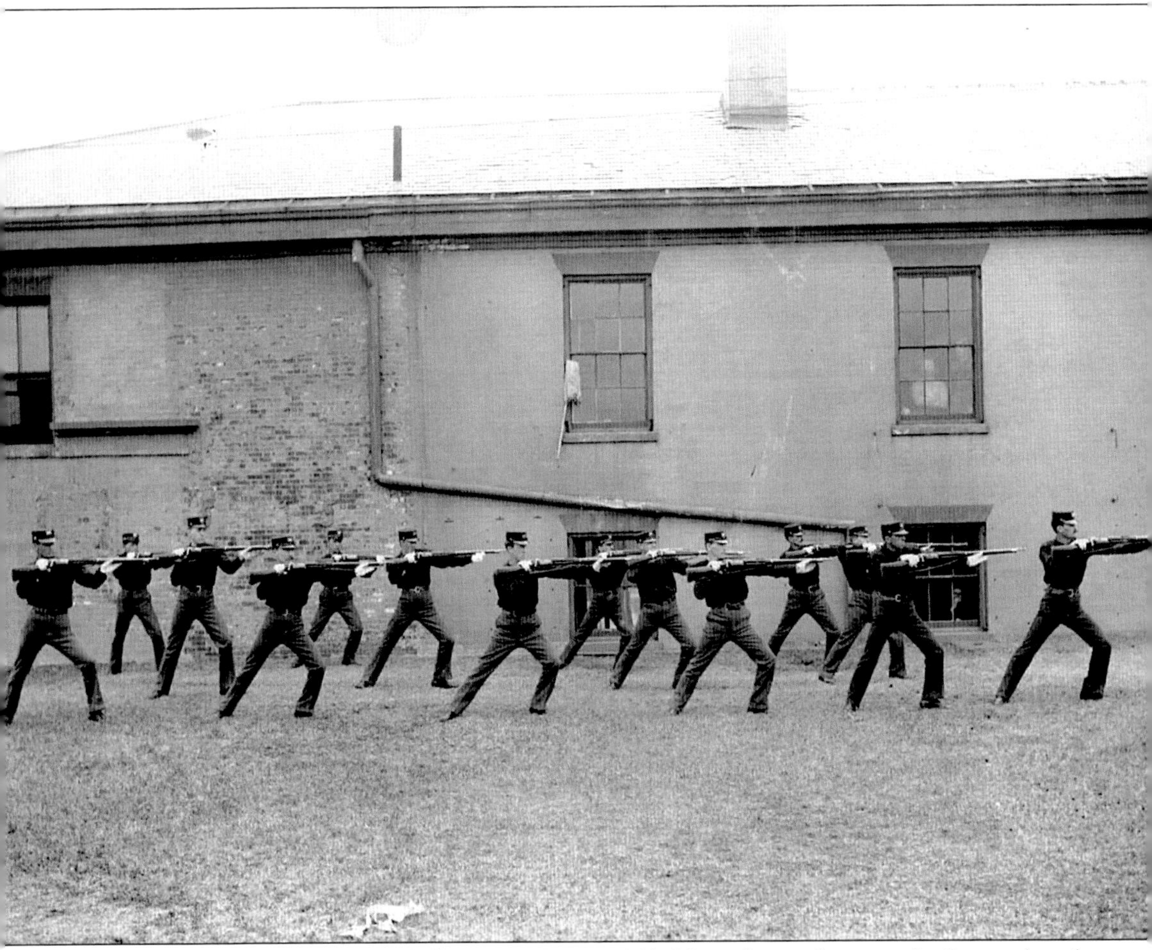

Soldiers are seen practicing drills at Fort Jay in 1902. Note the uniforms and rifles used at the time. (Courtesy of Governors Island National Monument Collection.)

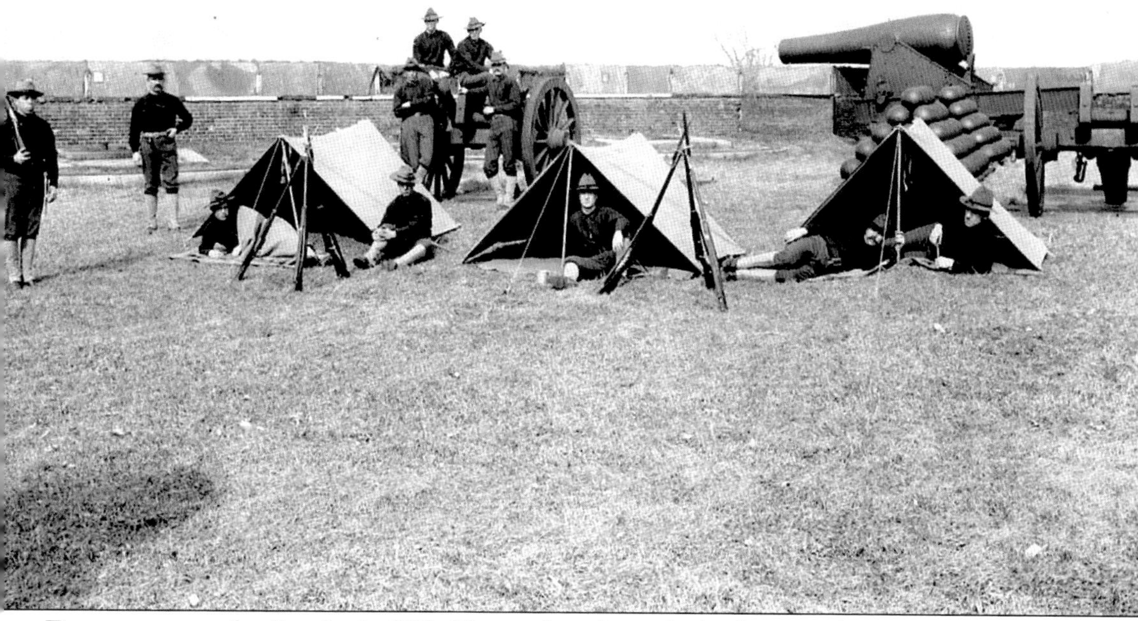

Tents were erected at Fort Jay in 1902. The quadrangle inside the fort was often the site of such encampments. (Courtesy of Governors Island National Monument Collection.)

The Governors Island

Gazette

Mayor's Hotline Page 2 | Housing Issues Page 6 | Sports Page 7

Friday, Sept. 24, 1993 | Your hometown newspaper | Volume 28, No. 38

Lead paint in island homes poses minimal health risks

by LCDR Paul Milligan, CWO3 Frank Libby, and CWO2 Barry Tate

Pollution index highest this summer
Asbestos keeps schools closed
Lead paint found in GI housing

The headlines go on and on, drastically raising our concerns for the health of our families.

Lead-bearing paint is found in the majority of Governors Island housing units, with the exception of the apartments in Liberty Village and New Brick Village. The older units were all painted with lead-bearing paints at some time in the past, the paint applied primarily to the wood trim around the exterior doors and window frames. Some of the exterior surfaces of the wooden homes and the exterior trim are also affected; however, this situation is gradually changing with ongoing renovations in progress.

The cost to remove all traces of this paint at one time is prohibitive as it entails complete removal of sheetrock and other surfaces on which the paint was originally placed. Furthermore, it is not necessary for maintaining the health and well-being of our residents.

The circumstances are not as bleak as the headlines might make them appear. Proper maintenance and repair techniques will allow residents to coexist with this paint without shutting down the housing on Governors Island for complete renovations.

The accepted practice is to scrape flaking areas back to where the paint firmly adheres to the surface, collect the chips for proper disposal, and, if required patch the damaged area with suitable patching material. The repaired area can then be repainted with a non-lead-bearing paint such as latex, latex enamel or oil-base paint.

Practically speaking, lead paint only poses a problem when it is ingested into the body. This normally occurs when a person eats paint chips that have flaked loose from the surface they are supposed to be covering. The principle concern is with infants and toddlers who, in their inquisitive way, place things like paint chips in their mouths.

Overall, lead-bearing paint poses minimal health risks to our residents. CWO3 Frank Libby of the Environmental Safety Office and LTJG Sam Bryant, Environmental Engineer at Facilities Engineering Division, are developing a comprehensive lead-abatement program for Governors Island.

Weekly inspections of facilities and close liaison with the housing inspection staff will immediately identify areas of concern and will initiate appropriate corrective action.

The following steps may be taken to further minimize any perceived risk:

- Clean/inspect your quarters regularly, paying particular attention to the interior trim work and other areas that show signs of paint deterioration.
- Sweep up loose paint chips that are flaking from the walls and bag them separately. Call the Environmental Safety Office at 668-4974 for direction on proper disposal.
- Contact the work reception desk at Facilities Engineering Division at 668-7373 to place a work order for repair of the deteriorating area.
- If you believe a member of your family has ingested lead-bearing paint, contact the Health Services Clinic at 668-7243.

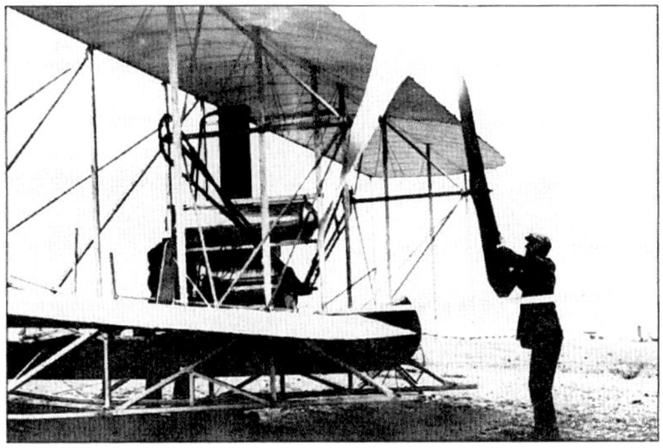

Wilbur Wright starts his airplane on Governors Island.

Aviation history made here 84 years ago

Wilbur Wright makes first flight over U.S. water

by Sue Glen
Contributing Writer

Looking at the playground between the Star of the Sea Chapel and the Child Development Center, one would not realize the history that occurred there 84 years ago. Between Sept. 25 and Oct. 9, 1909, there were several airplane flights of great significance launched from two airplane sheds constructed at that site.

The Hudson-Fulton Celebration was occurring in the 'Big Apple,' and a contract had been made with both Wilbur Wright and Glenn Curtiss for several flights to be made in and around the city. Aviation was just beginning and the airplane was still an unseen marvel.

For additional photos see Page 4

Maj. Gen. Leonard Wood, Army commander of the Department of the East, had given permission for the use of 96 acres on Governors Island for the event. This acreage was part of the area recently filled and leveled with dirt and rocks from the construction of the new subway system and the dredging of Buttermilk Channel.

The Army had also agreed to establish a signaling system from the island to the Singer Building at 149 Broadway by which the public would be notified of the flights. These signals were then transmitted to the Met Life Building at 1 Madison Ave., the New York Times Building, the Brooklyn Eagle Building, the Williamsburg Bridge and the Queensborough Bridge. Signal bombs were also exploded to announce the flights.

Wilbur Wright had his new machine on Governors Island on Sept. 25 and it was properly 'tuned up' to begin his contract. With weather being ideal on Sept. 29, he gave the starting signal at 9:15 a.m. and launched, circling the launching area twice, then flying east to Buttermilk Channel, then to the northern end of the island, then westward and back to his starting point. This flight took seven minutes to cover about two miles and was met by the whistles of tugs, steamboats and factories. A second flight of five-minute duration began at 10:18 a.m. and went straight toward the Statue of Liberty over the departing ocean liner Lusitania and after circling Bedloe's Island returned to land. These were the first flights over American water.

At 5:19 that afternoon he made his third flight, which lasted 12 minutes.

A fourth and most spectacular flight occurred Oct. 4. After attaching American flags to the wing tips and the air-tight canoe that was lashed to the airplane, Wilbur Wright launched his airplane down the monorail at 9:53 a.m. With his life preserver near his feet, he headed straight for the water. Once in the air, he passed west of Castle William, about 25 feet higher, and up over the Hudson River, north toward Grant's Tomb. He reached the tomb at 10:13 a.m., climbed another 25 feet, and turned about 1000 feet north toward the New Jersey shore. Below him a fleet of international war vessels blew their whistles as he began the return flight to Governors Island.

Upon landing at 10:26 a.m., he had been in the air for 33 minutes, 33 seconds and had flown for 20 miles. This was one of the most perilous flights of the time at an average speed of 36 miles per hour and average height of 200 feet.

That afternoon, after nine attempts to restart the plane for another flight, there was an explosion as a cylinder head blew out and ended the flights in New York.

Glenn Curtis arrived Sept. 28 and at 7 a.m. on the Sept. 29 flew 300 yards in 26 seconds but was only observed by a personal friend and one officer on the island. On Oct. 3 he made another attempt and flew at an altitude of 60 to 100 feet toward the Statue of Liberty but rather than going out over the water, he turned in a semicircle and as the engine quit he landed. His plane was recrated to be shipped to St. Louis the following morning.

Wilbur and Orville Wright came to Governors Island for the Hudson-Fulton Celebration and flew from the island using the new flat land that had been added at the southern end. Wilbur Wright is shown starting his airplane on Governors Island. (Courtesy of the Gazette historical file.)

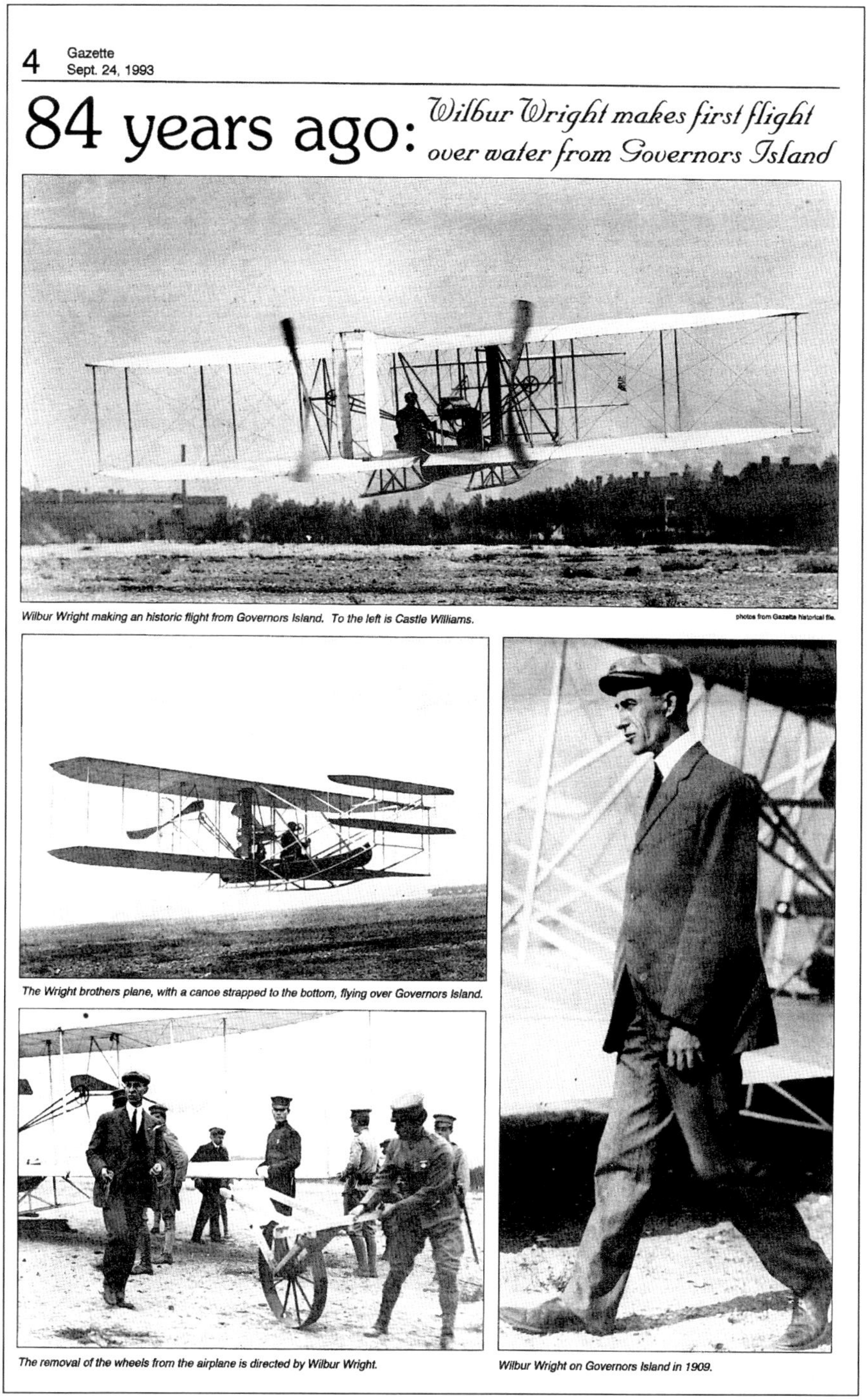

4 Gazette
Sept. 24, 1993

84 years ago: *Wilbur Wright makes first flight over water from Governors Island*

Wilbur Wright making an historic flight from Governors Island. To the left is Castle Williams.

photos from Gazette historical file.

The Wright brothers plane, with a canoe strapped to the bottom, flying over Governors Island.

The removal of the wheels from the airplane is directed by Wilbur Wright.

Wilbur Wright on Governors Island in 1909.

Wilbur Wright makes his historic flight from Governors Island (above). To the left is Castle Williams. The Wright brothers made a total of five flights from the island during the Hudson-Fulton Celebration. Their airplane (middle) is shown with a canoe strapped to the bottom, flying over Governors Island. Wilbur Wright (lower left) directs the removal of the wheels from the plane and (lower right) walks on the island. (Courtesy of the Gazette historical file.)

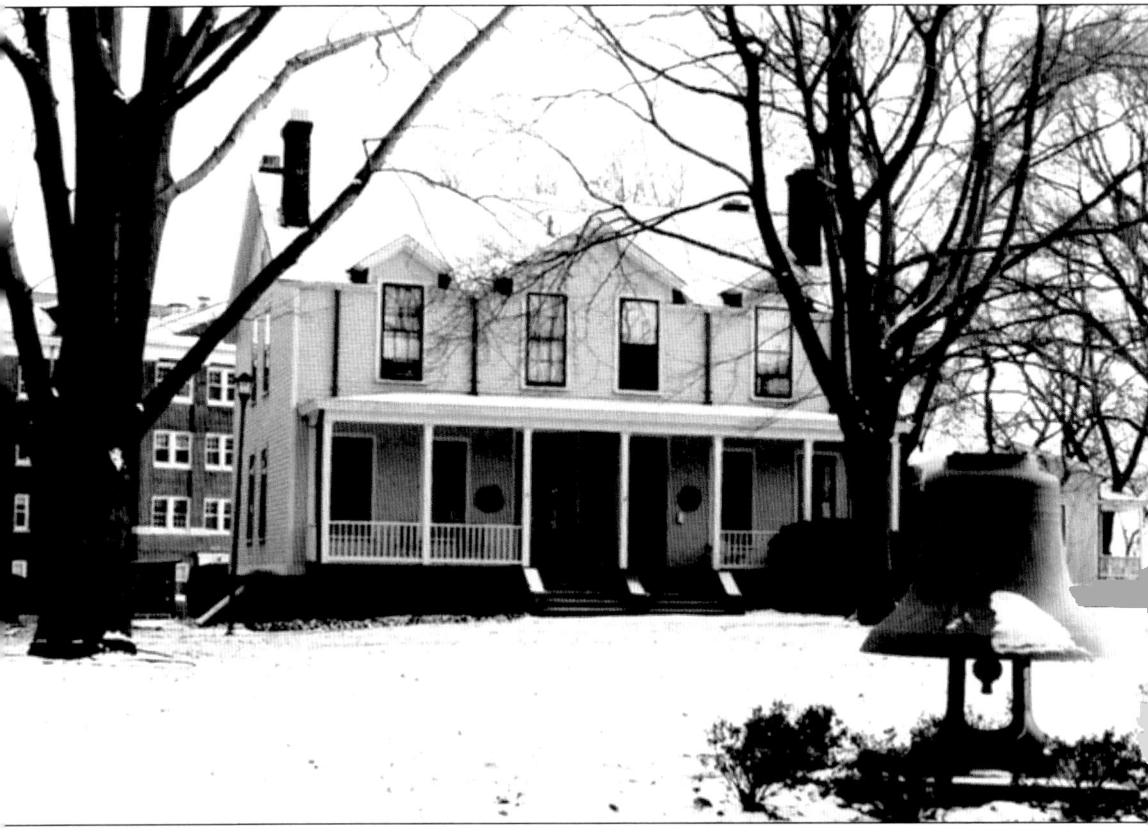

The blizzard of 1888 washed the first bell into the harbor. When the second bell was later replaced by a horn and light, it was erected and placed in Nolan Park. This bell was dated 1883.

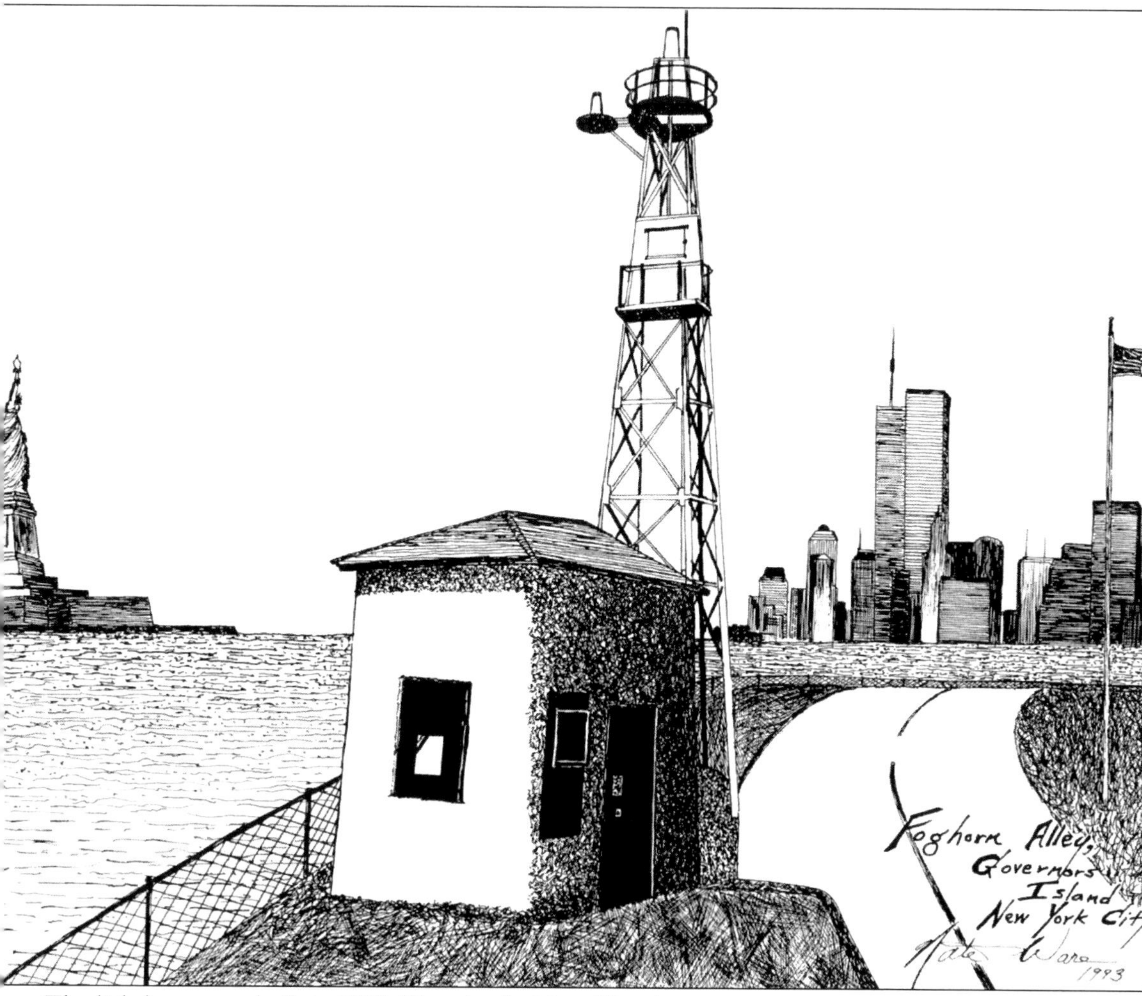

The lighthouse was built in 1910. (Drawing by Nate Ware.)

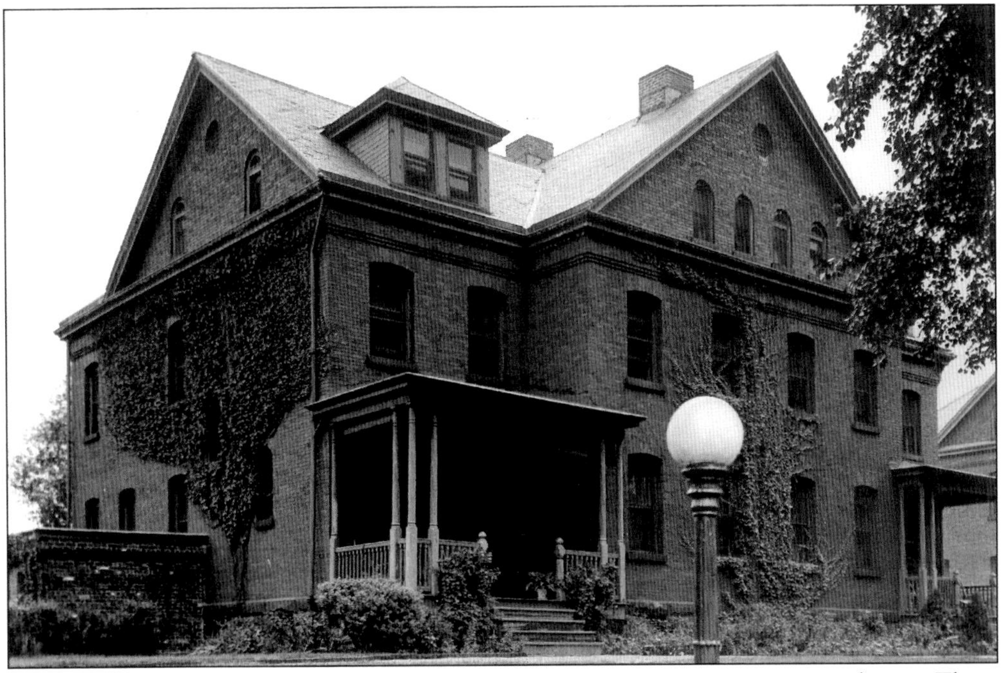

Additional houses were built on the western side of the island between 1893 and 1894. These one- and two-family residences were brick. This address was building 405.

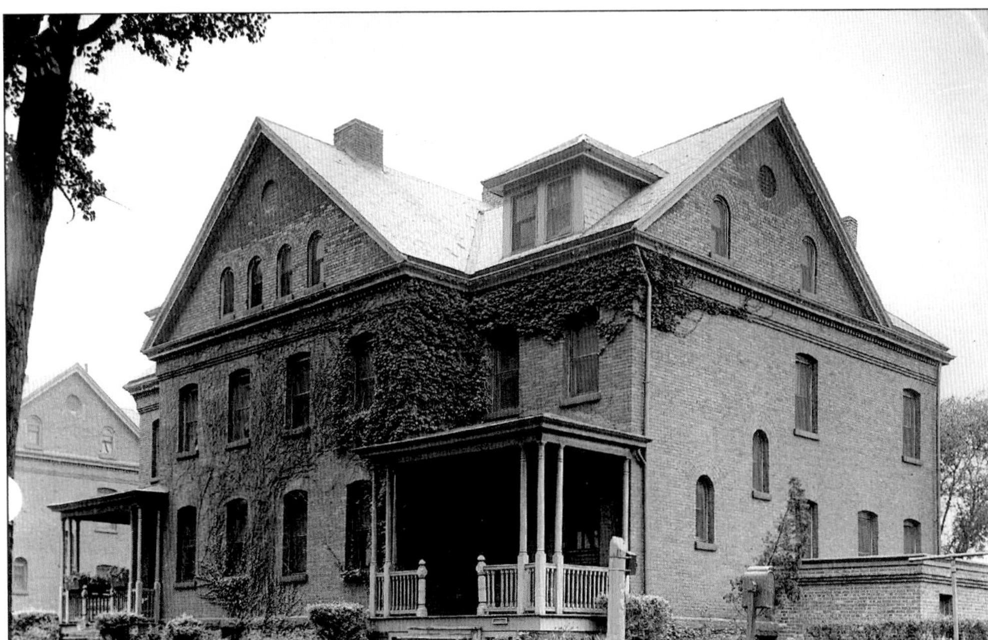

Building 406, another of the new officer's residences, was the next house on the row. The design for these residences came from the Office of the Quartermaster, U.S. Army.

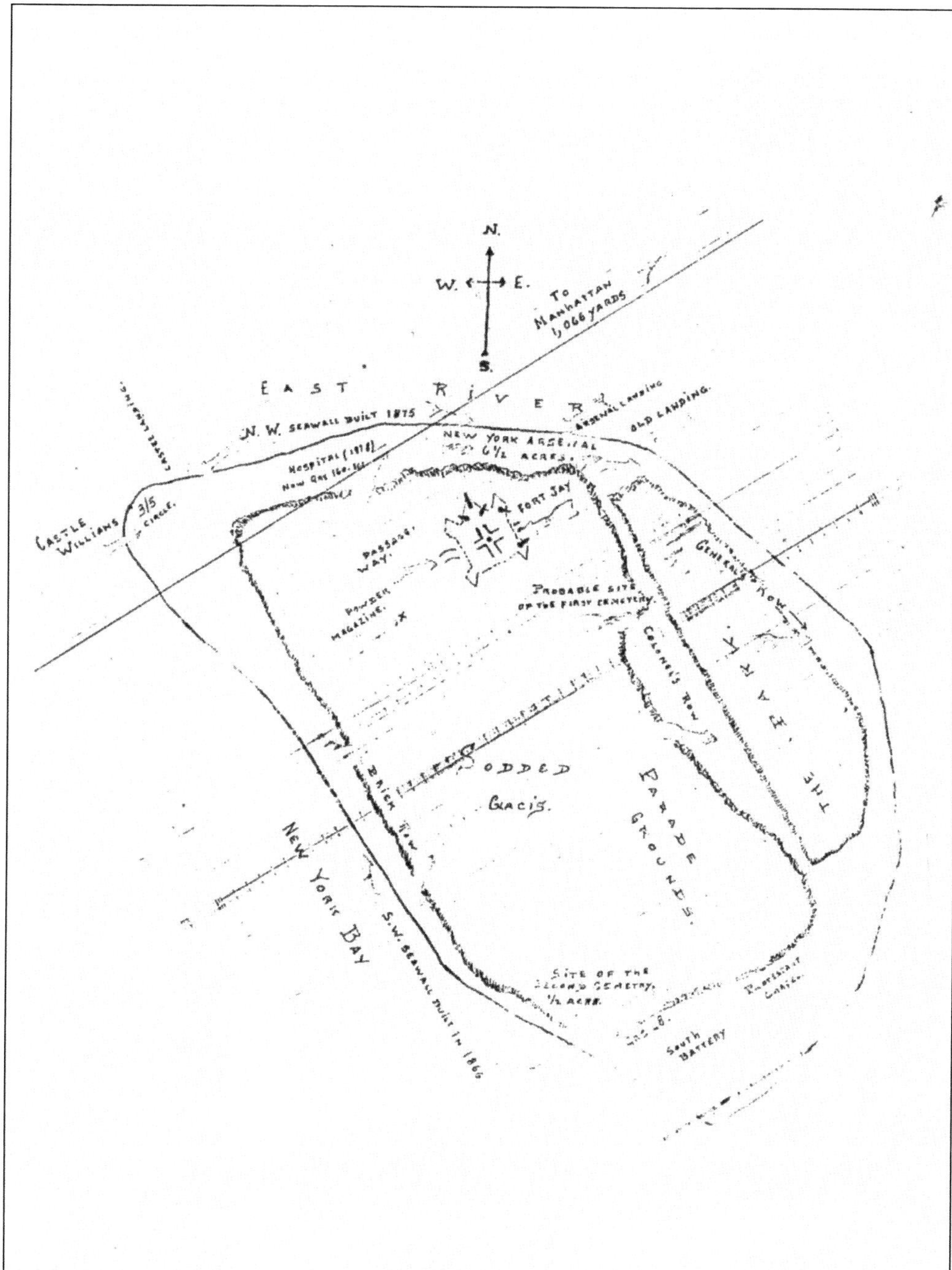

This map of Governors Island shows the island before it was enlarged. By 1900, the island had shrunk to about 70 acres. Dirt and rock from the building of the No. 4 subway tunnel was used to increase the island to its present size.

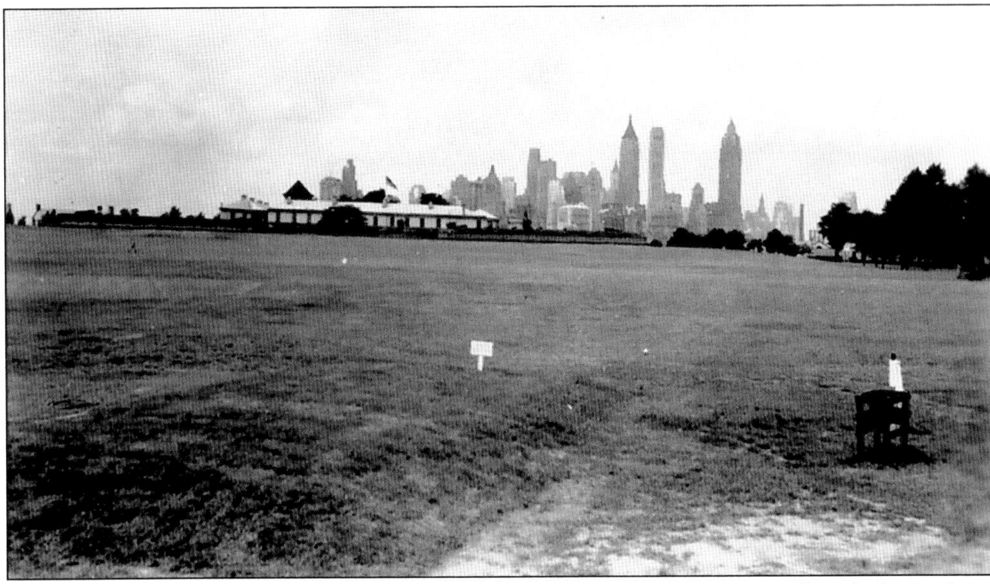

The nine-hole golf course, established in 1903 behind Fort Jay, was originally 3 holes and was also known as the Quadrangle. It had been used as a polo field in 1936 and was the probable site of the race course in the late 1700s.

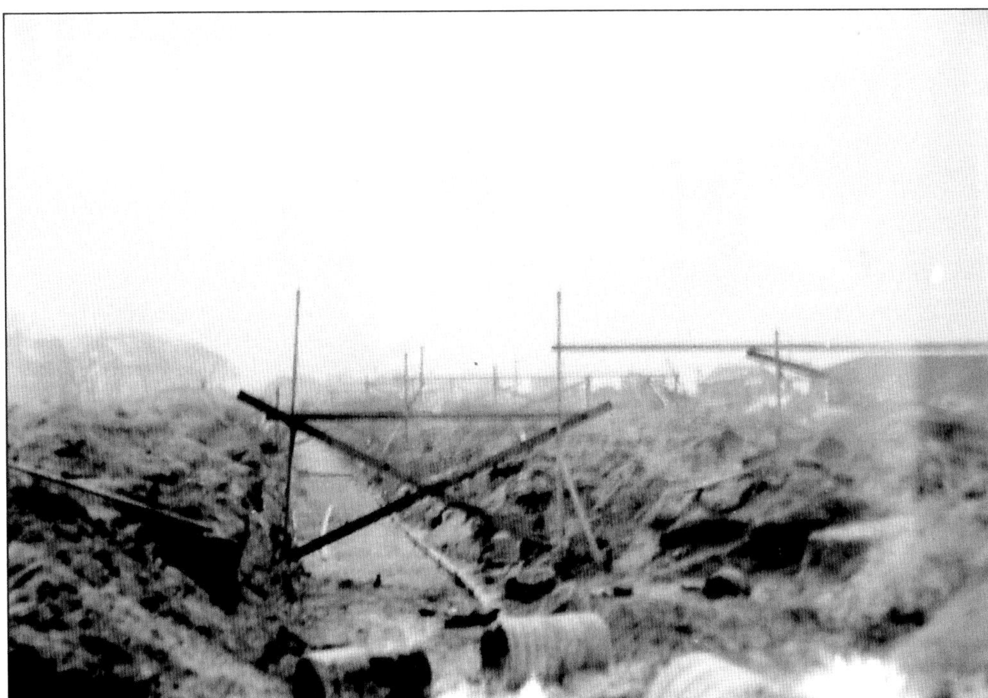

Construction of salt water mains across the island in 1910 was done for use in case of fire.

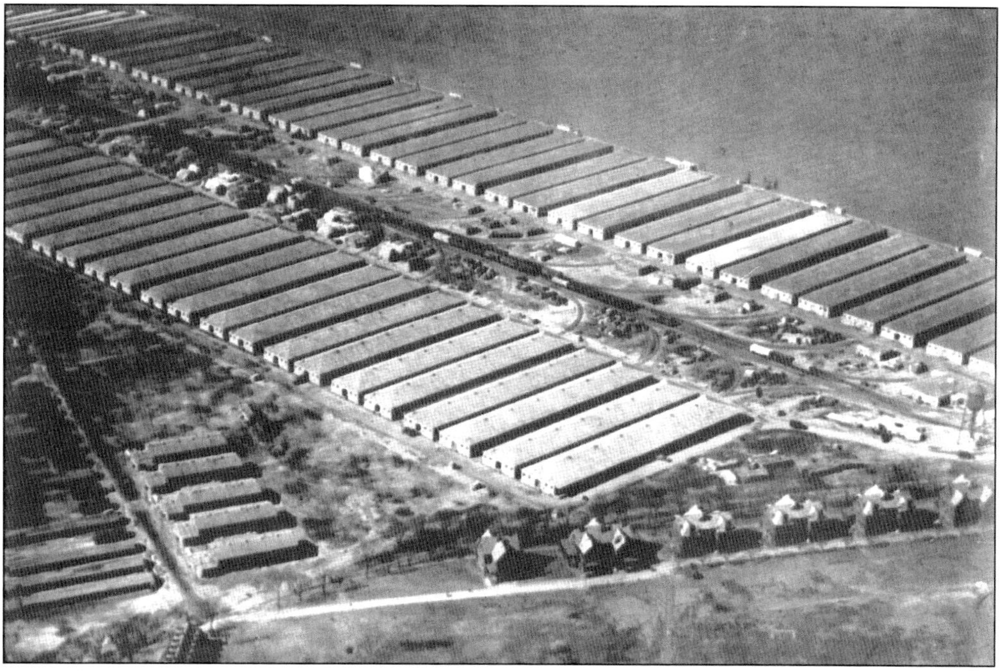

A total of 70 huge warehouses, a railroad, and five additional miles of vehicle roads were constructed as World War I broke out.

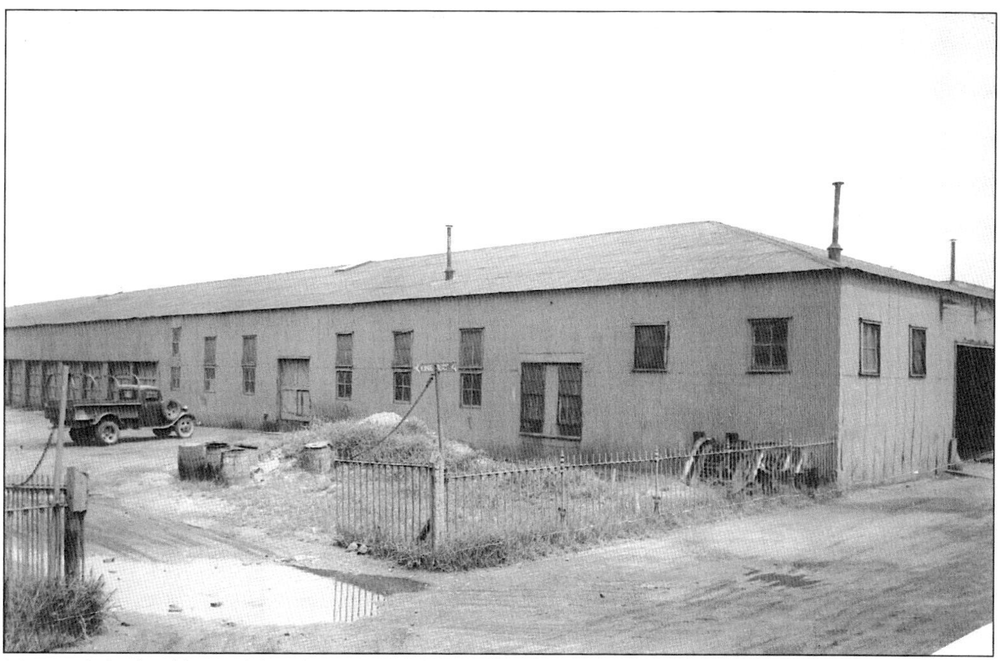

Many of the buildings, like this one, no longer exist.

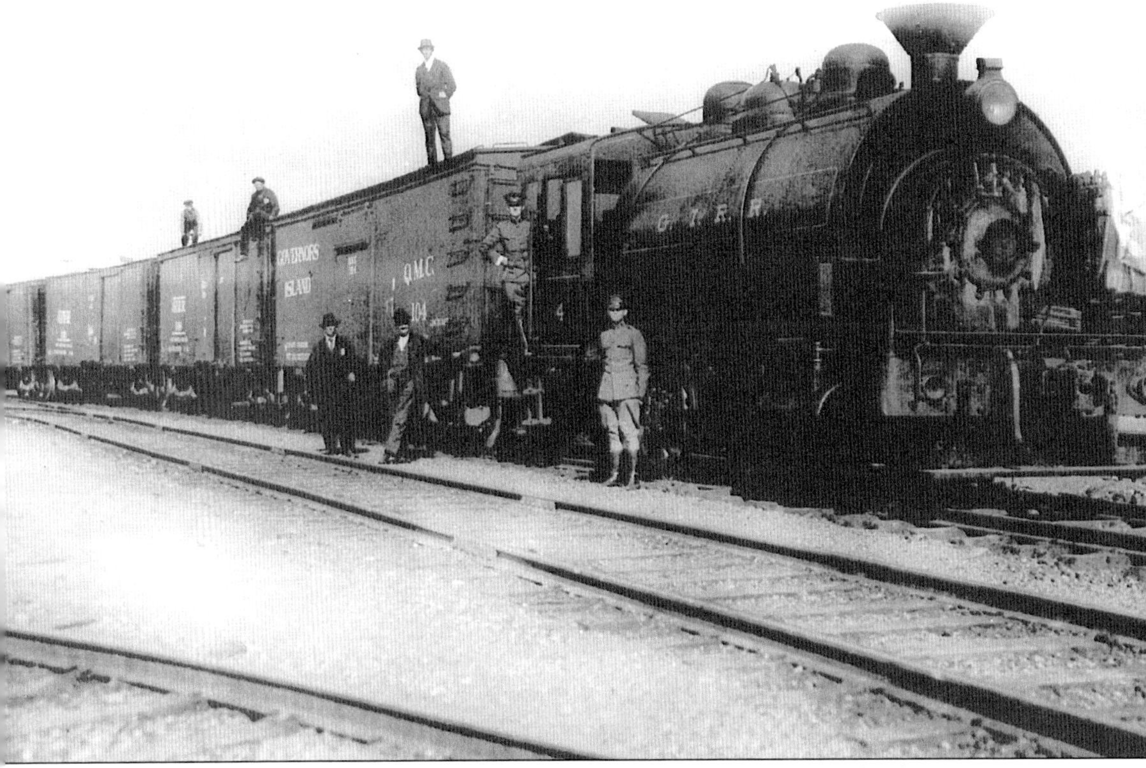

This steam locomotive was in use on the island's railroad. Governors Island was an important embarkation point for troops and supplies for the war. Known as the Governors Island Railroad, it was one of the world's shortest railroads at only eight miles in length.

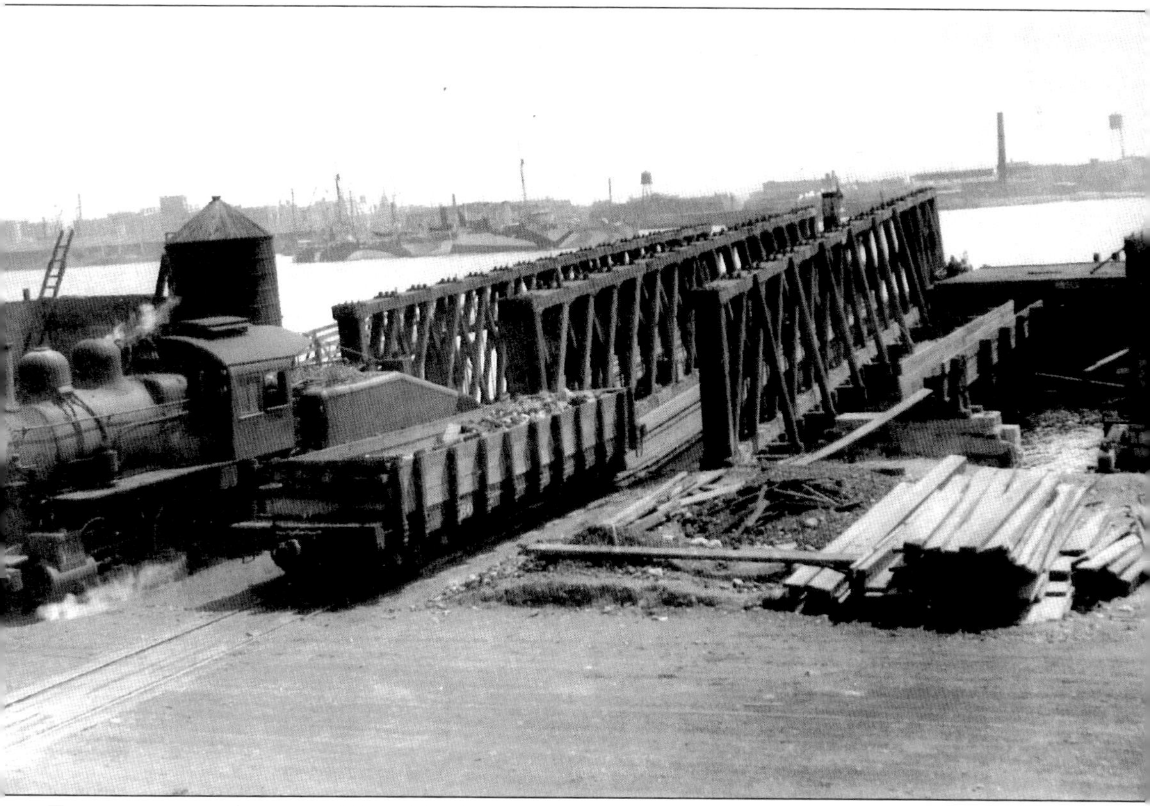

Train cars were taken to and from Manhattan by barge.

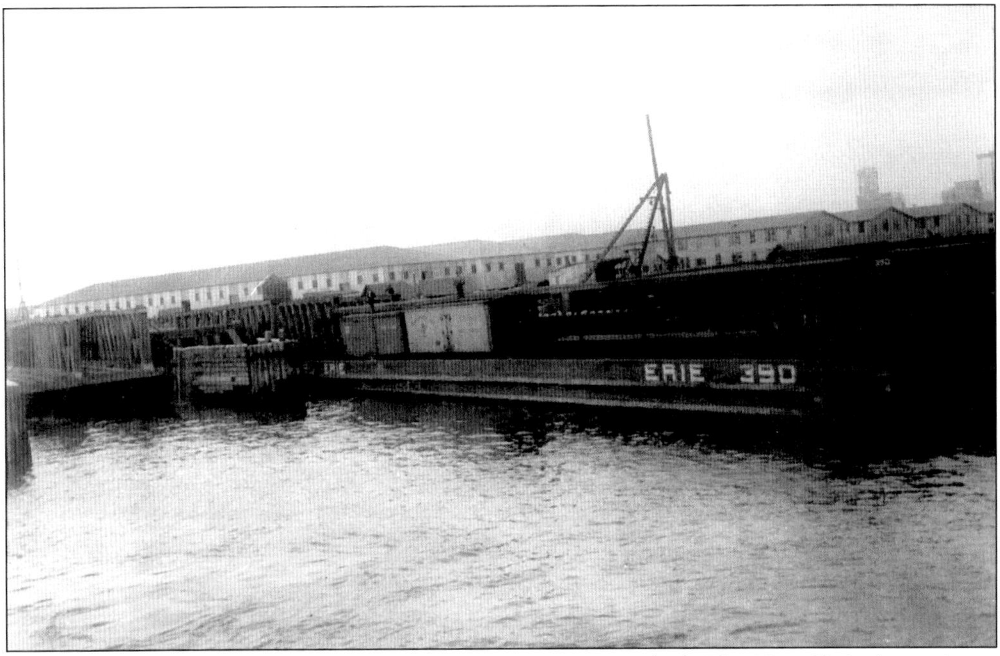

Barges of train cars filled with war material kept troops supplied. The New York Arsenal was located on the island during this time.

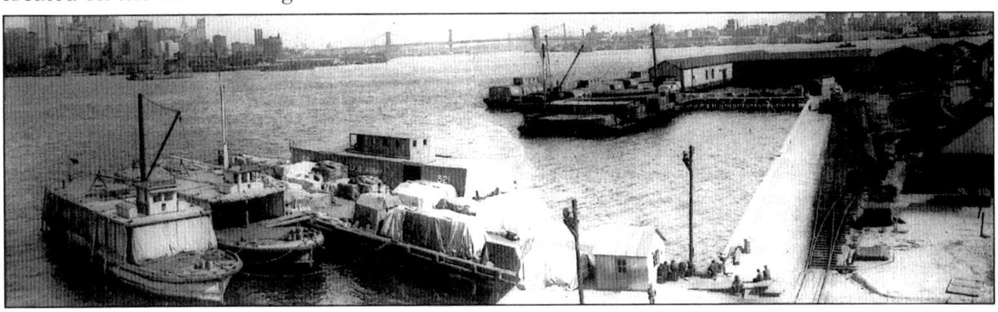

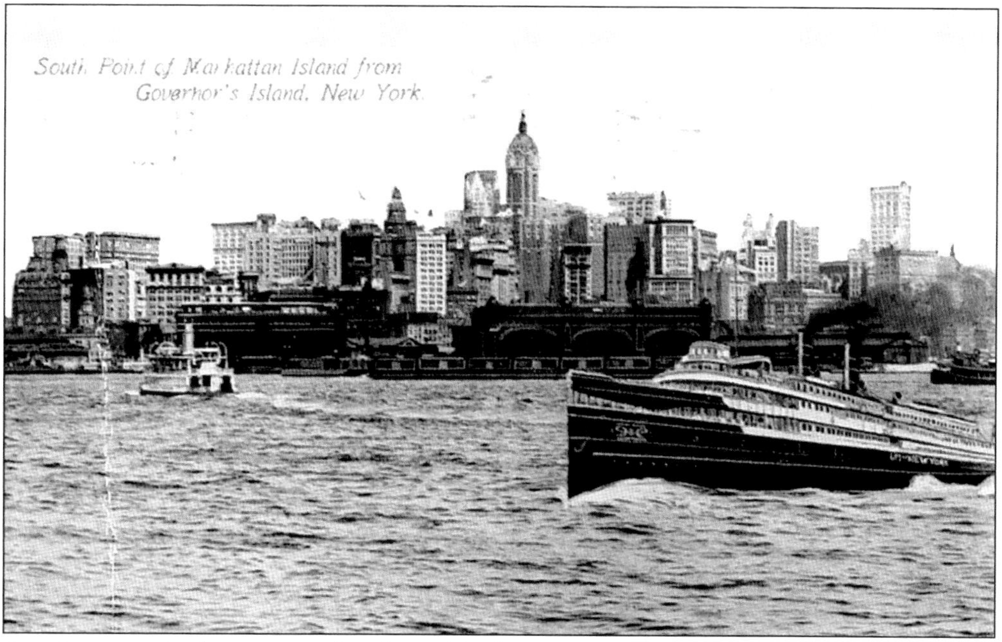

A train passes the ferry terminal on lower Manhattan.

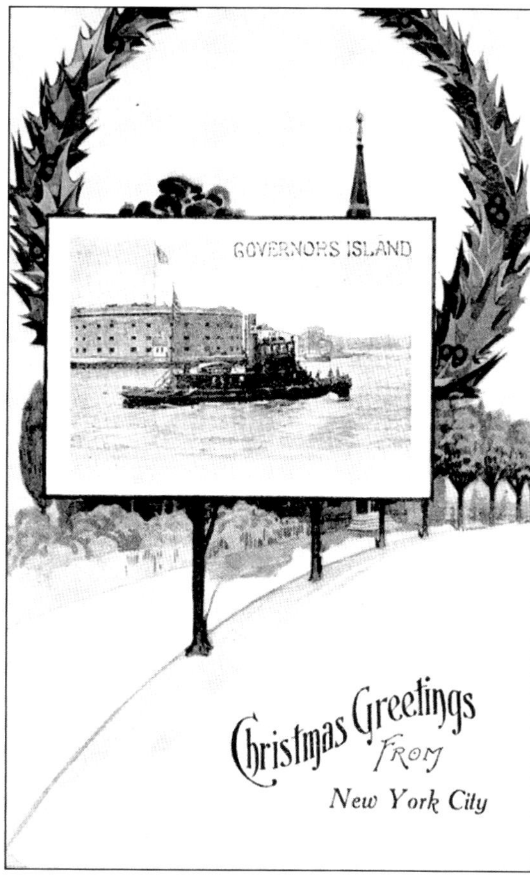

Castle Williams appeared on Christmas cards during World War I.

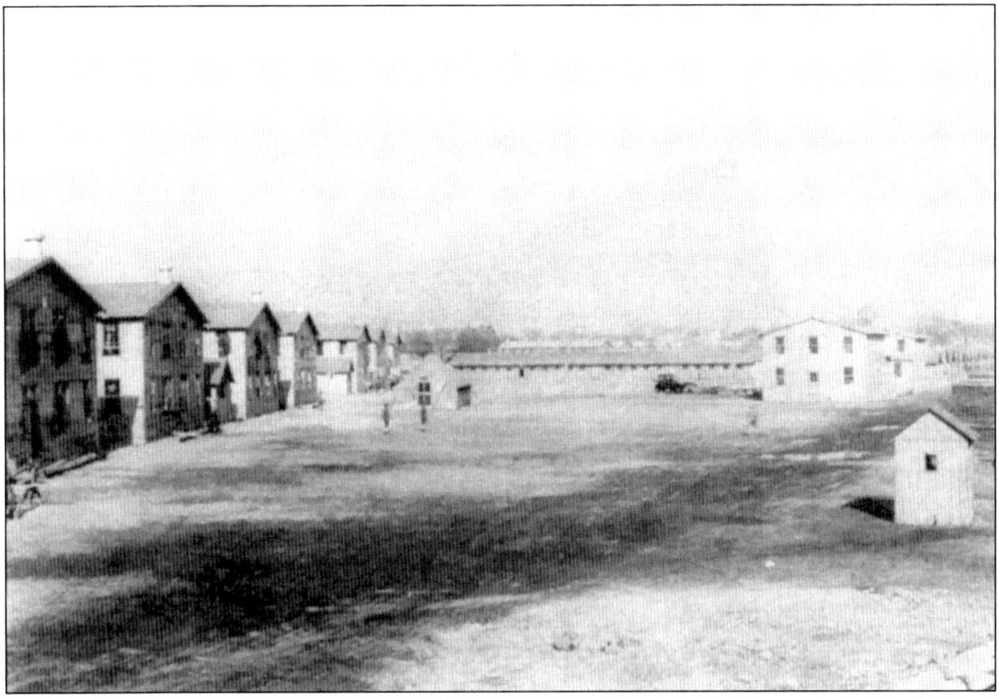

The treeless addition gave rise to many wooden structures that were used during both World War I and World War II, as the various Army units came and left the island. (U.S. Army photograph.)

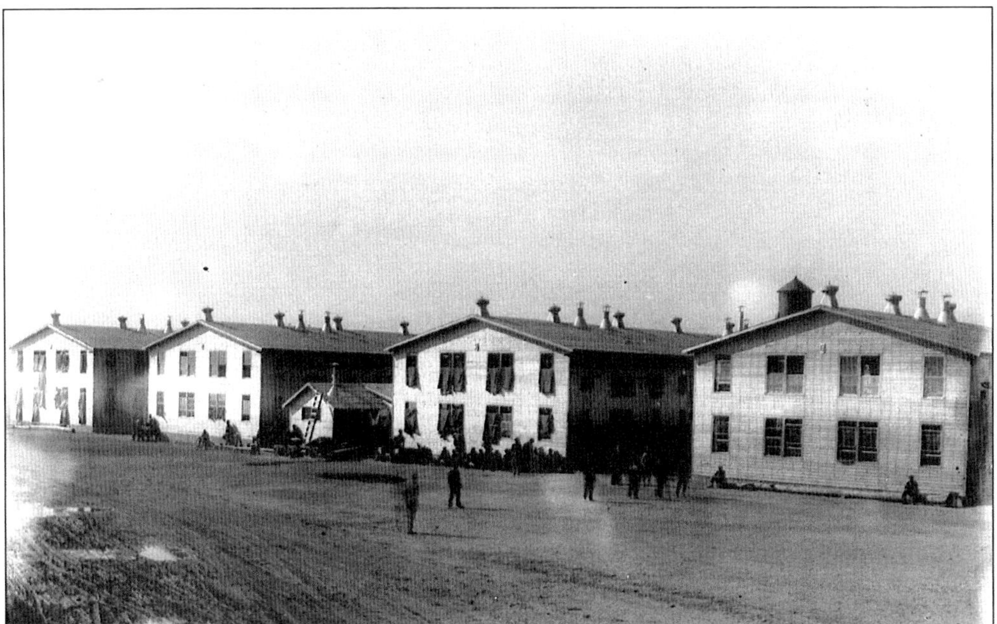

More barracks were erected to house the battalion of Infantry and other troops on the island. These buildings are no longer standing.

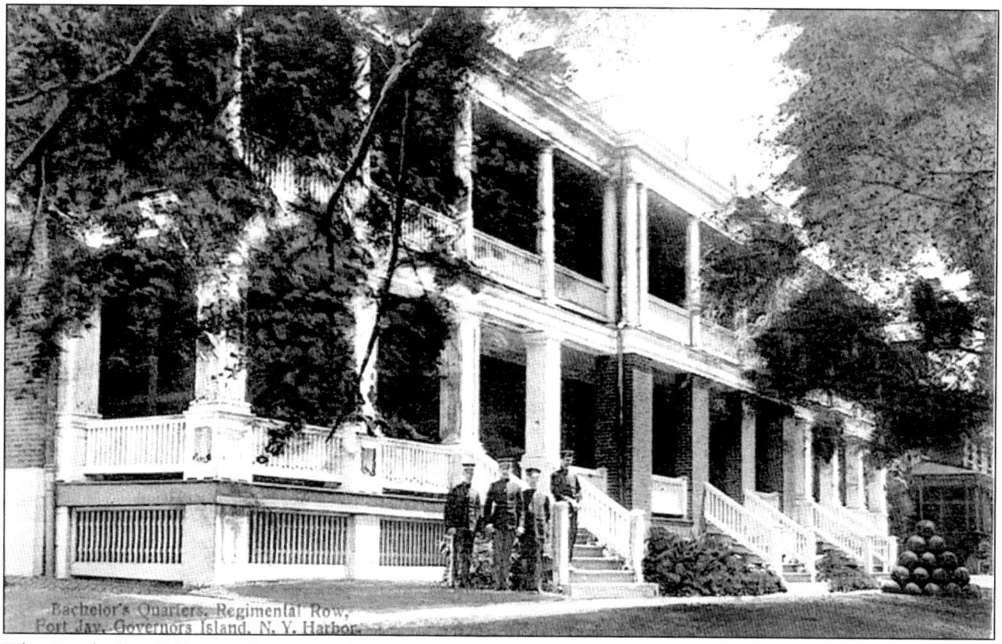

The Bachelor Officers' Quarters, known as Regimental Row, was built between Castle Williams and Fort Jay between 1907 and 1910.

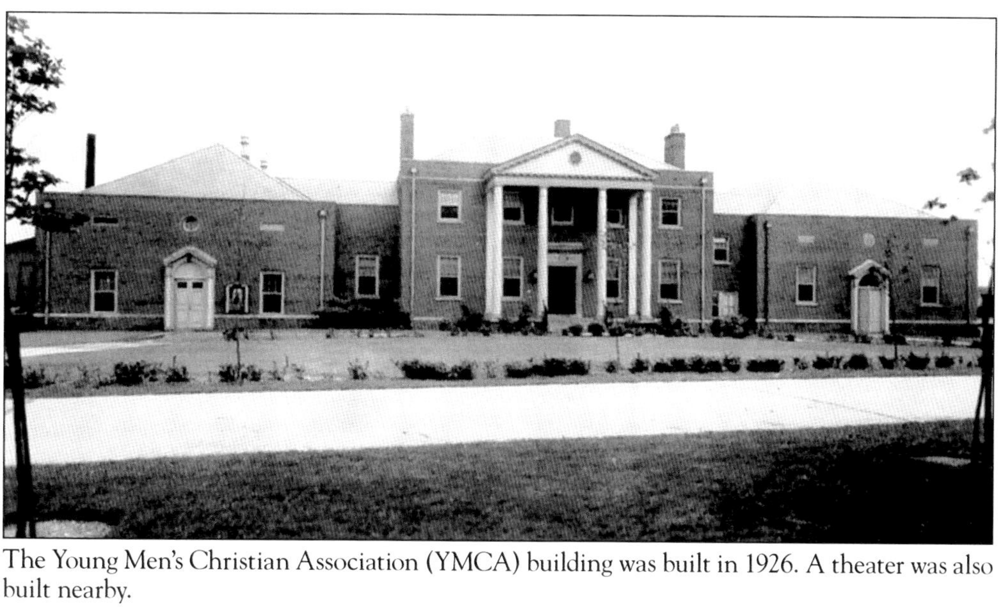

The Young Men's Christian Association (YMCA) building was built in 1926. A theater was also built nearby.

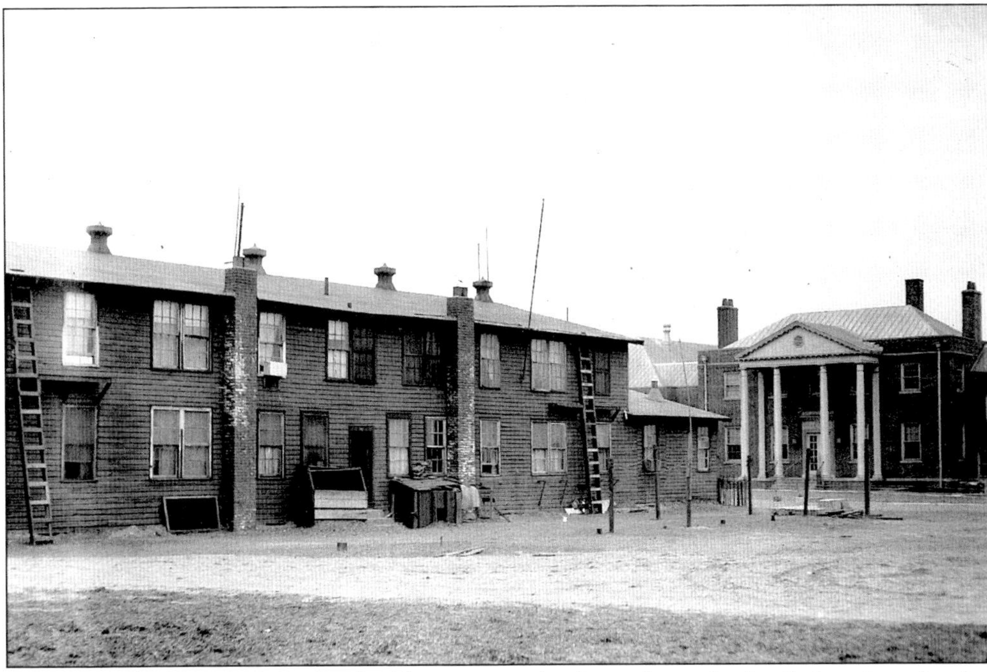

This is another group of wooden buildings, erected as barracks or for family housing, that has long since disappeared. Building 124 was near the YMCA. (U.S. Army photograph.)

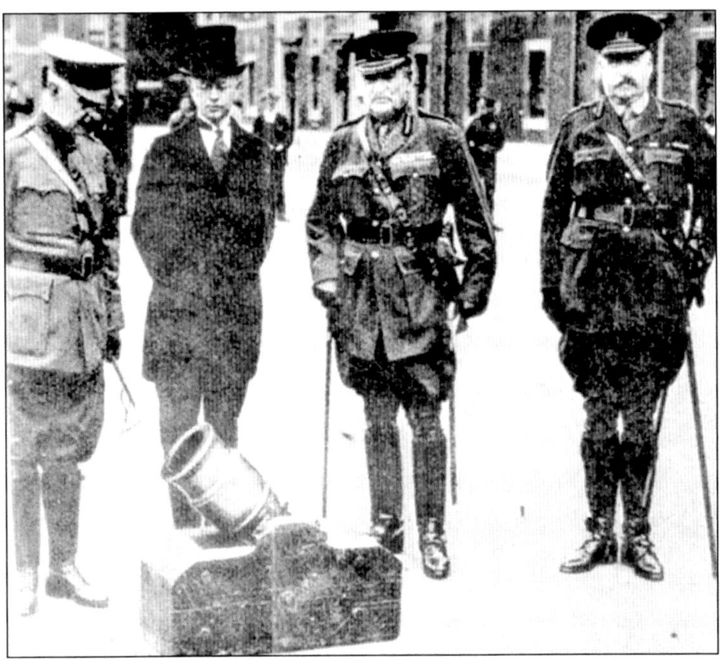

In 1921, to reciprocate the receipt of many banners from the British, which were hung in St. Cornelius chapel, the presentation of a Coehorn mortar, one of two remaining from when the island was a depot for the Royal Americans, was made to the British Regiment. Shown here from left to right are Chaplain Edmund Banks Smith, Secretary Thurston of the American Embassy, Lt. Gen. Sir Edward Hutton, and Lt. Gen. Sir W. Pitcairn Campbell, with the mortar.

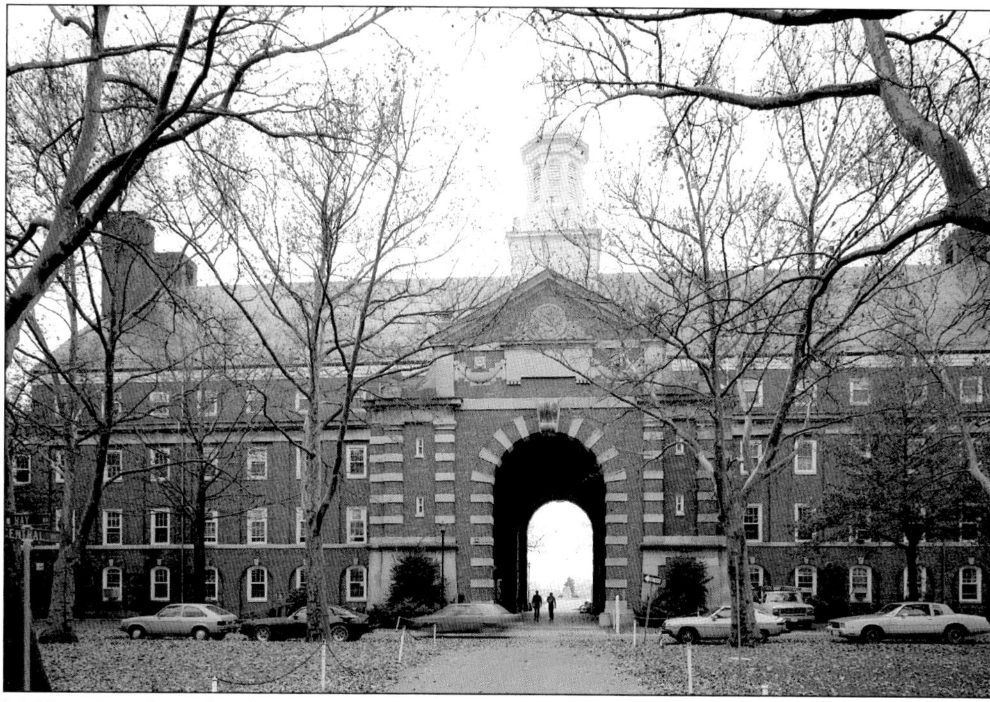

McKim, Meade and White designed building 100 in the early 1930s. It was designed to house the entire 16th Infantry Regiment, "New York's Own." It was later called Liggett Hall and renumbered as building 400. (Courtesy of John T. Lowe, National Park Service/Historic American Building Survey.)

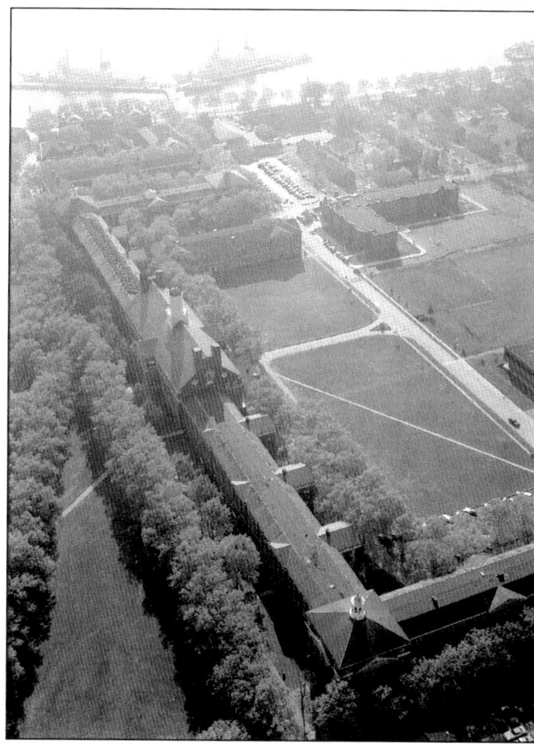

This aerial view shows the size of building 100 upon completion. (Courtesy of John T. Lowe, National Park Service/ Historic American Building Survey.)

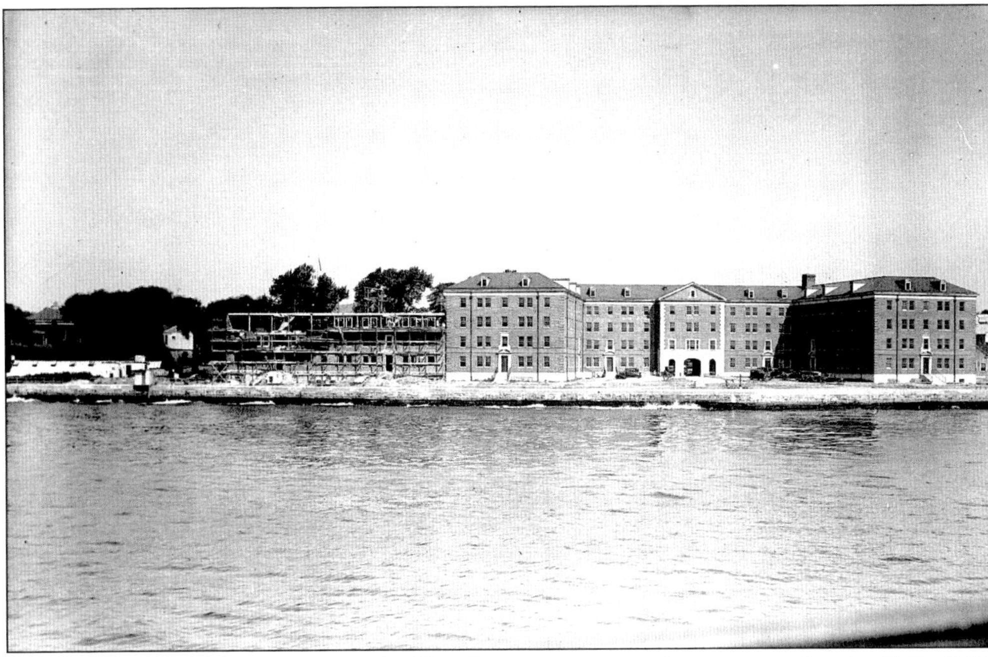

This building for noncommissioned officers' quarters was under construction in 1931. (U.S. Army photograph.)

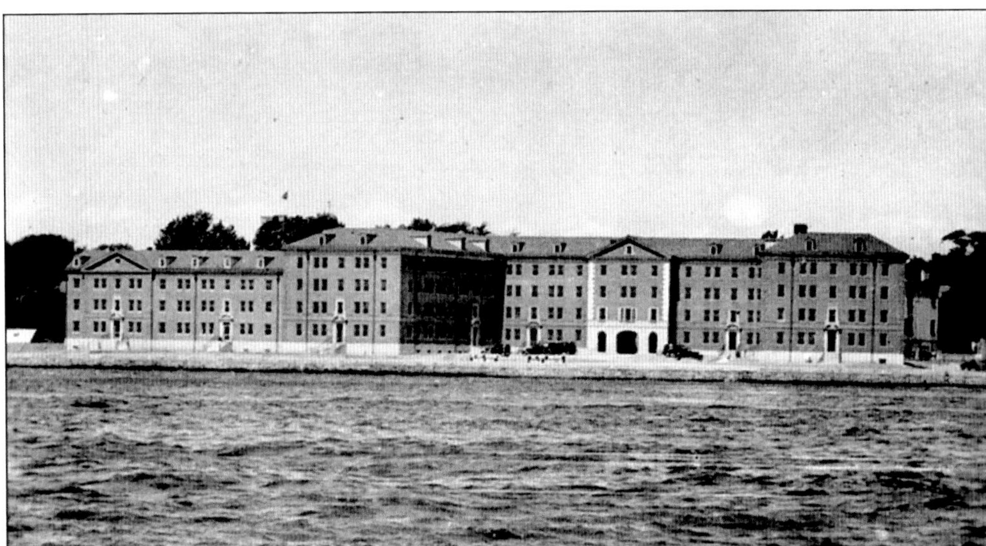

The building following completion is shown here. Built on the eastern side of the island, it can be seen from the Brooklyn waterfront.

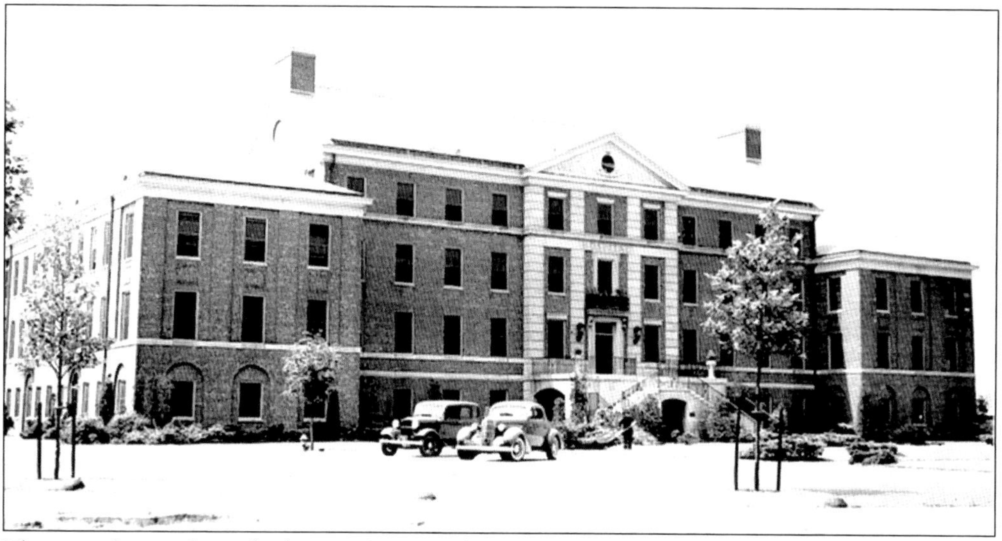

This post hospital was built in 1933 to replace the wooden structure on the opposite side of the island.

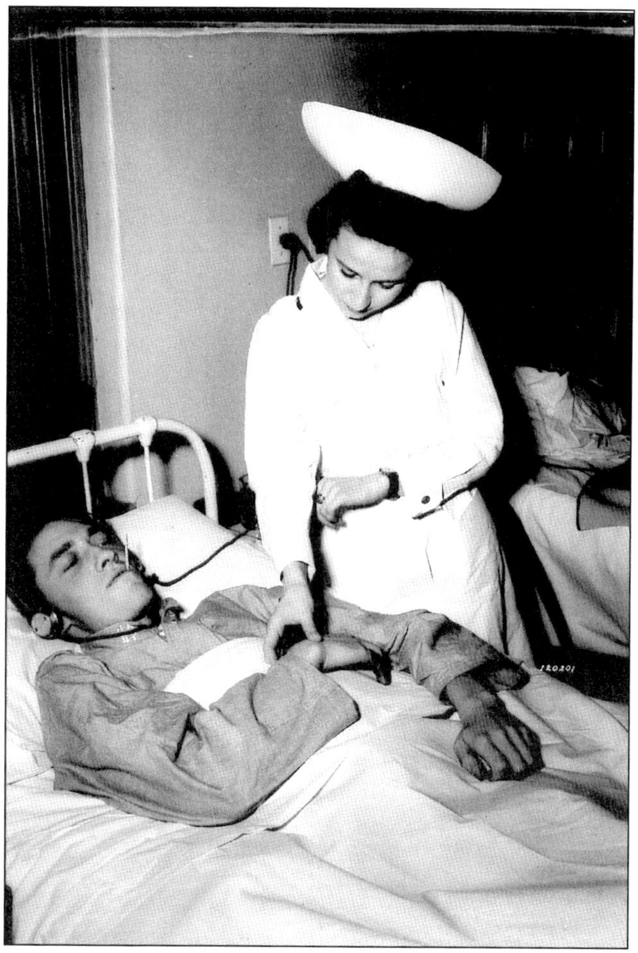

Nurses cared for the patients there. (U.S. Army photograph.)

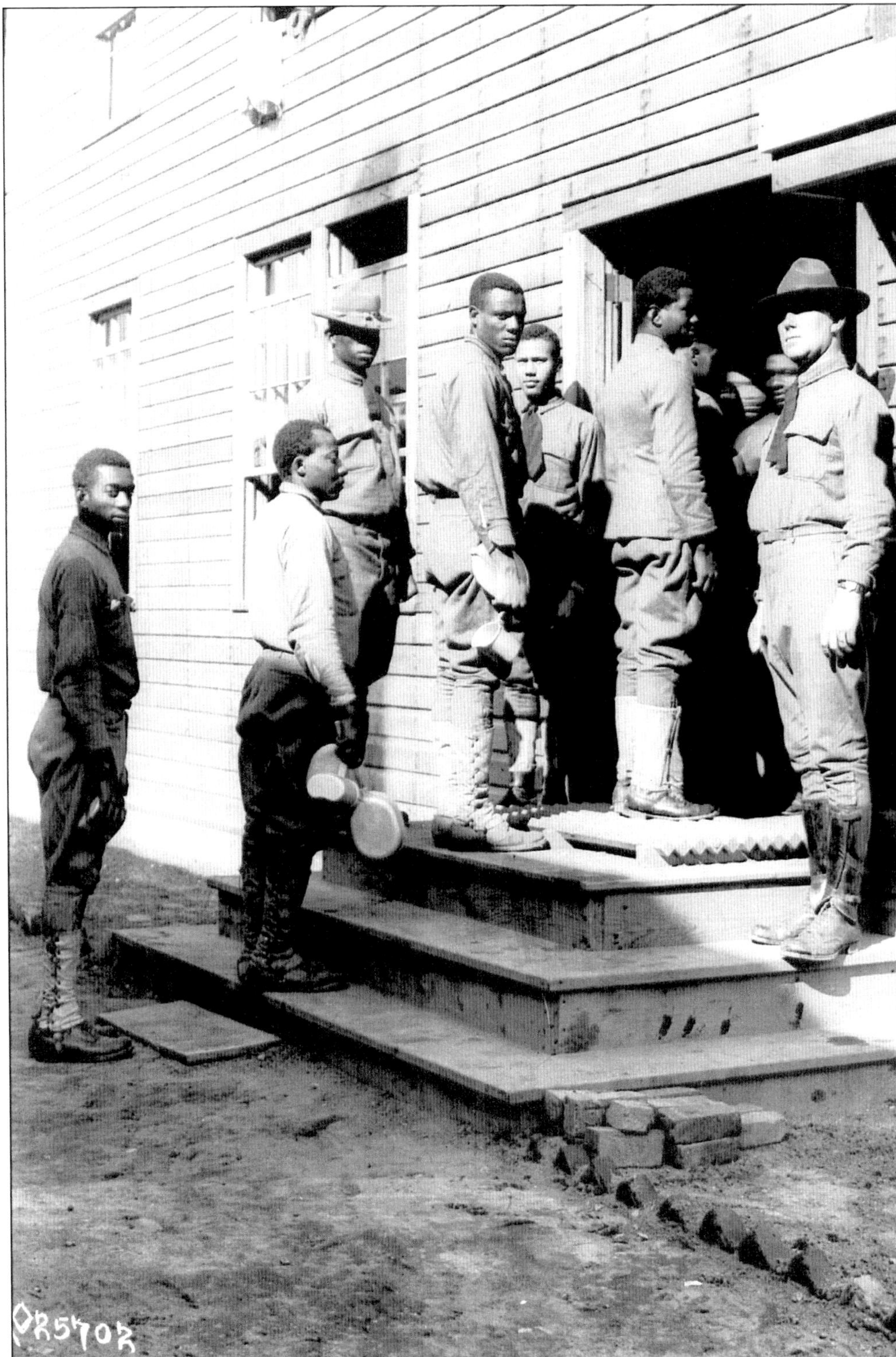

Lines of soldiers could be seen outside many of the buildings.

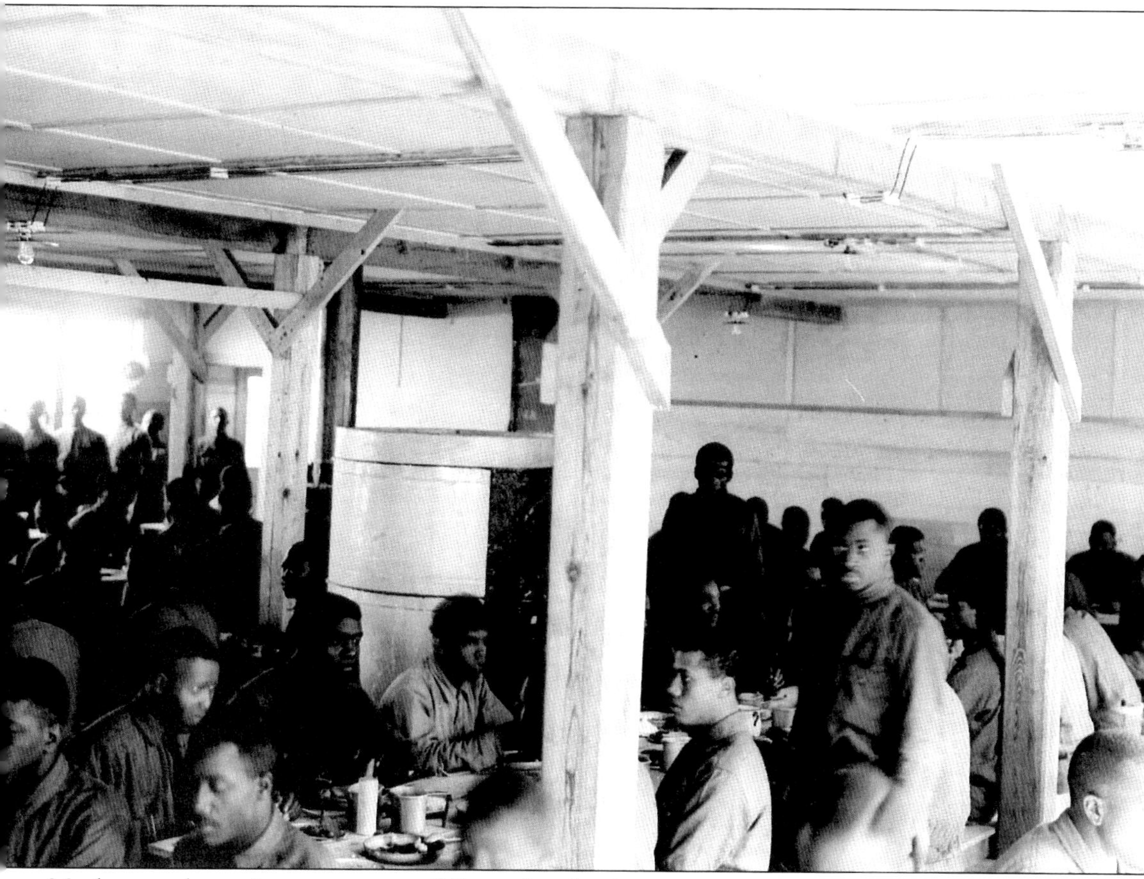

Meals were also an important part of life on the island.

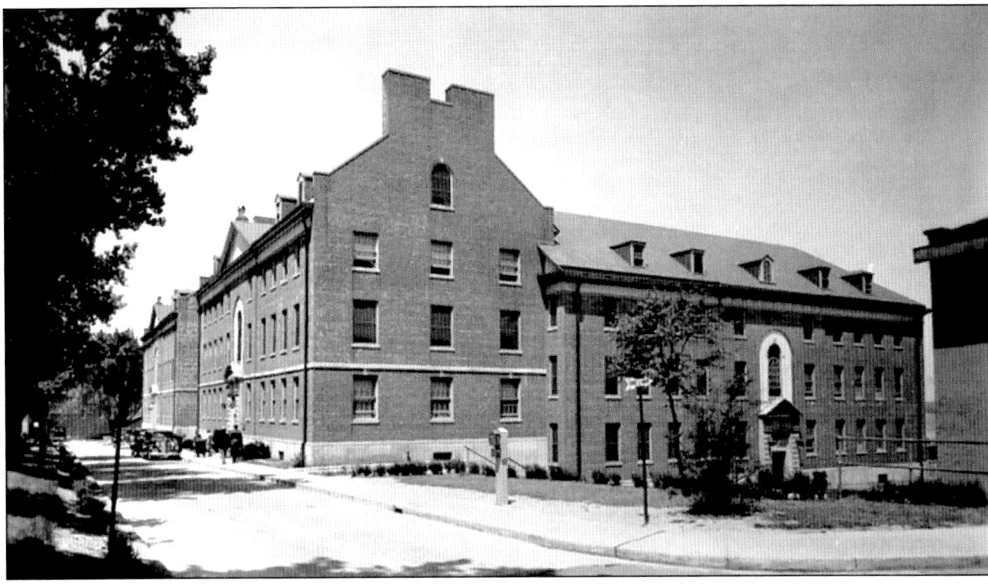

The multi-family officer's quarters designed by Rogers and Poor that are seen here were built in 1934. These buildings are on the northern end of the island overlooking New York Harbor.

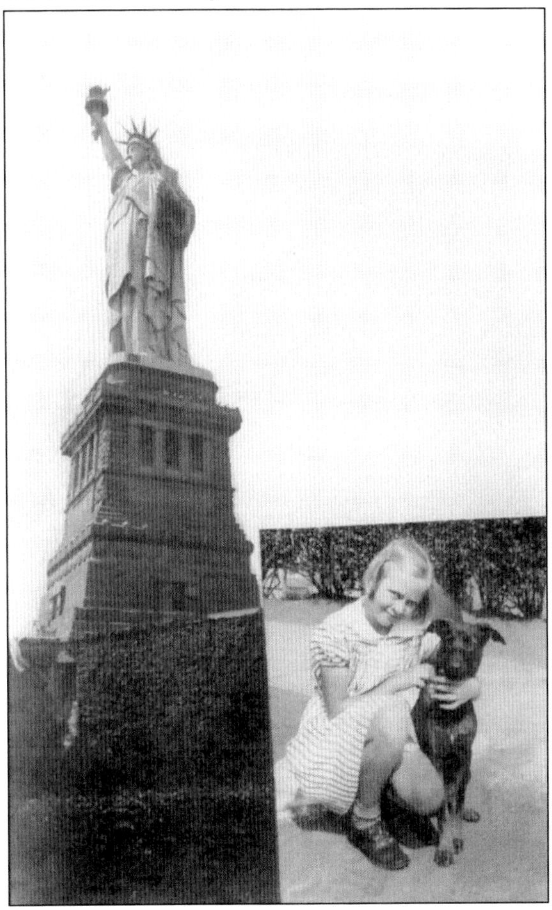

Children and pets were always an important part of life on the island and would often be superimposed against the backdrop of the Statue of Liberty, which is just to the west of the island.

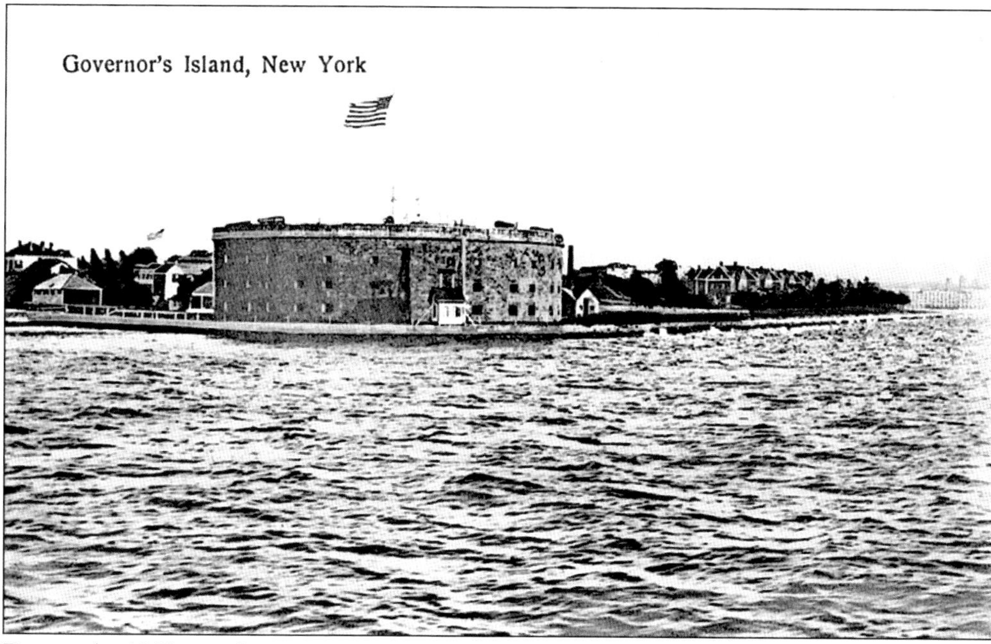

During the 1940s, modern renovations were made to the fort. The following pictures show this work being done.

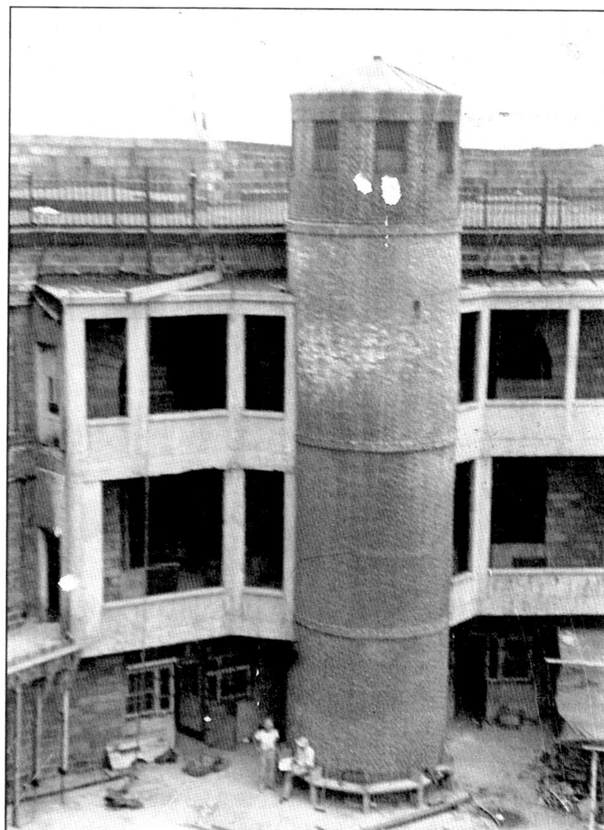

This is Castle Williams from the east showing the "crooked tower." The tower is no longer in the fort.

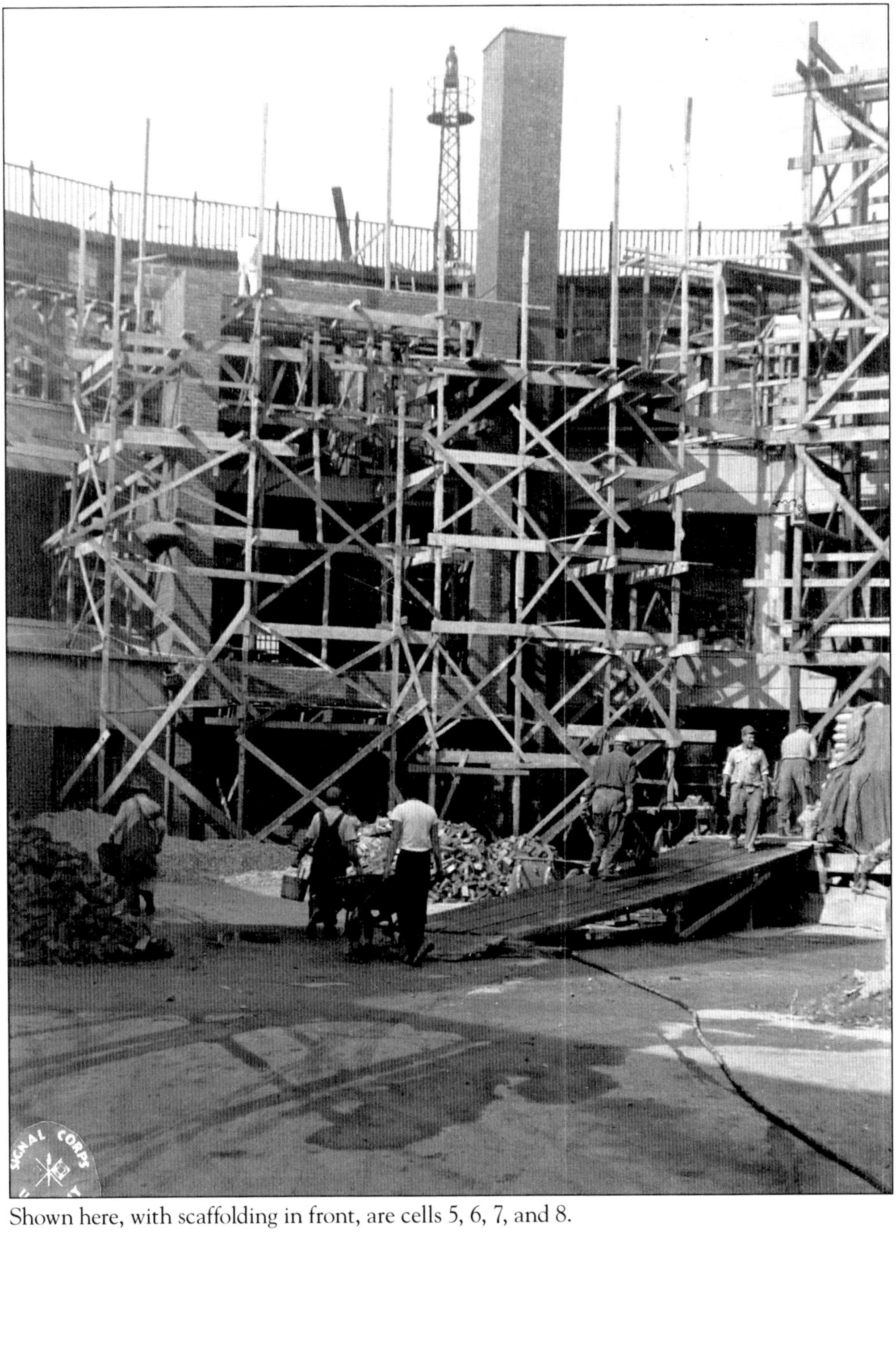

Shown here, with scaffolding in front, are cells 5, 6, 7, and 8.

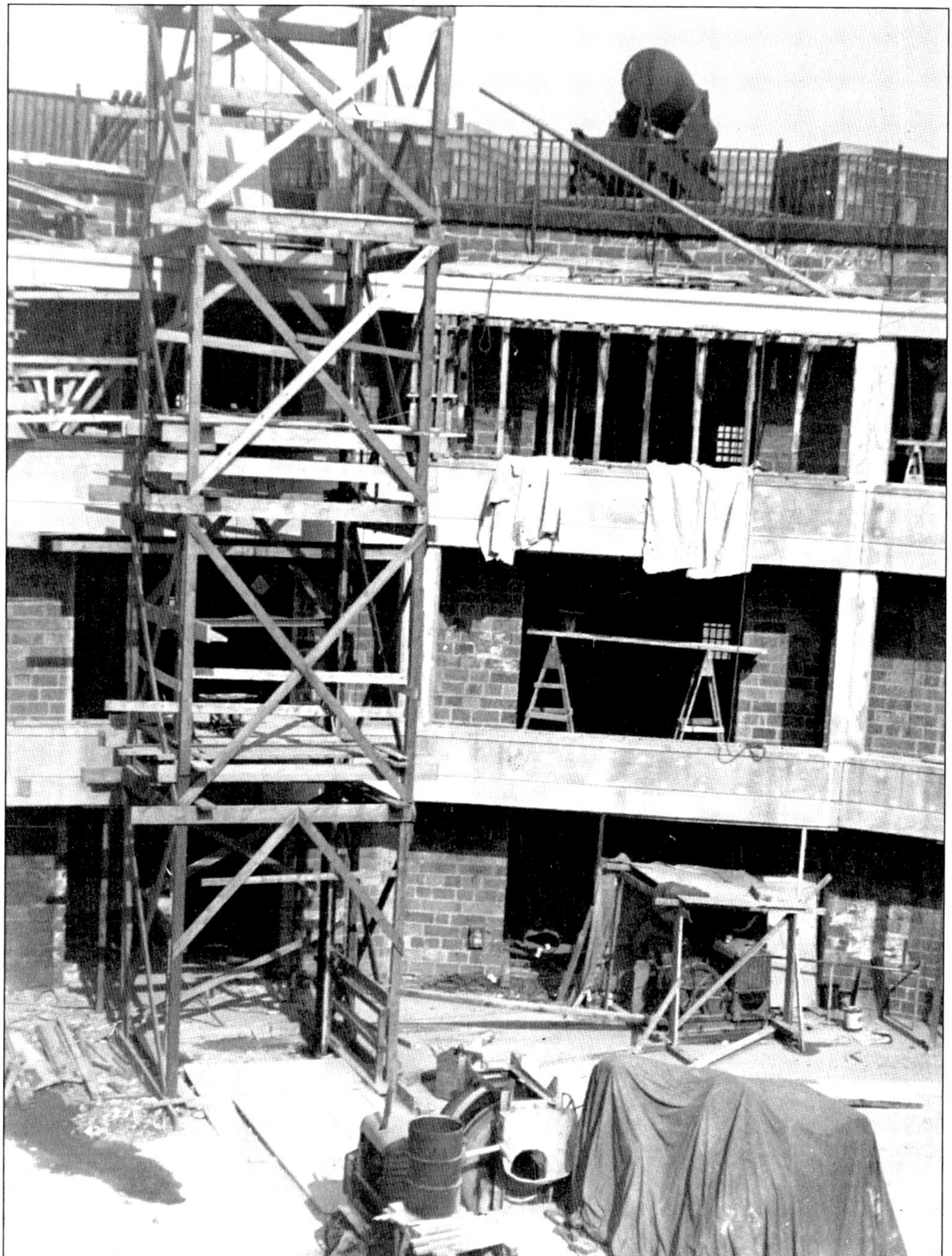

Cells 8 and 9 are seen here from the roof of Castle Williams.

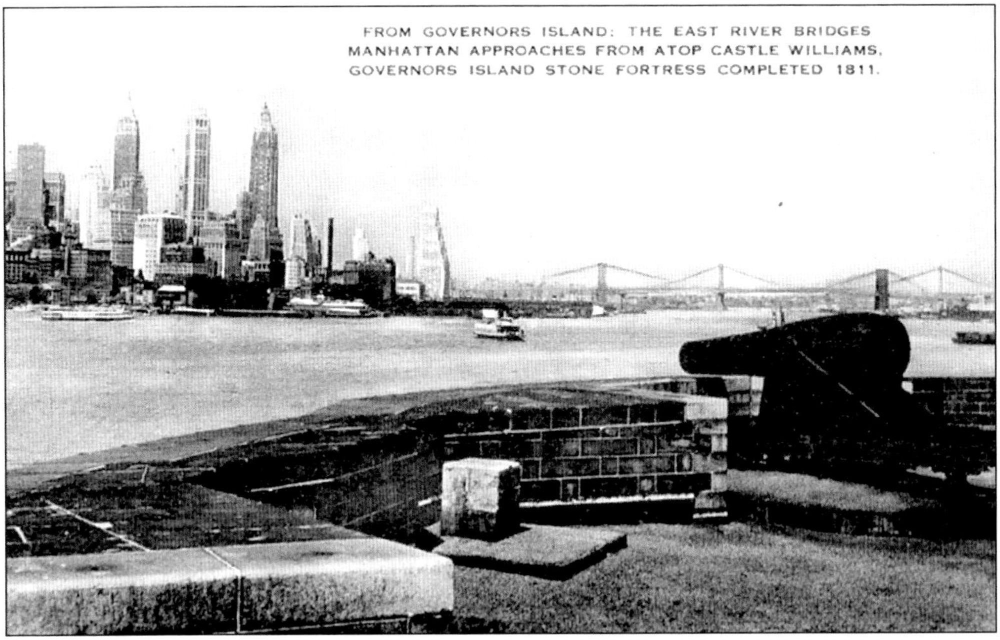

Cannon atop Castle Williams guard New York Harbor.

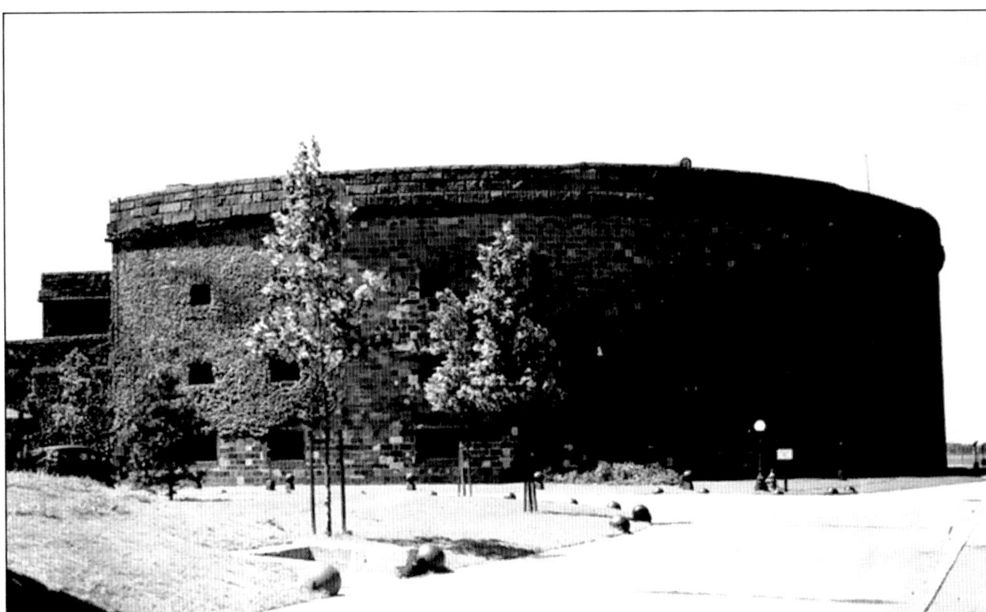

Following World War II, the cannon atop Castle Williams became less visible, but their cannon balls were still scattered throughout the island.

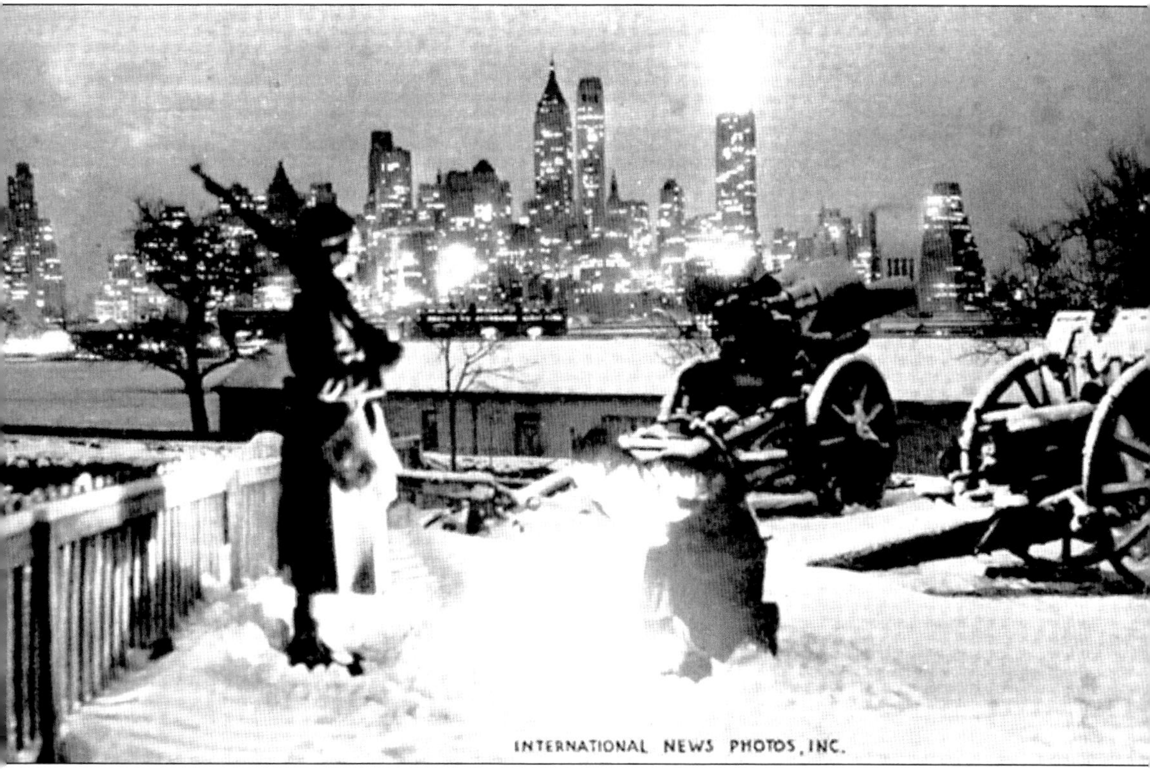

Cannon and guards were always at the ready atop Fort Jay.

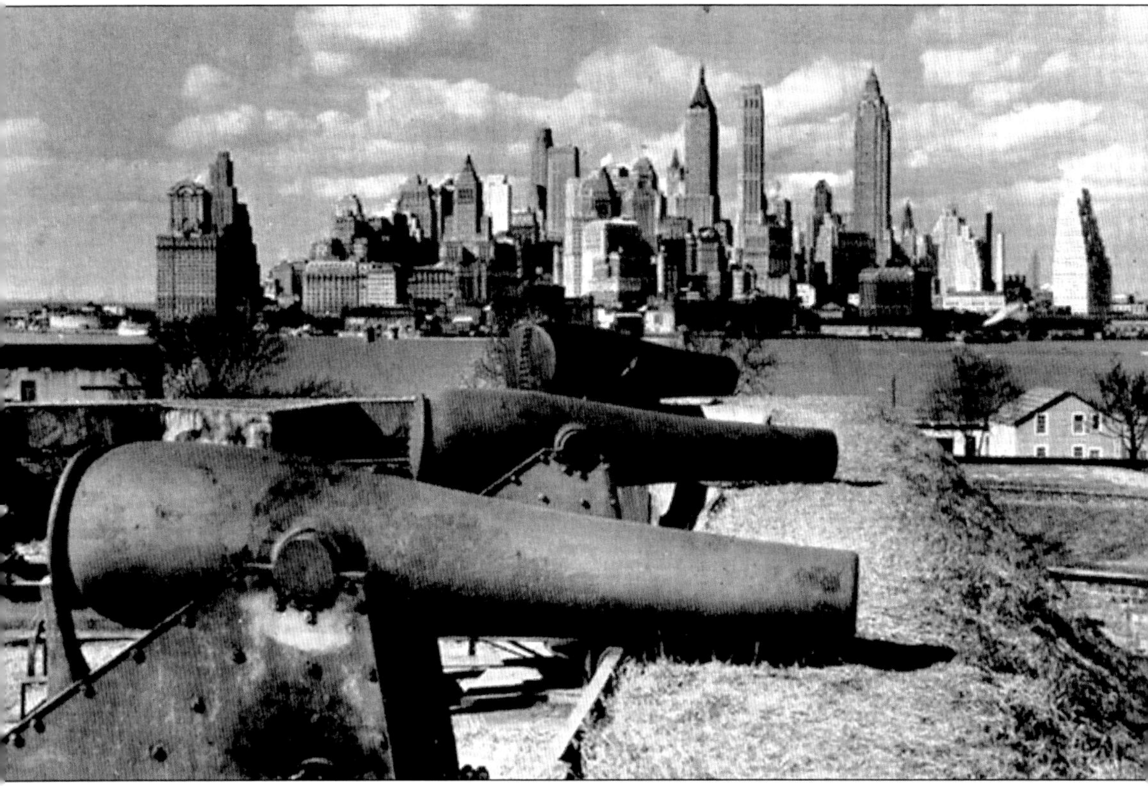

A group of 10 inch Rodman guns lined the top of Fort Jay. Several of these guns are still present around the top of the fort.

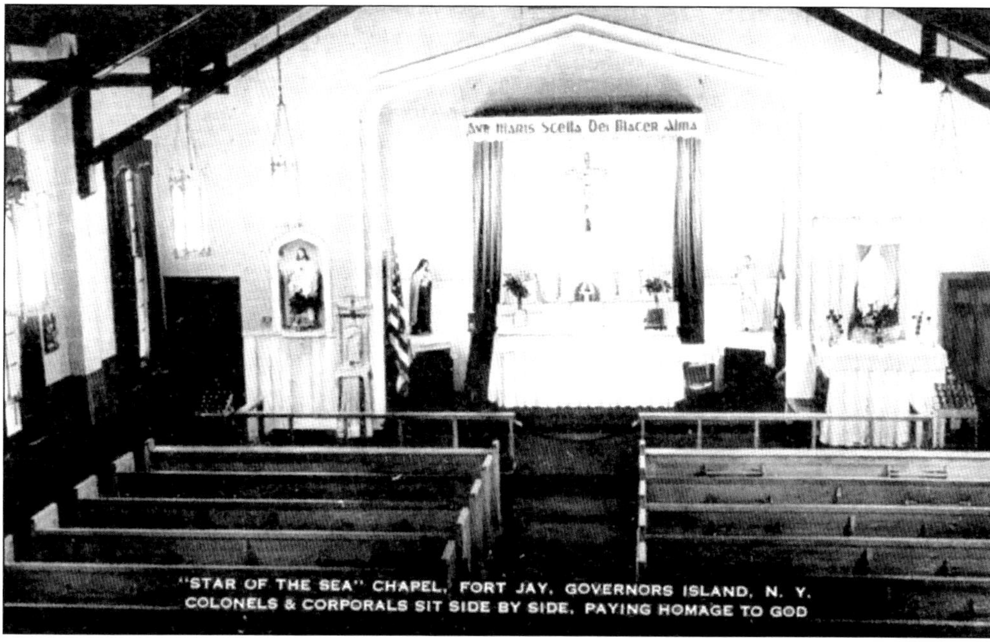

Roman Catholic Church services were held at Our Lady Star of the Sea. Shown here is the interior of the Our Lady Star of the Sea Chapel built in 1942.

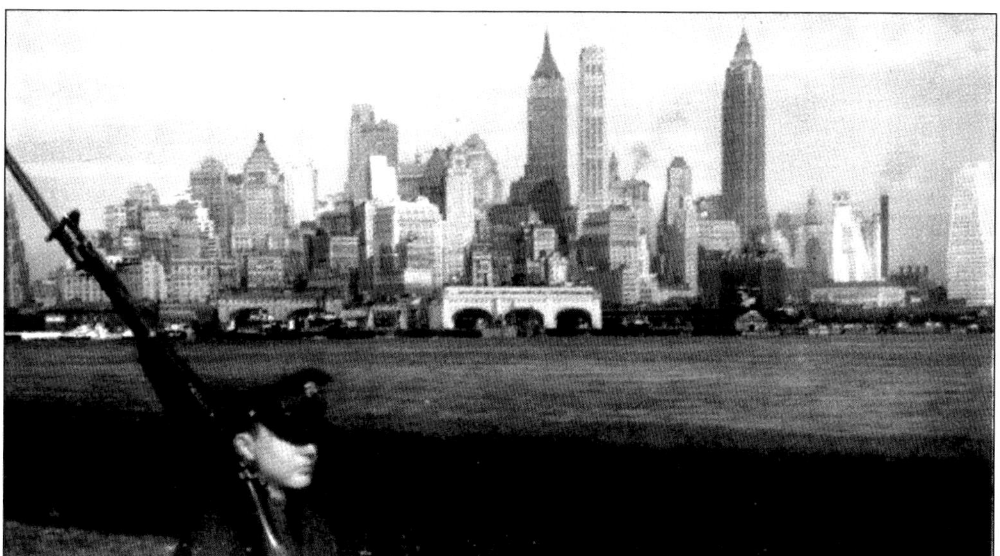

Throughout the years, Army personnel walked the perimeter of the island within sight of the ever changing skyline of Manhattan. The ferry terminal is in the background.

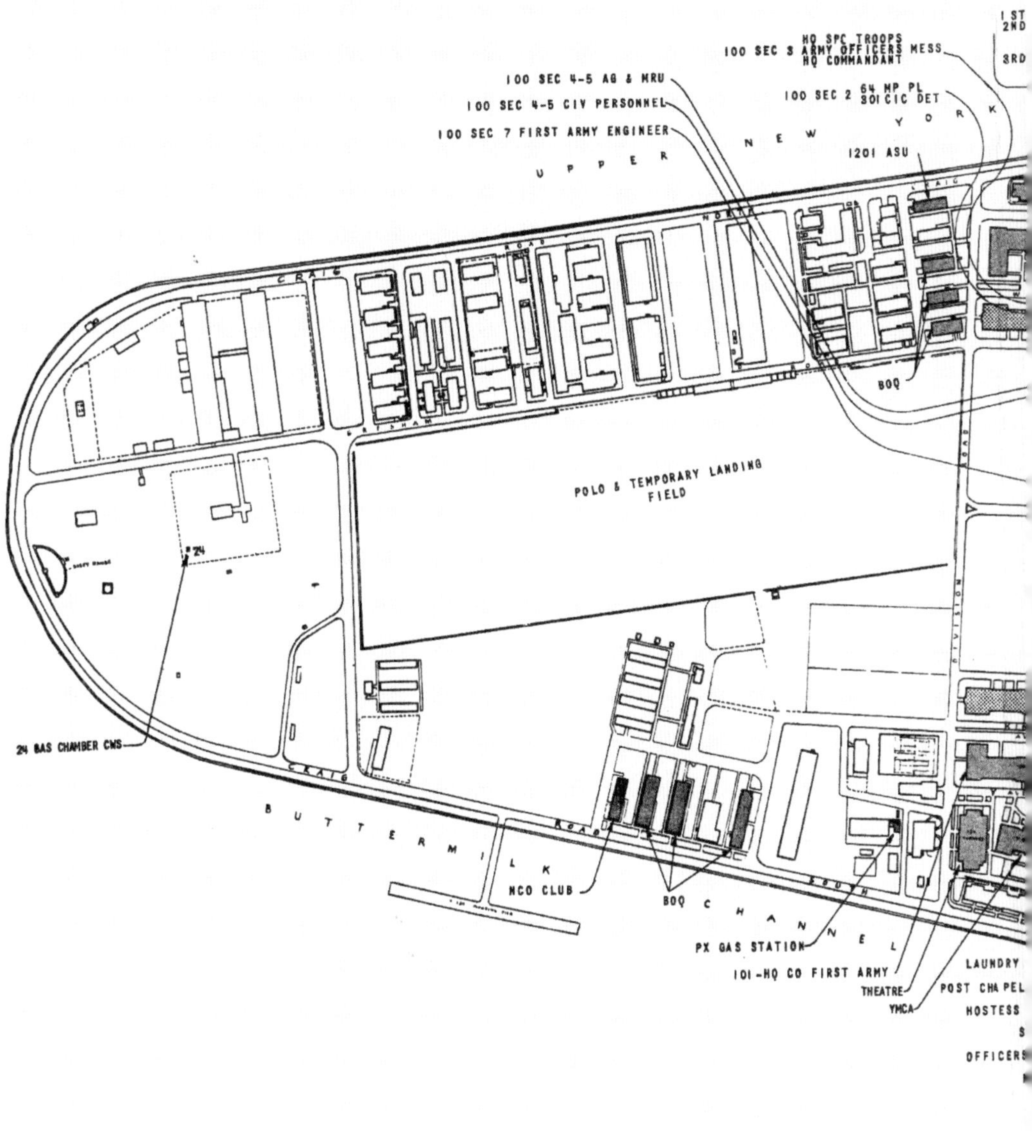
HQ SPC TROOPS
100 SEC 3 ARMY OFFICERS MESS
HQ COMMANDANT
100 SEC 4-5 AG & MRU
100 SEC 4-5 CIV PERSONNEL
100 SEC 7 FIRST ARMY ENGINEER
100 SEC 2 64 MP PL
301 CIC DET
1201 ASU
UPPER NEW YORK
CRAIG
NORTH
ROAD
BOQ
POLO & TEMPORARY LANDING
FIELD
24
24 GAS CHAMBER CWS
BUTTERMILK
CHANNEL
NCO CLUB
BOQ
PX GAS STATION
101-HQ CO FIRST ARMY
THEATRE
YMCA
LAUNDRY
POST CHAPEL
HOSTESS
OFFICERS

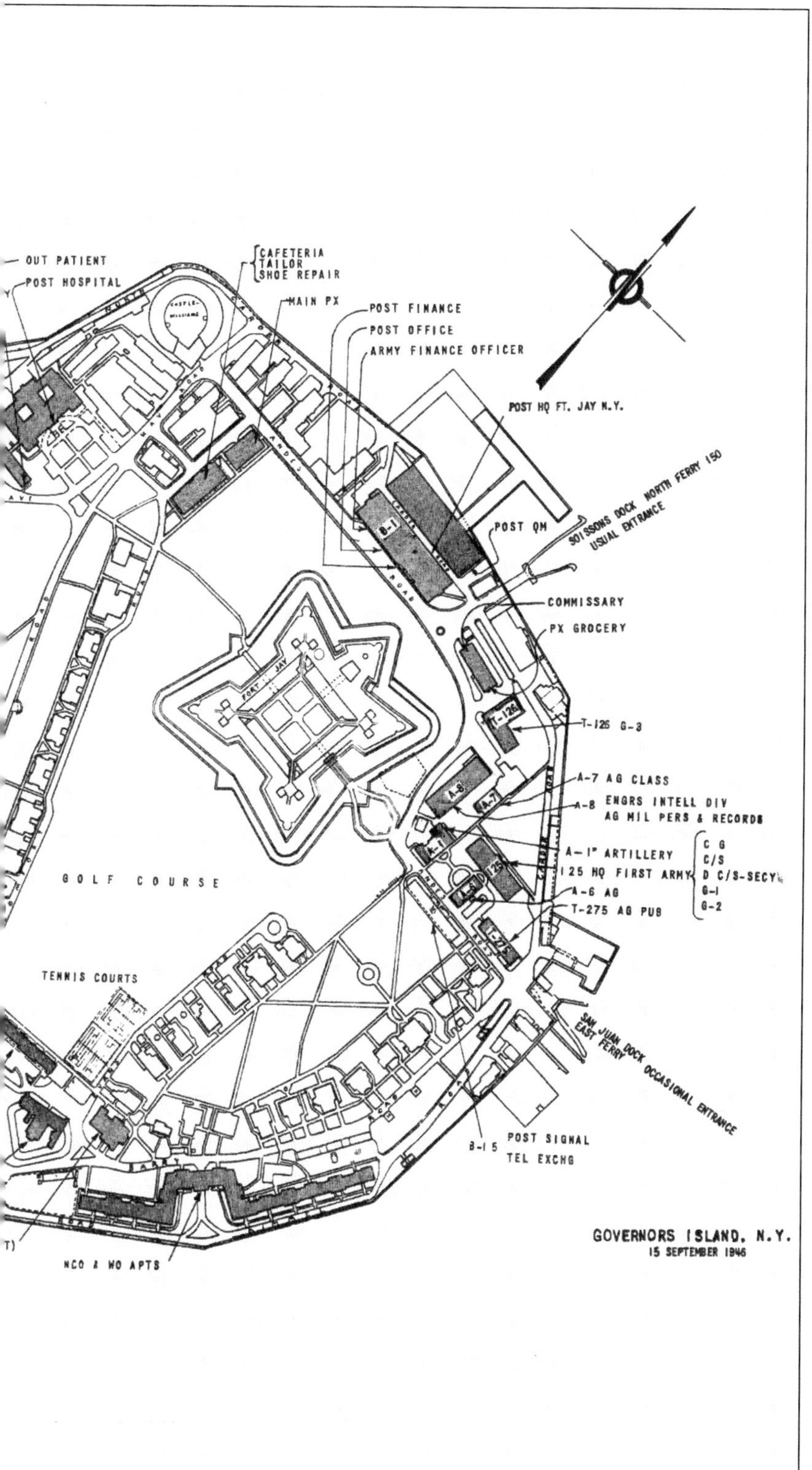

This U.S. Army map of the island dates from 1946.

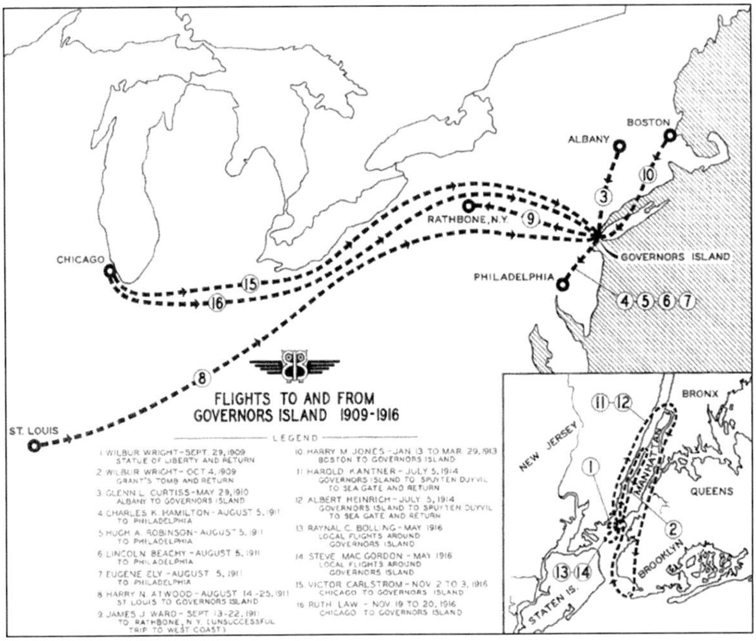

On December 17, 1954, in a ceremony on the grounds in front of Building 100, a monument was dedicated to The Early Birds, an organization of those who flew solo before December 17, 1916. It was from here that many aviators flew. This map shows the routes flown from Governors Island from 1909 to 1916. (U.S. Army photographs.)

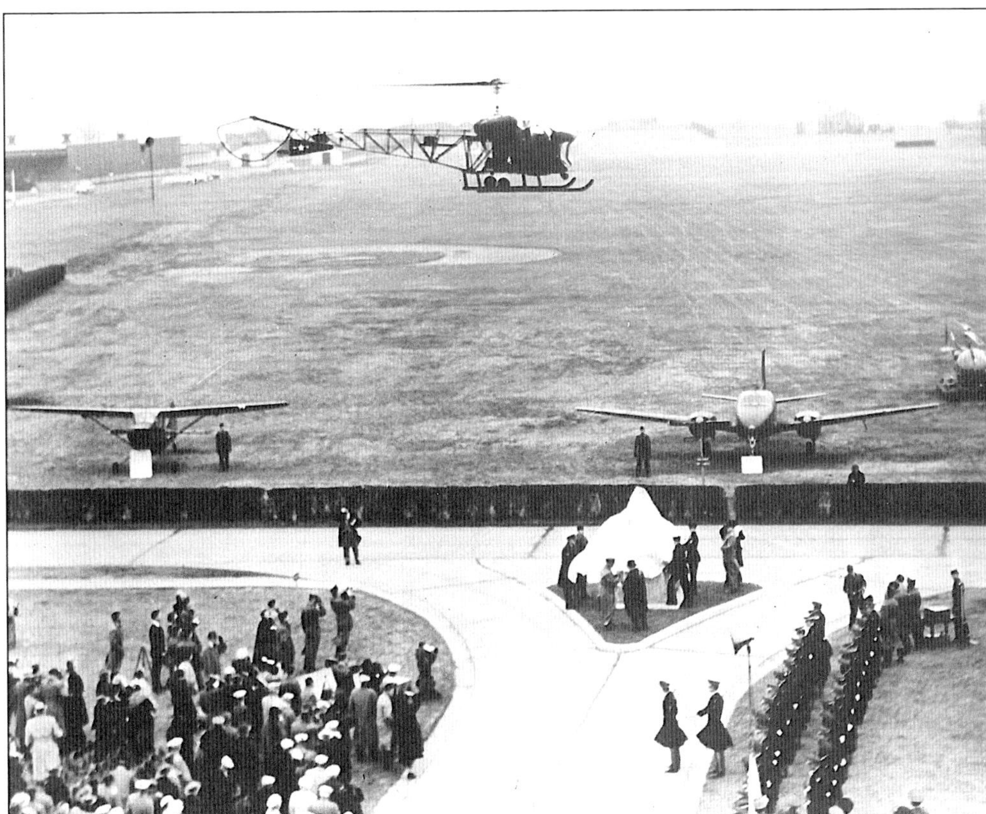

This flat expanse had been used as an aviation school and the site of much aviation activity. It was also the site of the dedication of the monument.

This is the program used that day.

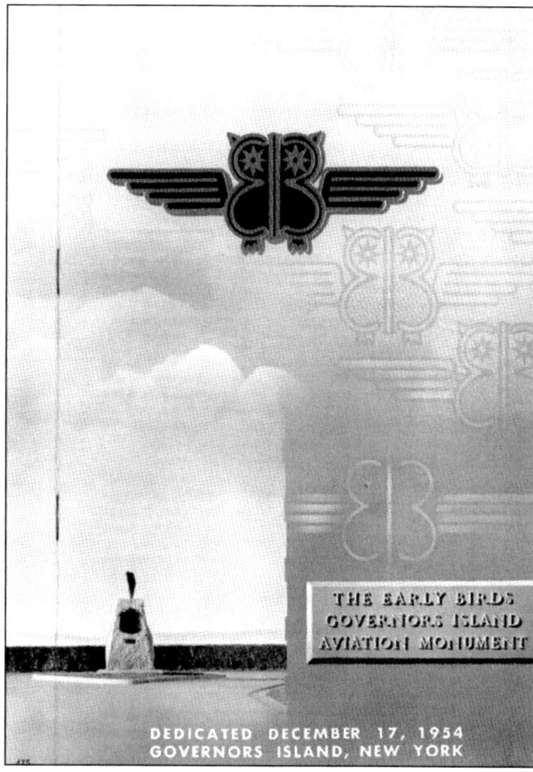

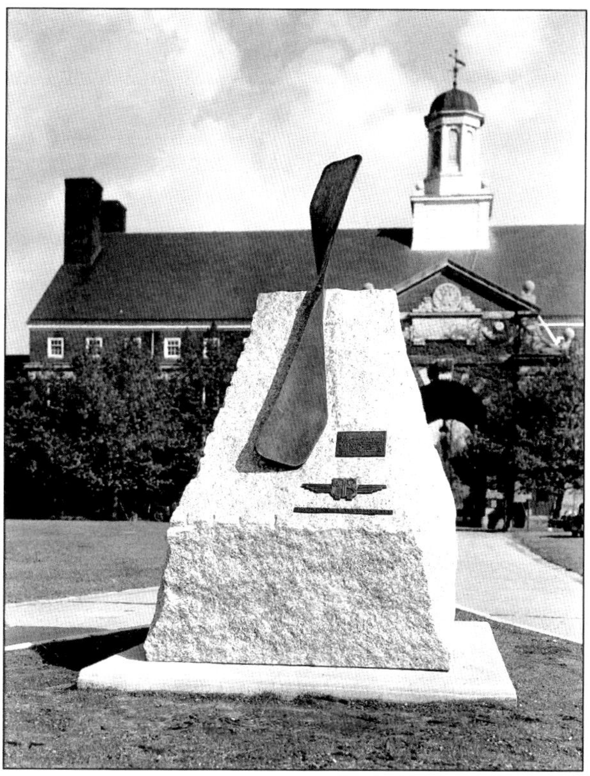

Shown here is the monument with a replica propeller.

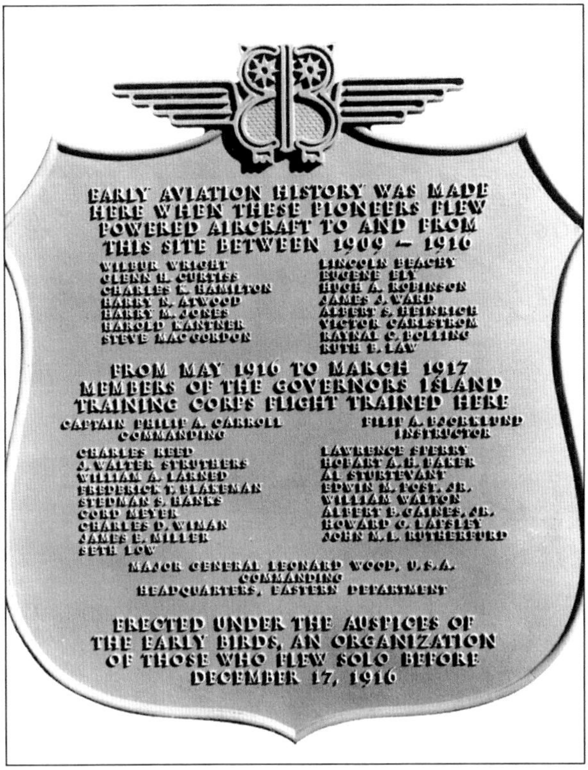

These are the plaques on the front and back of the monument.

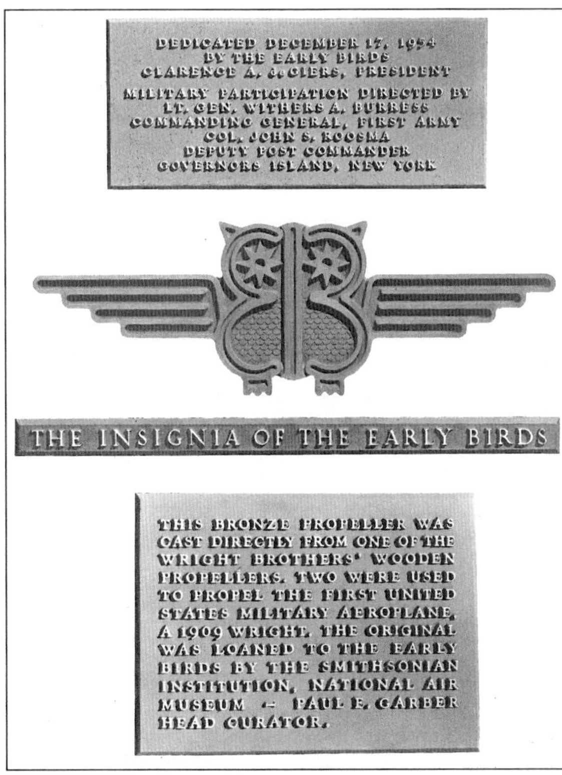

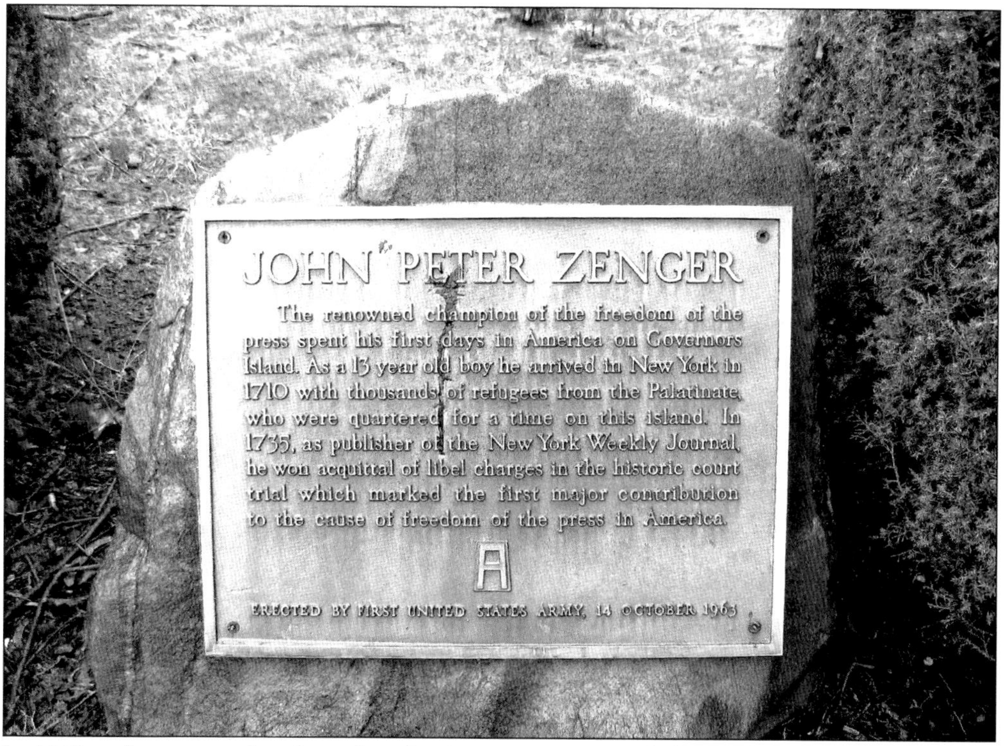

In 1963 a plaque was placed on the island to commemorate John Peter Zenger, "champion of the freedom of the press." He was one of the thousands of refugees from the Palantine who were quartered on the island in 1710.

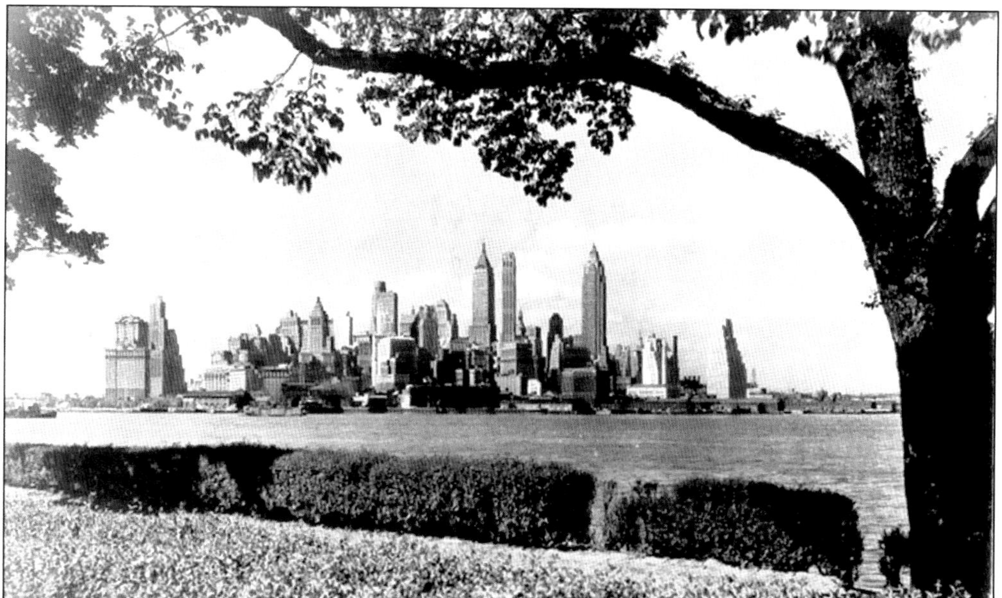

This is the Manhattan Skyline as seen from Governors Island in 1946. At night, the lights of the city glittered, and on holidays many of the islands inhabitants would sit on the lawn here to watch the fireworks displays over the harbor beyond.

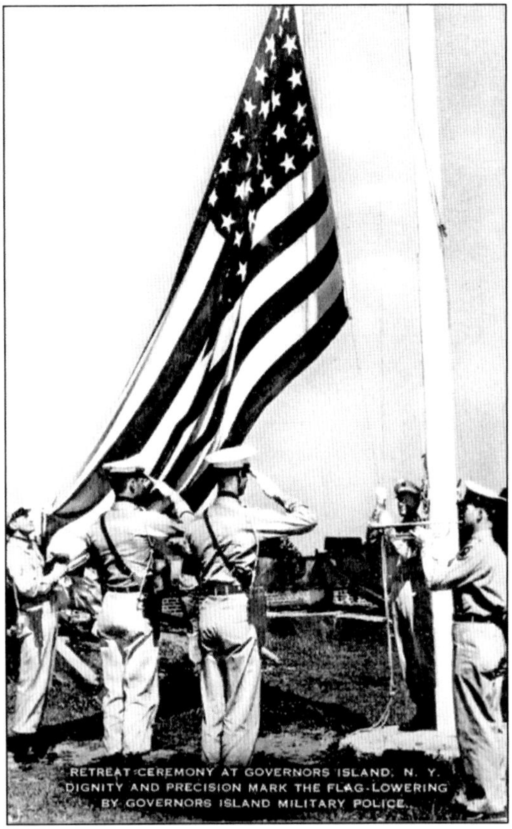

Each evening the retreat ceremony would be performed by the Governors Island military police.

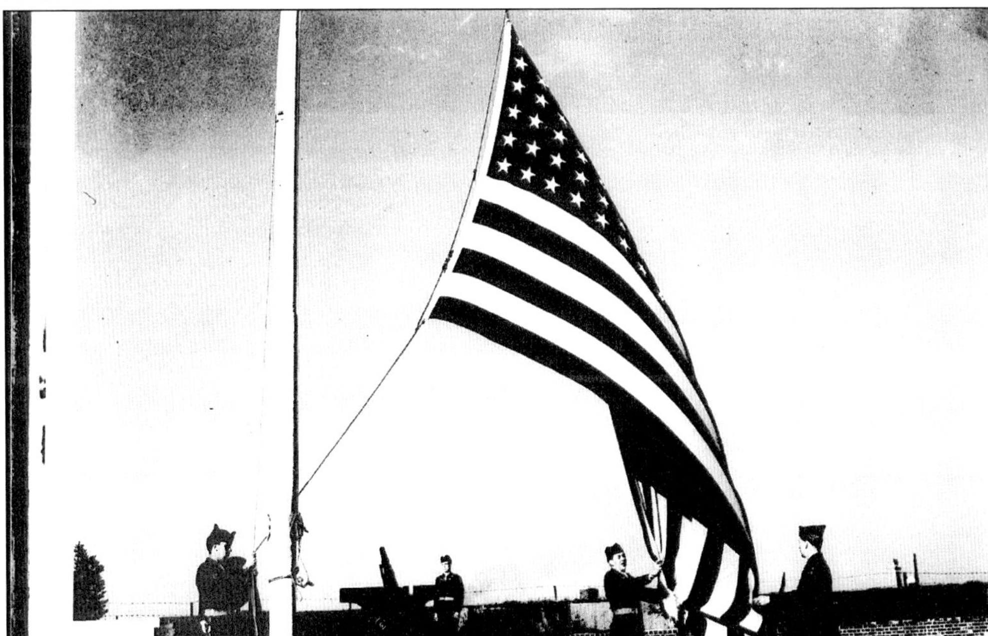

The raising and lowering of colors has been a daily event on Governors Island throughout its military history.

Three

The U.S. Coast Guard

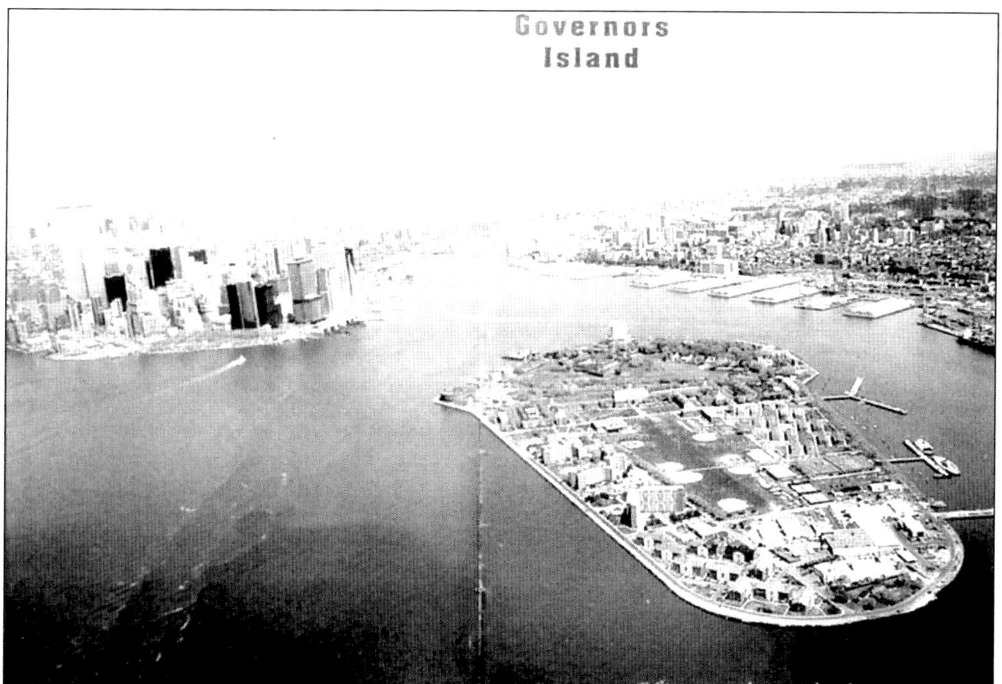

This cover of a brochure printed by the U.S. Coast Guard shows an aerial view of the island.

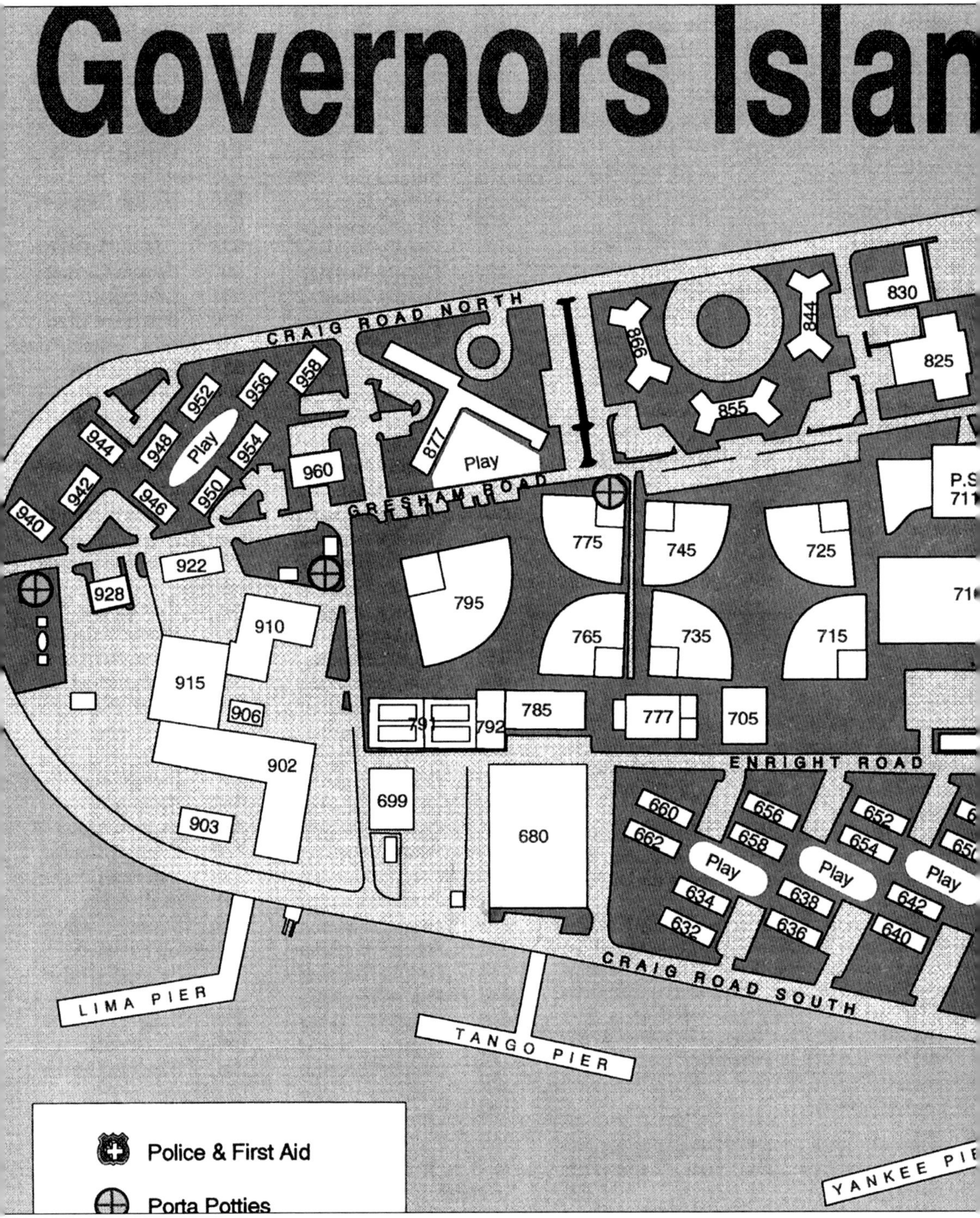

This 1990–1991 map of the island was given out by U.S. Coast Guard personnel to visitors of the island. The reverse side of the map notes buildings of specific interest and historical significance. Among those buildings and their numbered locations are (1) the 27-room Admiral's House, built in 1840; (2) the Governors House, the oldest building on the island, built in 1708 for the British

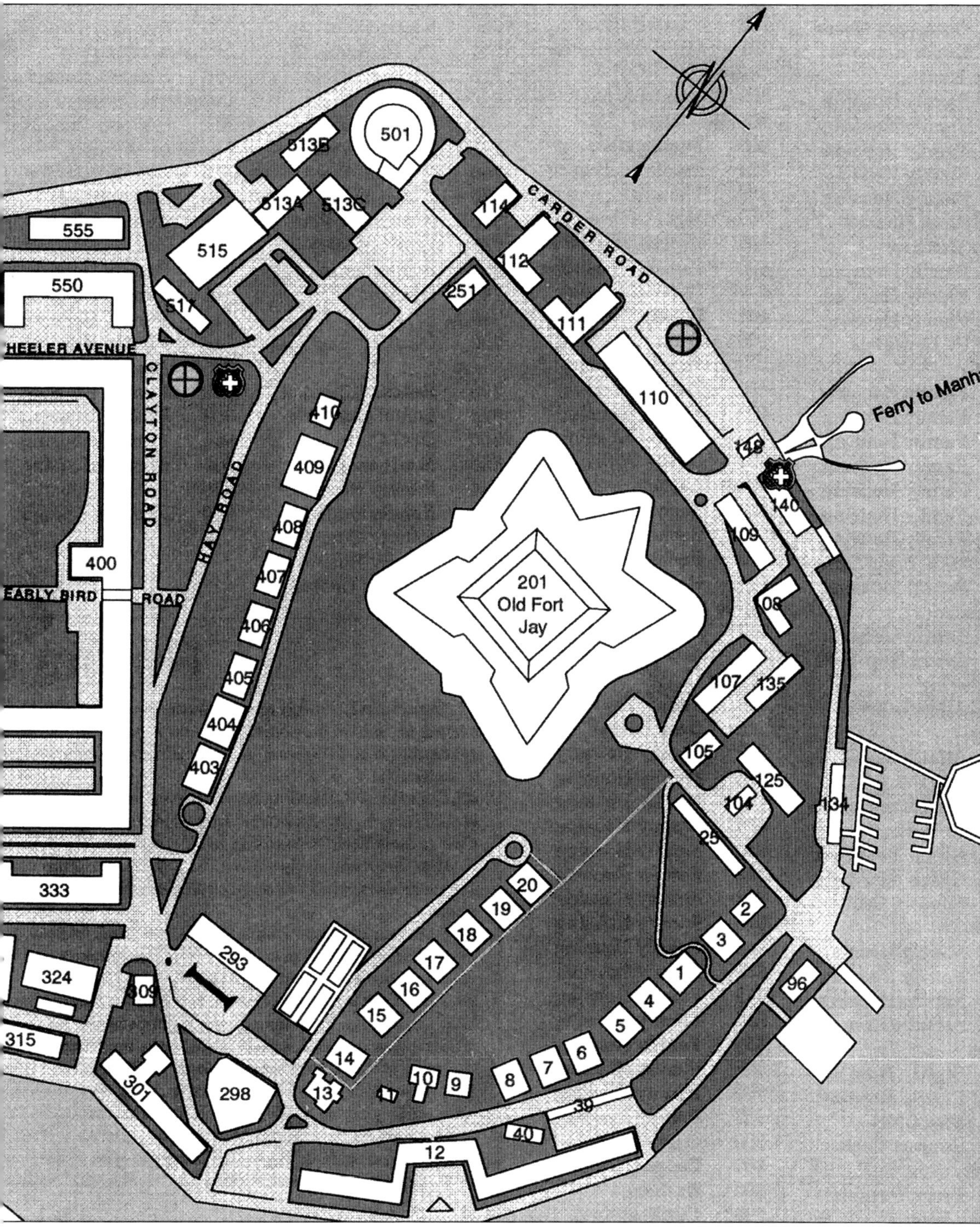

governor of the New York Colony; (3) the Dutch House, built in 1845; (9) the Blockhouse, built in the 1840s; (13) St. Cornelius chapel, built in the 1840s; (201) Fort Jay, completed in 1798; (298) the South Battery, erected in 1812; and (501) Castle Williams, completed in 1811. (By PA1 Christopher A. Haley.)

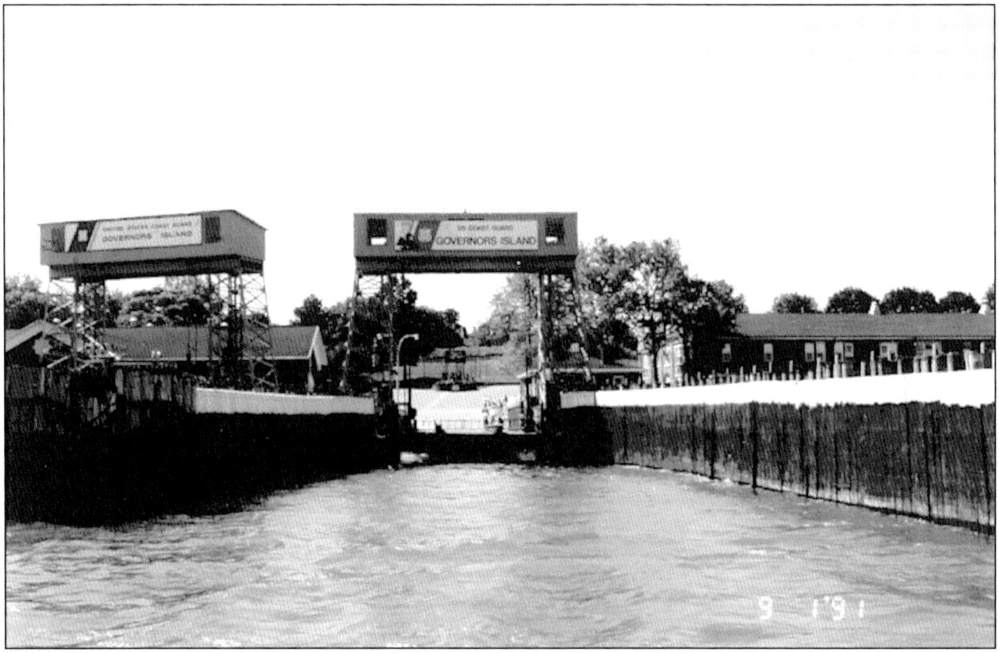

The ferry arrives at Soissons Dock. This entry point to the island was named as a memorial to the heroic service of the 16th Infantry Regiment in the successful offensive against German forces near Soissons, France, July 18, 1918. More than 57 percent of the regiment's men were casualties.

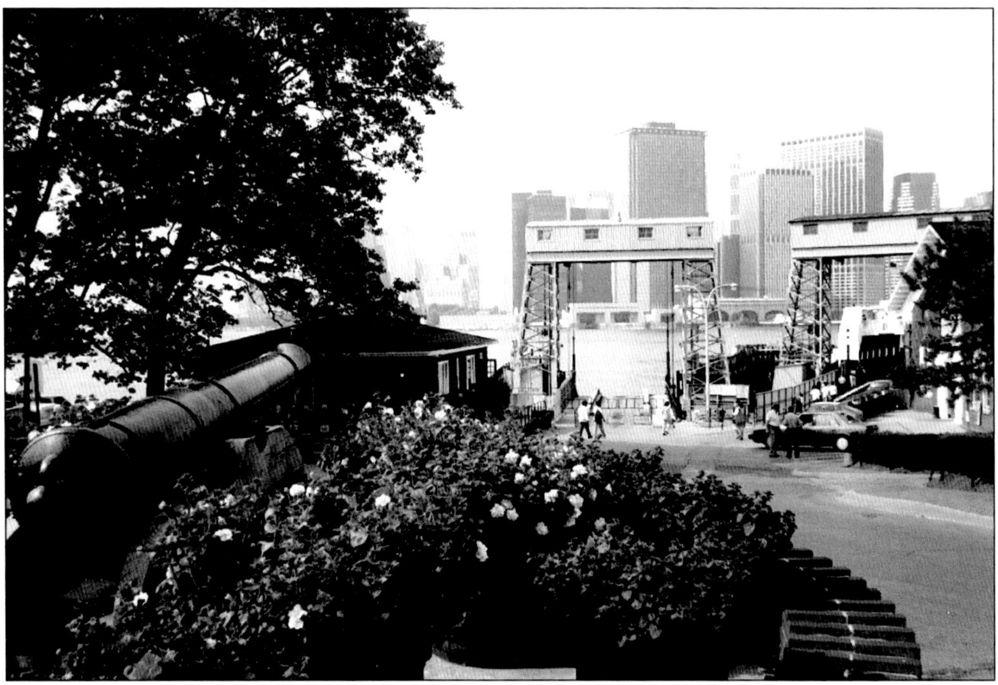

A British cannon welcomes visitors to the island. It dates from the 18th century and is plainly marked on the barrel with the royal crown and monogram G. R. (George Rex). It is painted black and is mounted on a concrete carriage. It is the only cannon remaining from the British occupation at the time of the Revolutionary War.

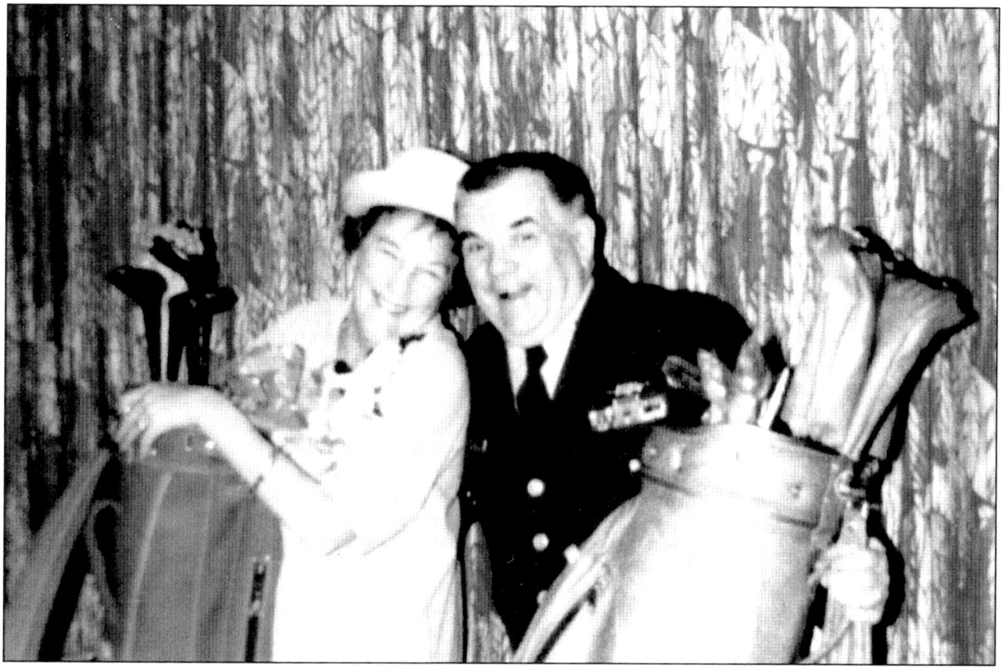

Vice Admiral William Rea and his wife Ruth are seen here. Admiral Rea was commander of the Atlantic Area and lived in the Commanding Officer's Quarters from 1974 to 1978. (Courtesy of Ruth Rea.)

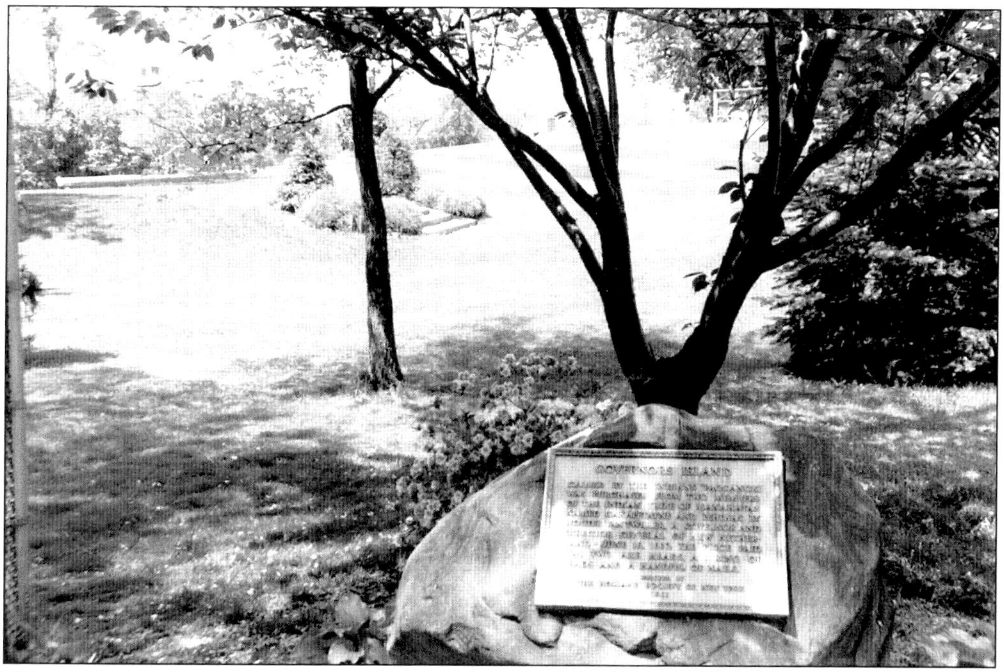

This plaque commemorates the purchase of the island for the price of "certain parcels of goods," believed to be two axe handles, a string of beads, and a handful of nails. The original deed, written in Dutch and Latin, was dated June 16, 1637.

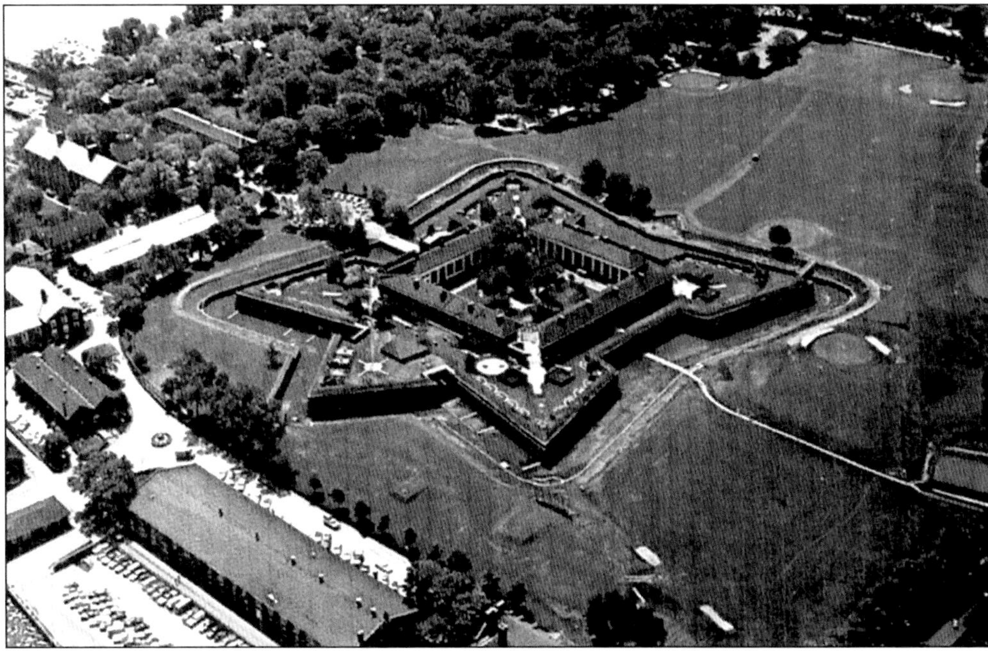

This aerial view of Fort Jay shows the wide expanse used as a nine-hole golf course.

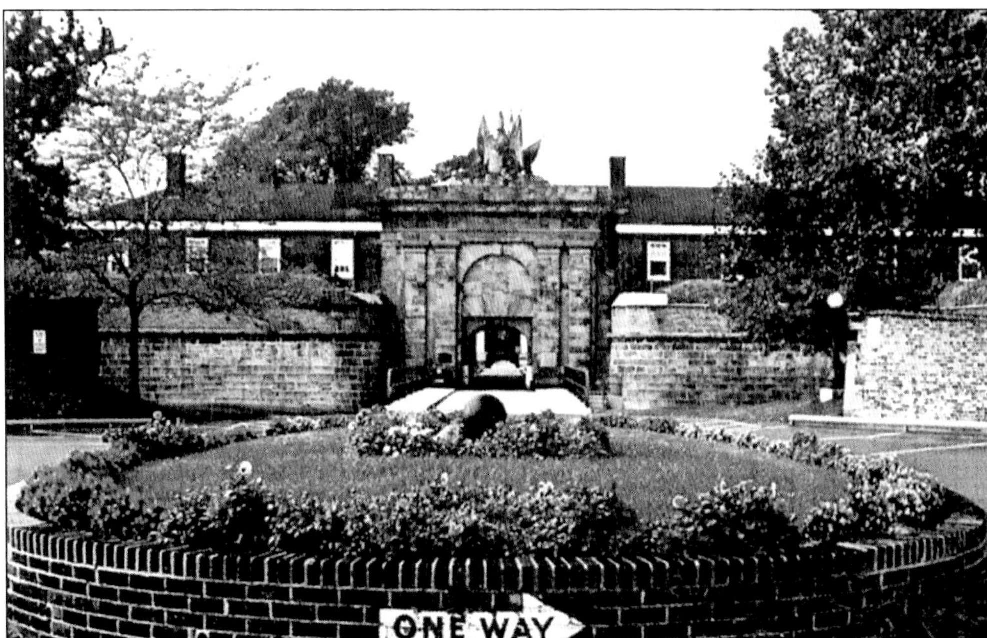

The entrance to Fort Jay was resplendent with flowers during most of the year.

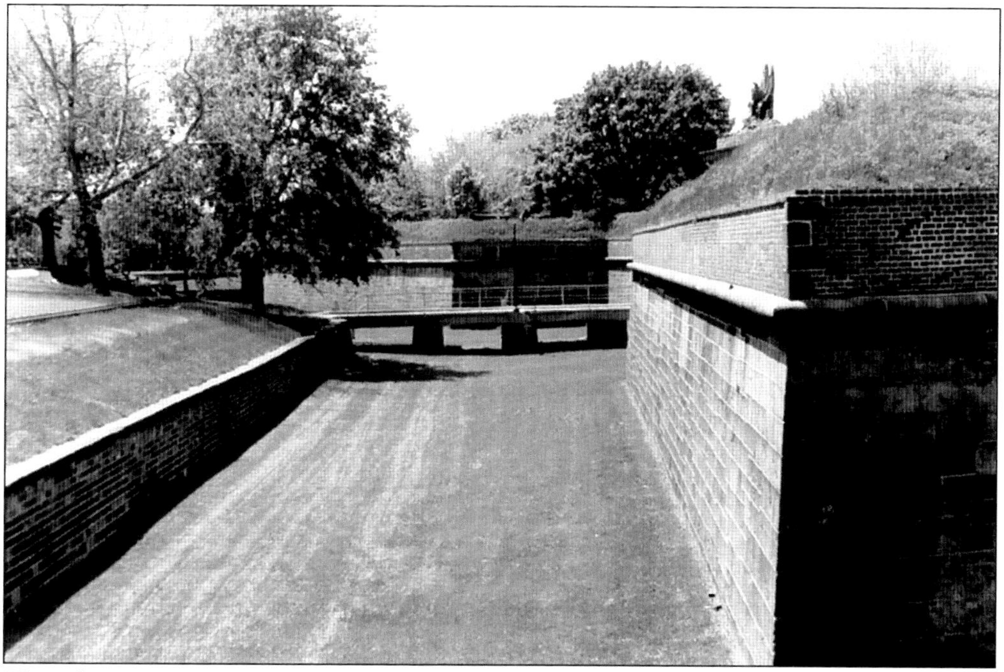

The sally moat outside Fort Jay was the site of pony rides for children in the 1970s.

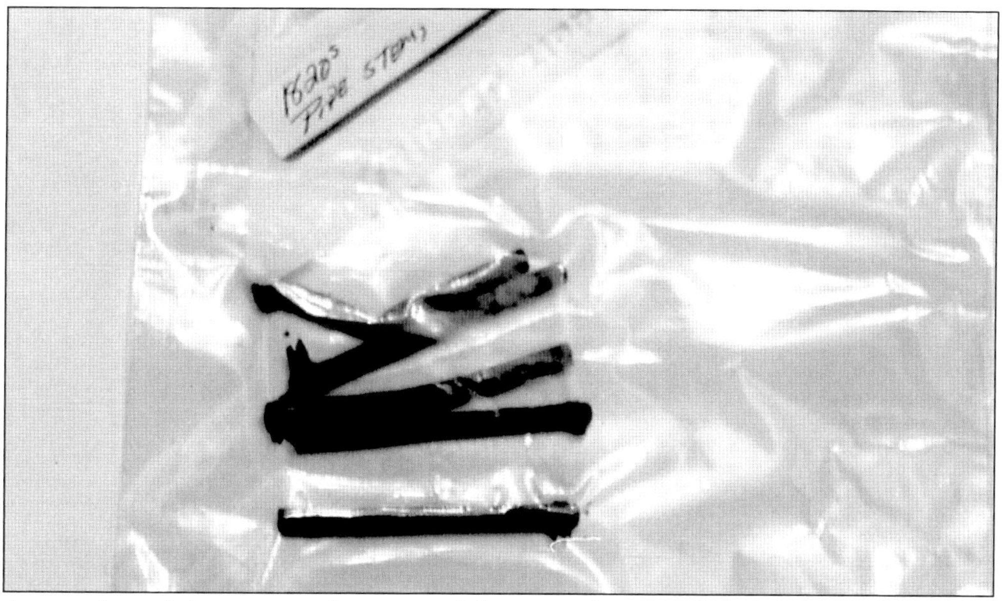

Approved metal detecting in the moat and digs in gardens revealed many artifacts from ages past. These are pipe stems from the 1820s found by one detector. All the finds were cataloged and turned over to the base commander.

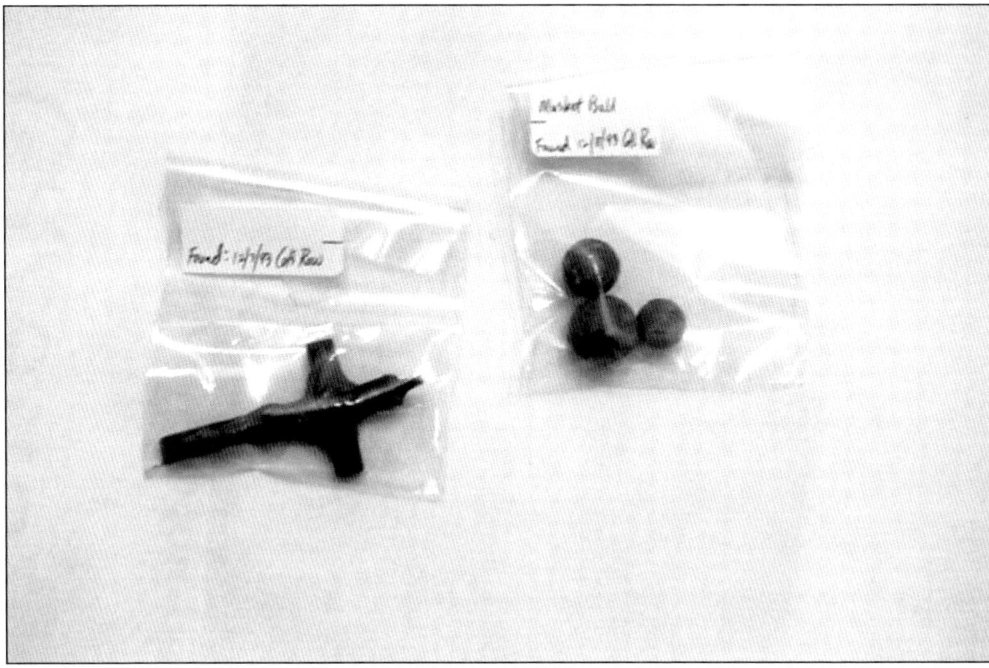

Musket balls used during the Revolutionary and Civil Wars as well as an old cross were also found.

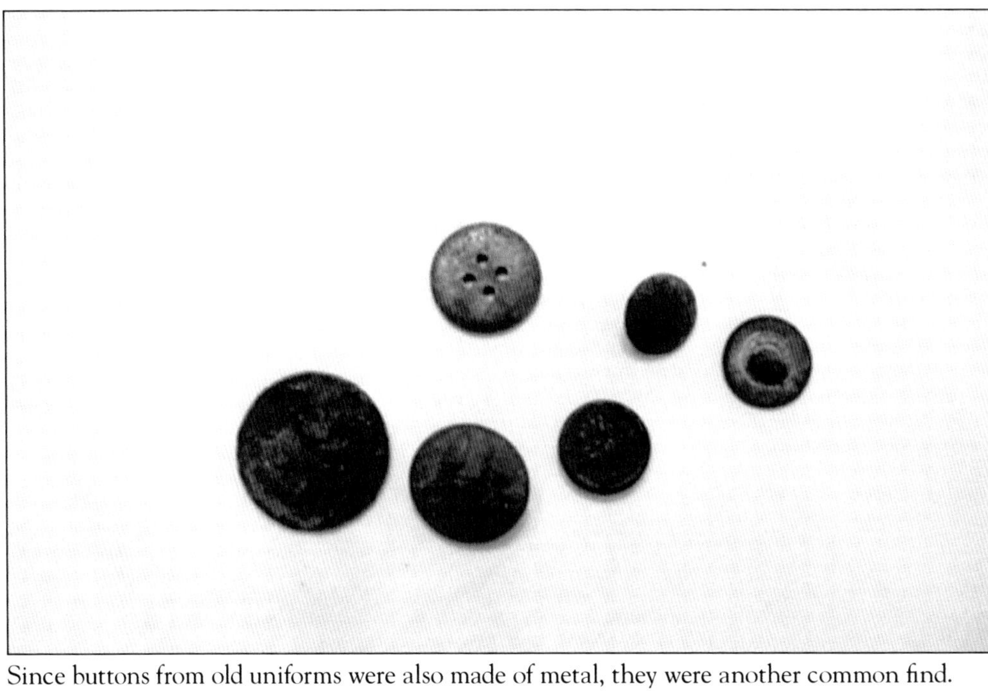

Since buttons from old uniforms were also made of metal, they were another common find.

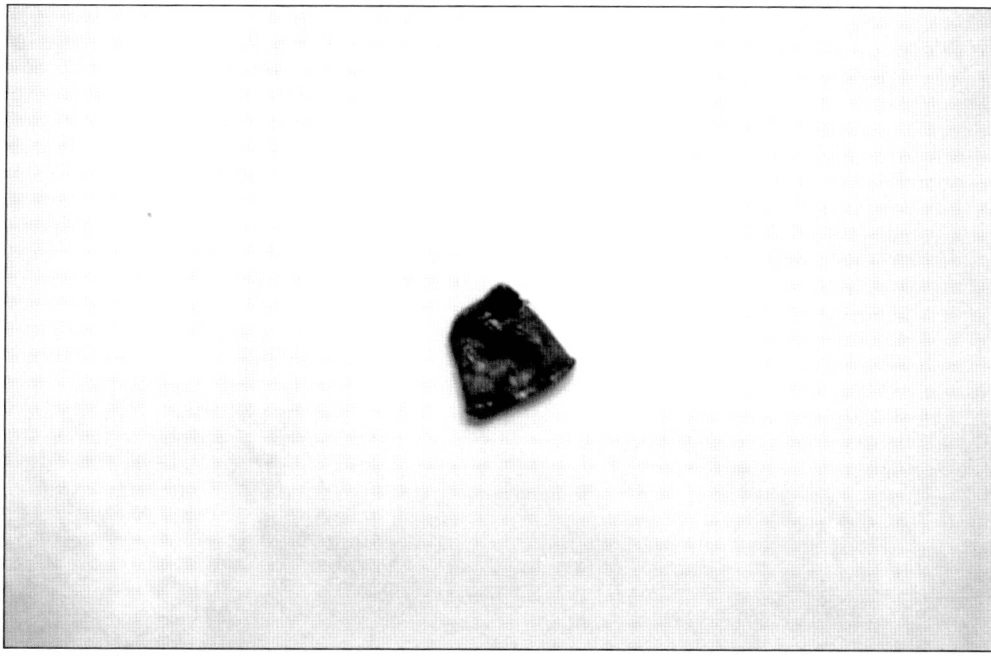
A flattened silver thimble was found on the Quadrangle.

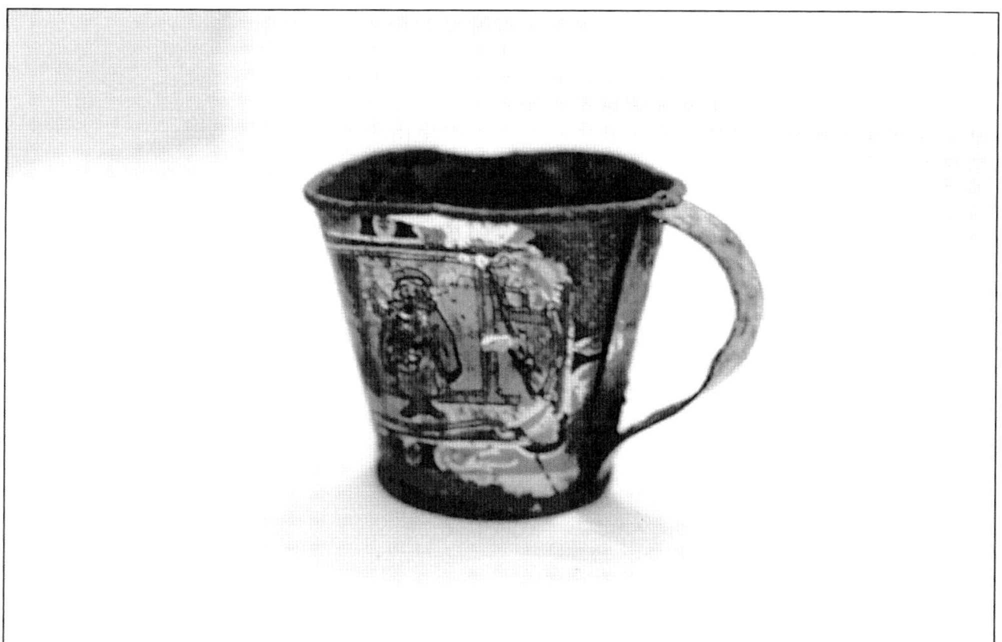
A child's tin toy cup was found beneath the kitchen that had been added on to Quarters 4 in 1932.

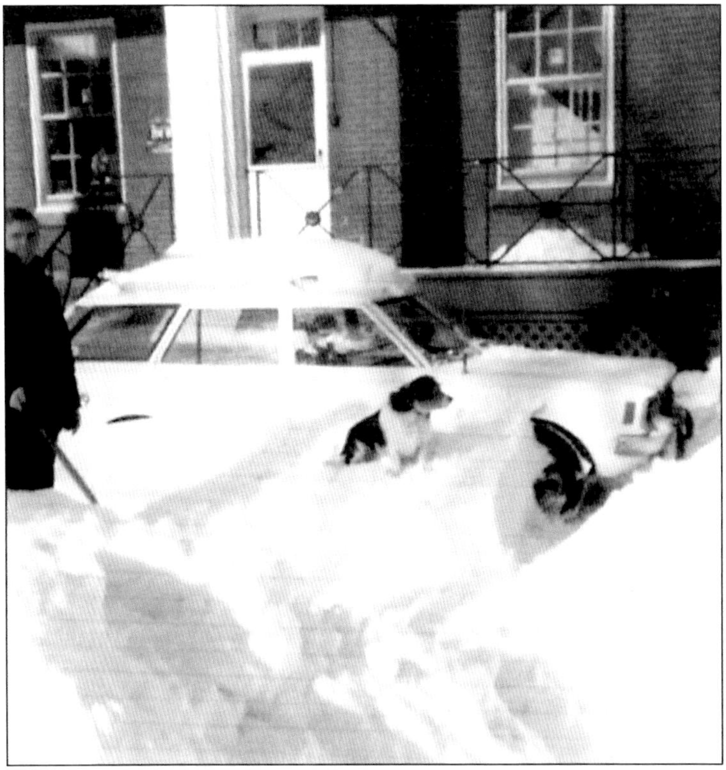

In 1978, a winter snow storm turned the interior of Fort Jay into a winter wonderland. (Courtesy of J. Packard.)

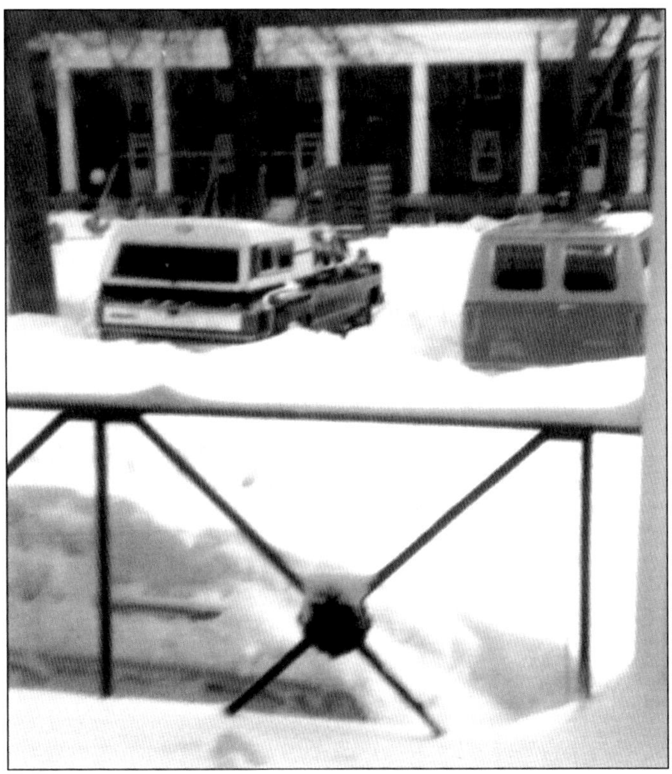

It was the responsibility of those living within the fort to dig themselves out.

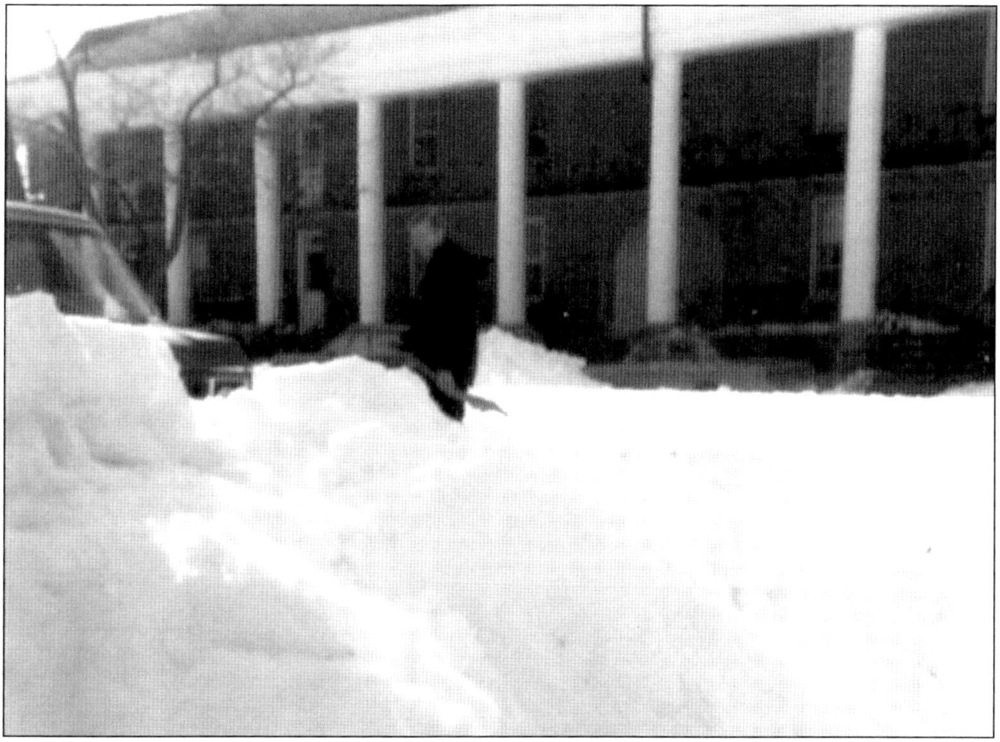

The same snowstorm left drifts as high as the fences and covered the cars inside the fort. Since the access to the fort was through the narrow passage over the sally port, large snowplows or sanding trucks had to be replaced by snow shovels for clearing away the snow.

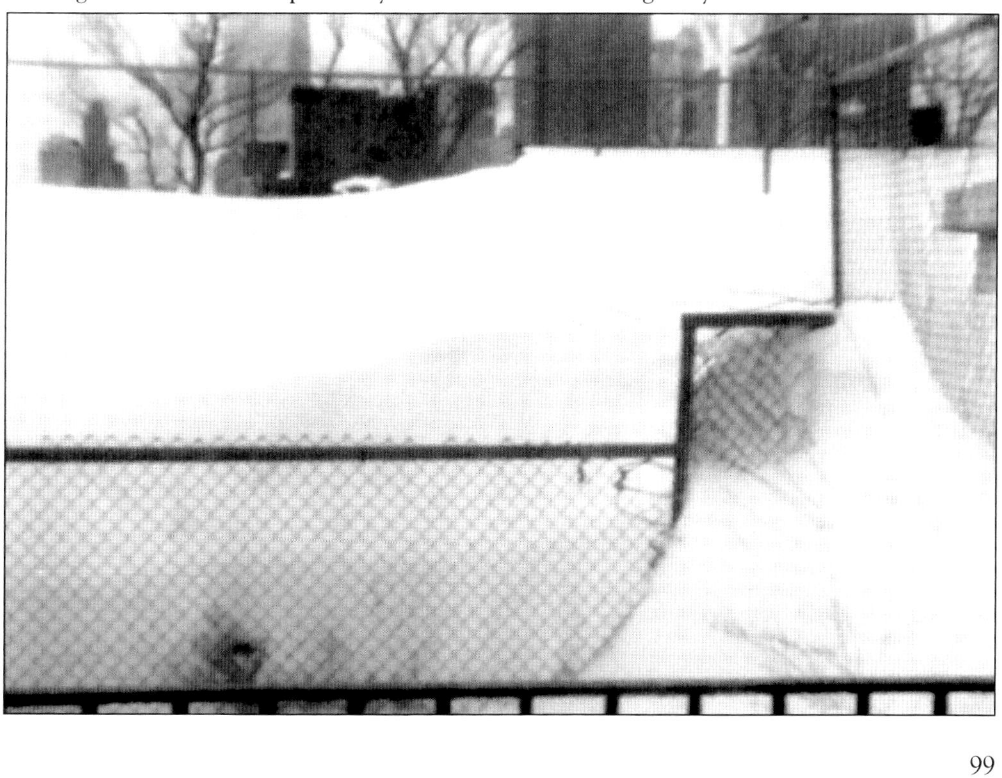

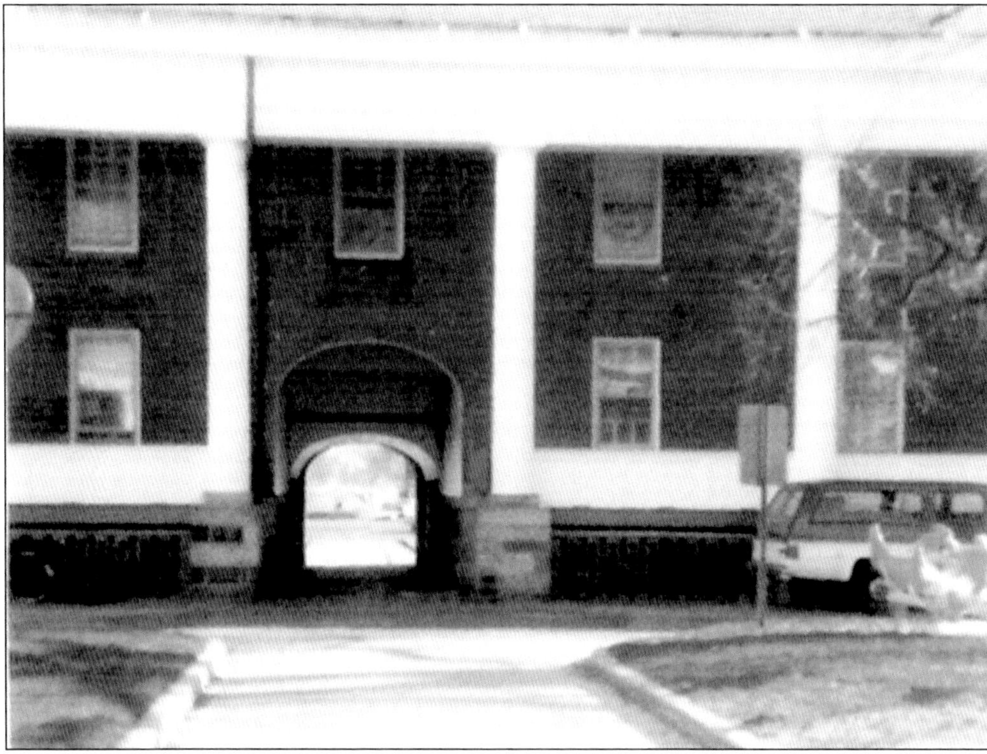

This is the Fort Jay quadrangle looking out through the back entrance. At one time there was a pathway that went from here to Castle Williams.

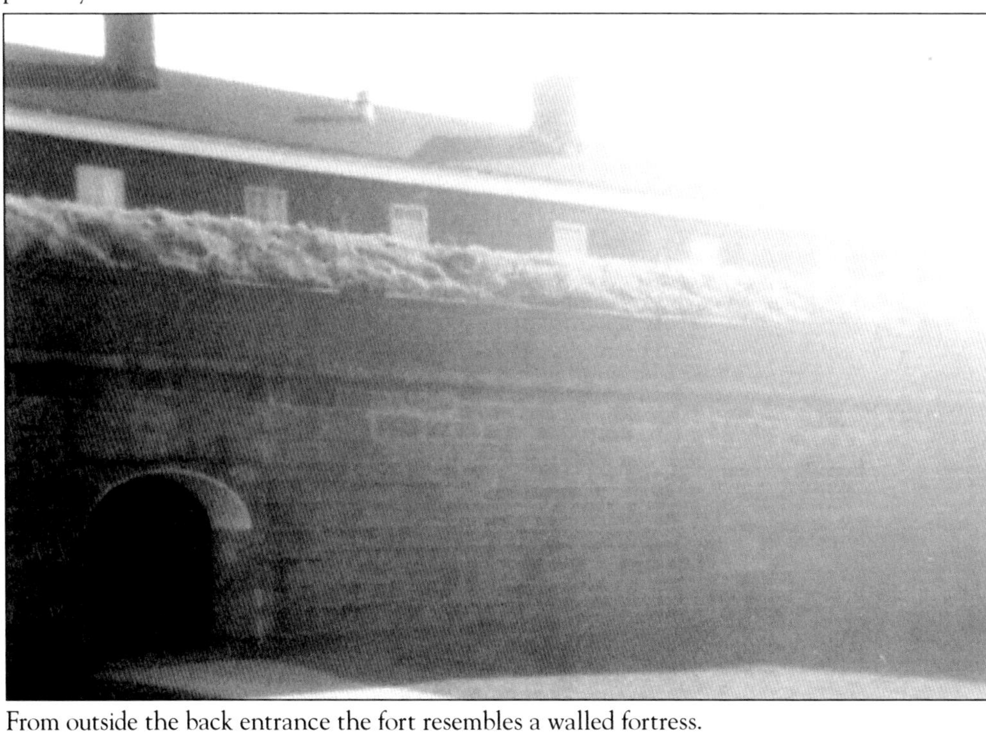

From outside the back entrance the fort resembles a walled fortress.

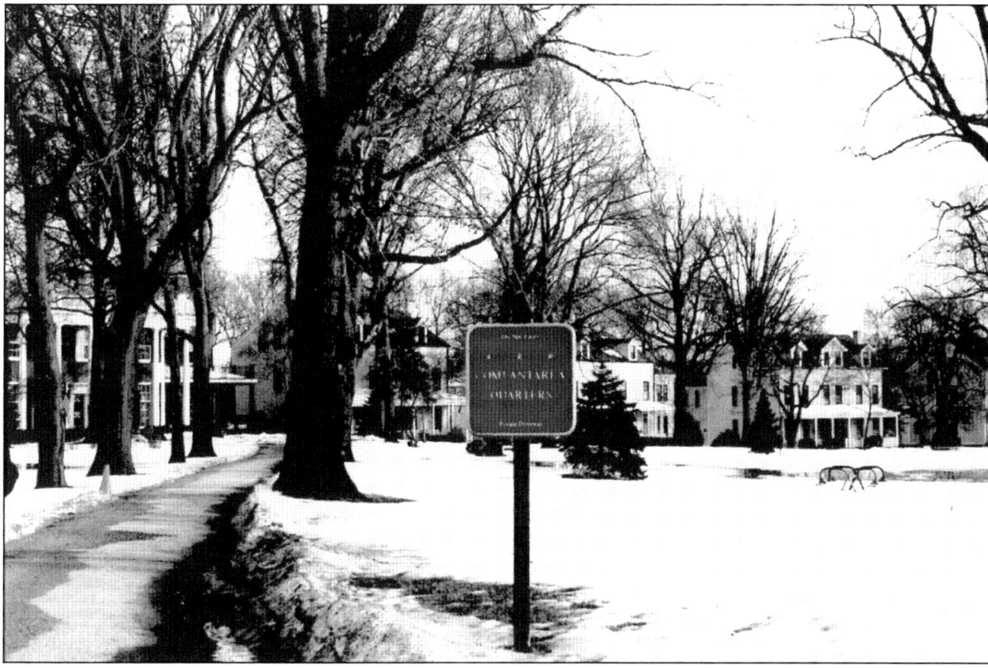

The sign, commanding officers quarters, is at the beginning of Nolan Park and just south of the National Park Monument offices. Following the wide brick walkway you pass the houses built from 1838 to 1904, or if you exit the park at the southern end you will come to St. Cornelius chapel and the South Battery.

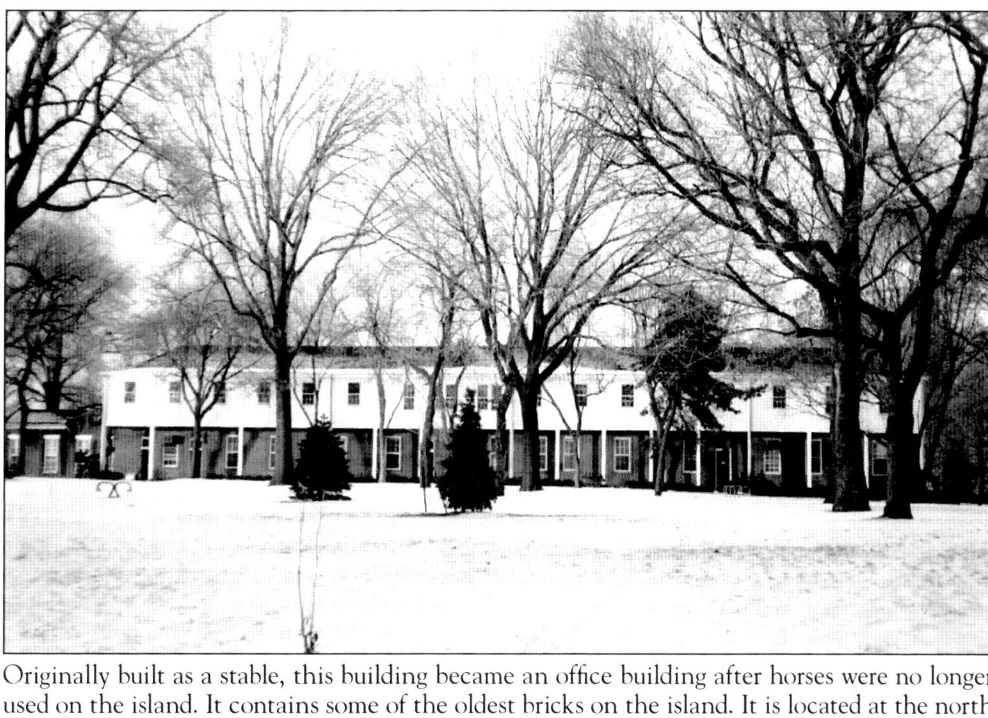

Originally built as a stable, this building became an office building after horses were no longer used on the island. It contains some of the oldest bricks on the island. It is located at the north end of Nolan Park.

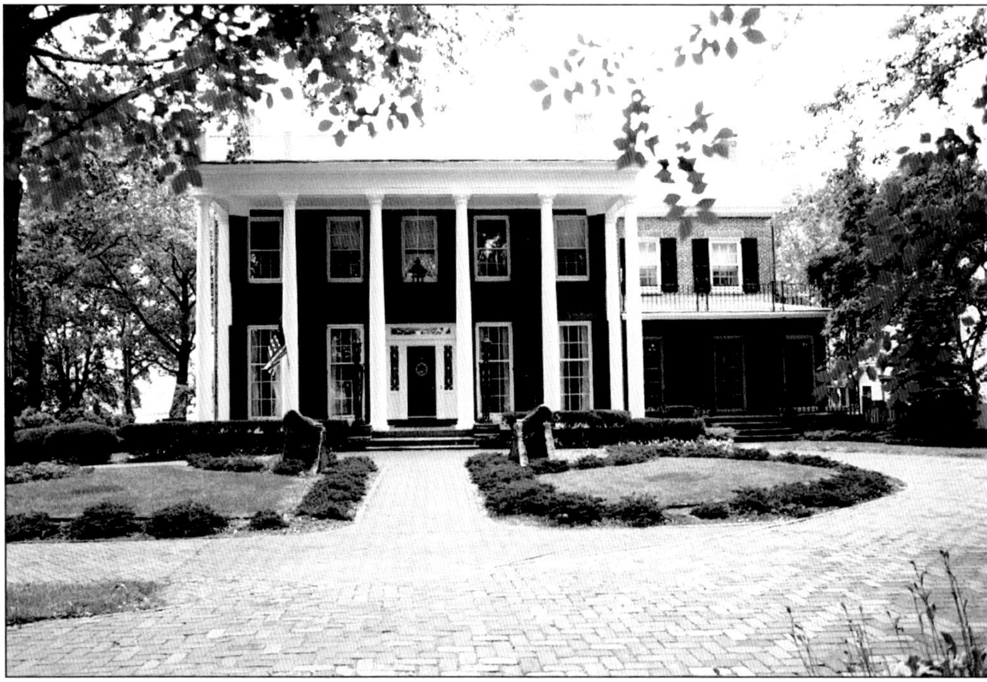

The commanding officer's quarters is the third, and largest, house on the east side of the park. Inside there is a black stone fireplace mantle and a parquet floor as well as old wall and ceiling moldings.

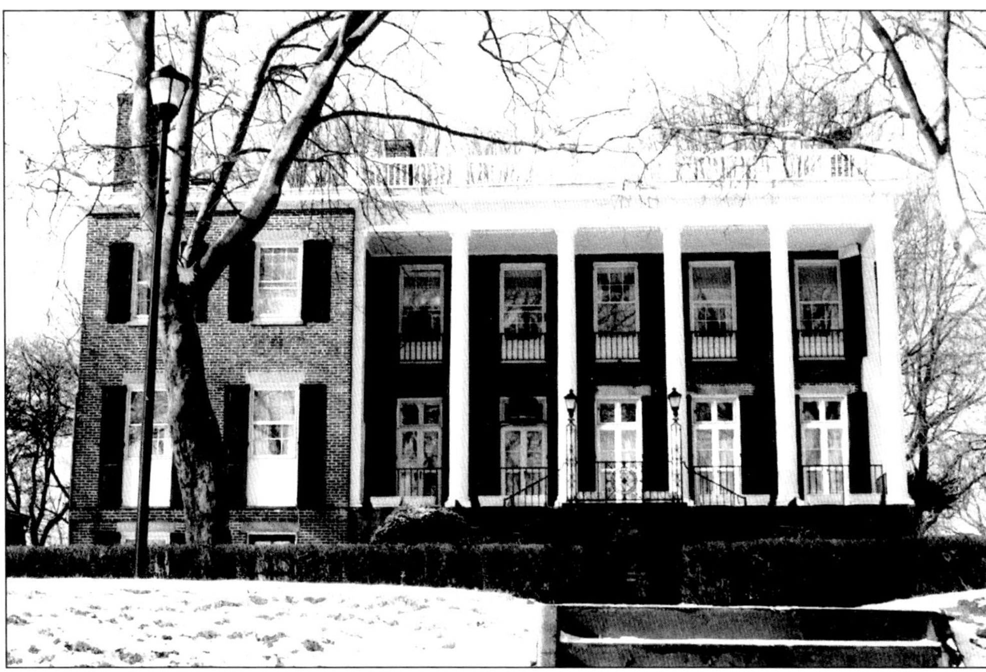

The back of the commanding officer's quarters overlooks Buttermilk Channel and Brooklyn.

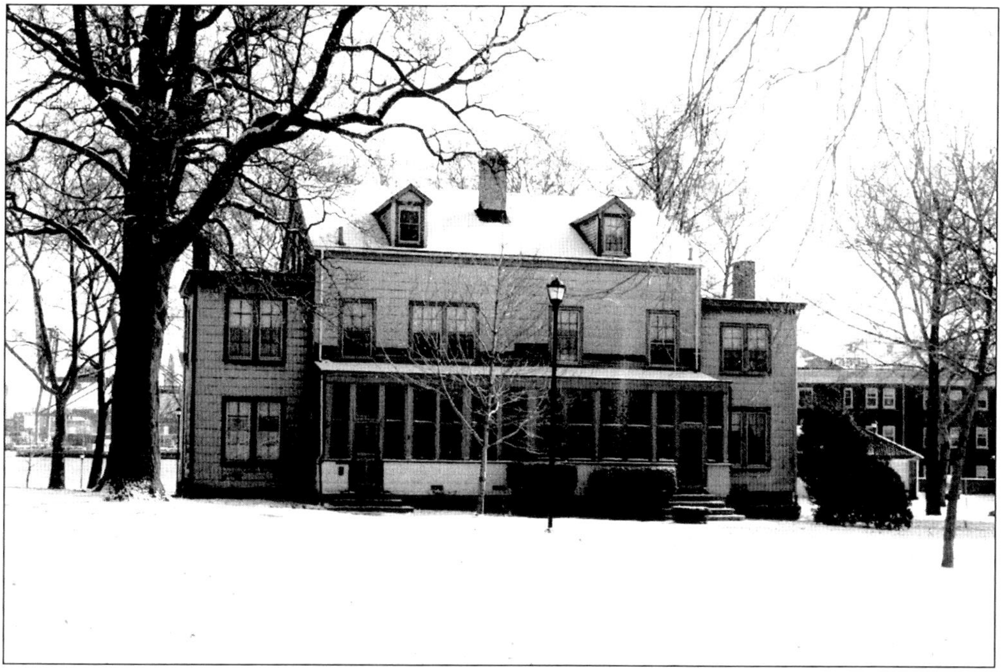

Asbestos siding was added to the houses in Nolan Park sometime in the 1930s. In the spring of 1992, work was begun to remove the siding and restore the original look of the houses. Shown here is Quarters 5.

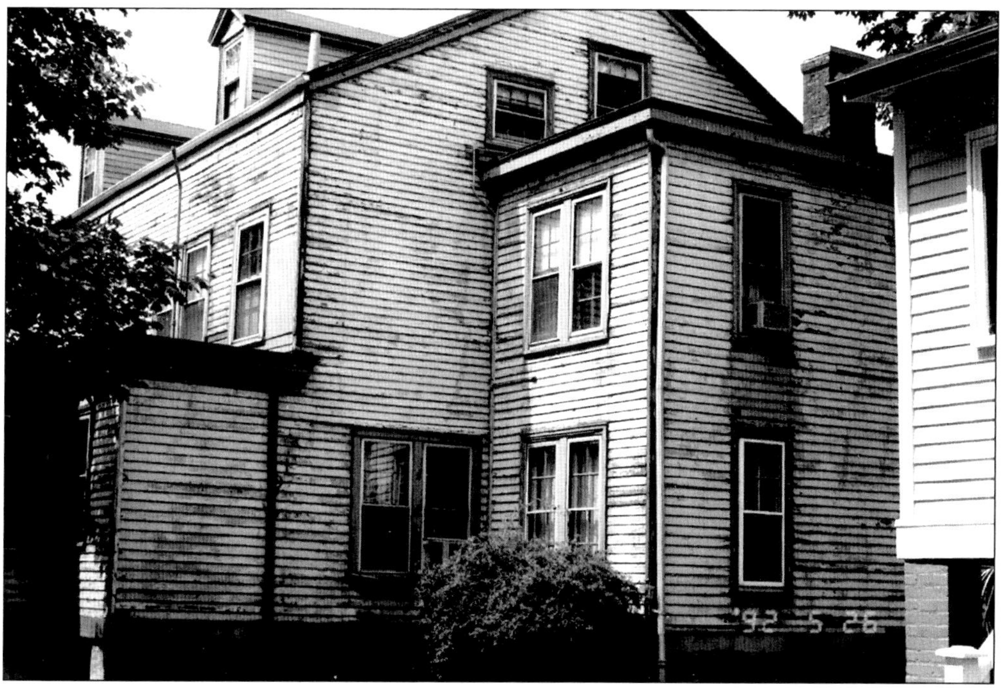

Beneath the siding, many clapboards were found to be rotten and in need of replacement. Plywood sheeting is shown covering the rotten areas that needed to be replaced.

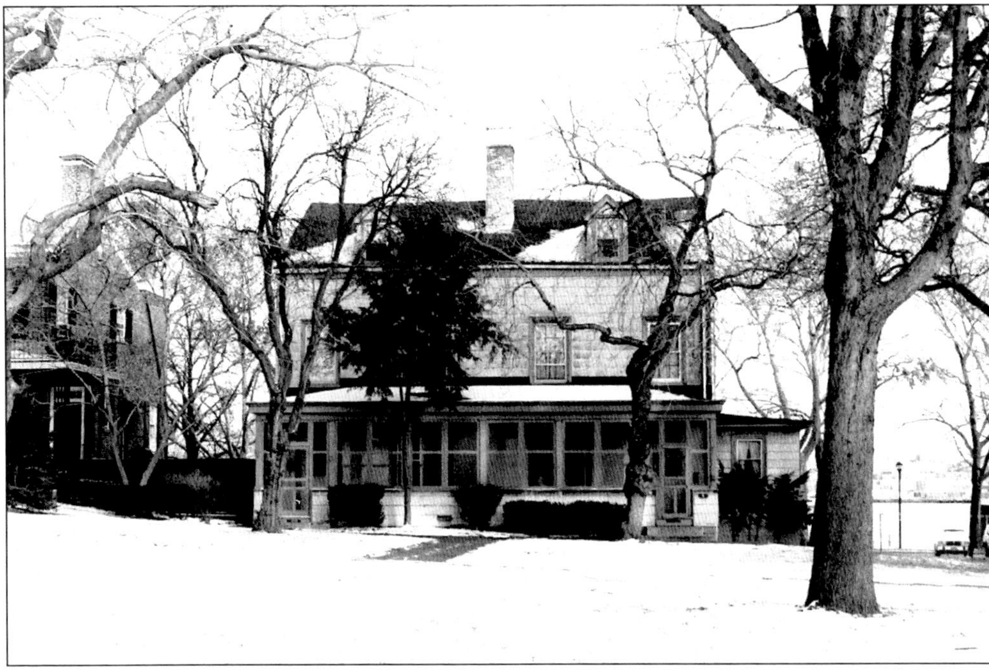

These two views show the front and back of Quarters 4 before the siding was removed.

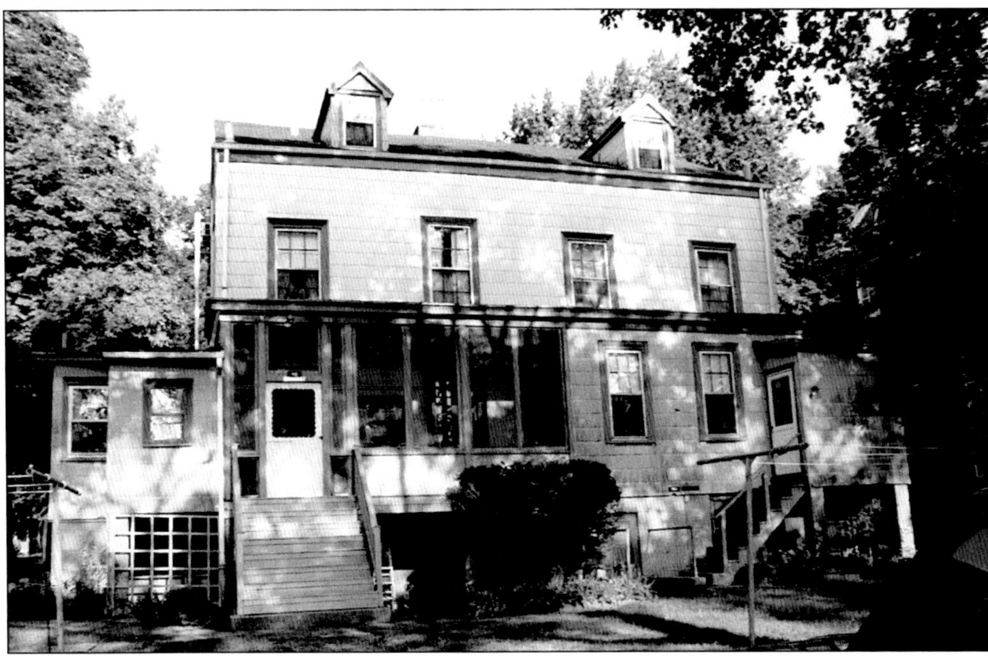

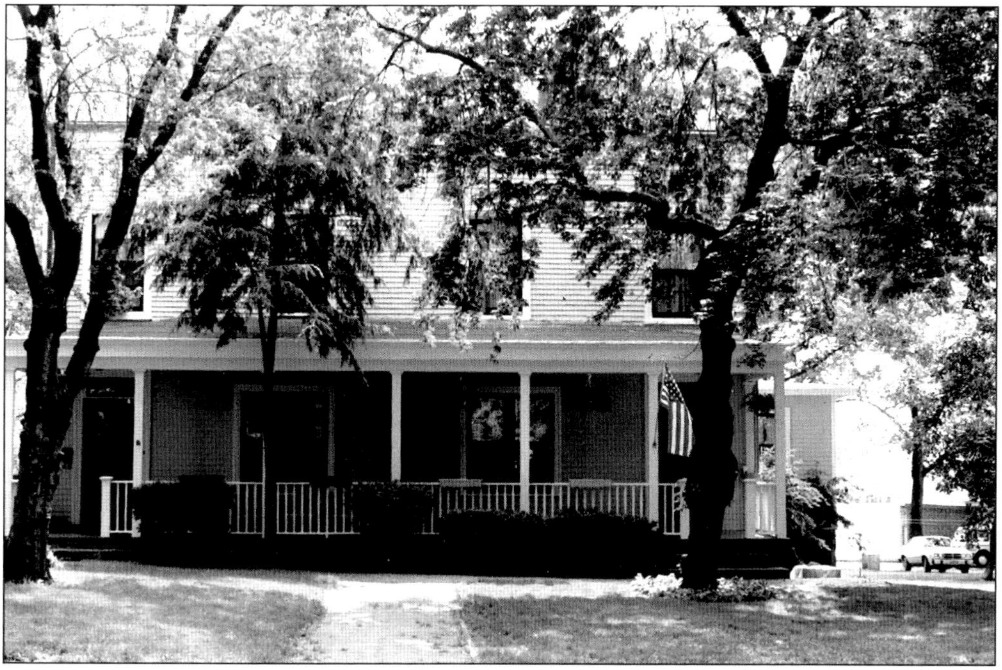

Quarters 4 is shown after the renovation. Copper gutters and downspouts were added to replace the old ones and a new coat of yellow paint, similar to the original 1850 paint, completed the renovation. The side addition of a kitchen had been added in about 1932. This was a two family quarters and has 92 inch original French doors leading off the dining room onto the screened porch. The enclosed front porches were also removed.

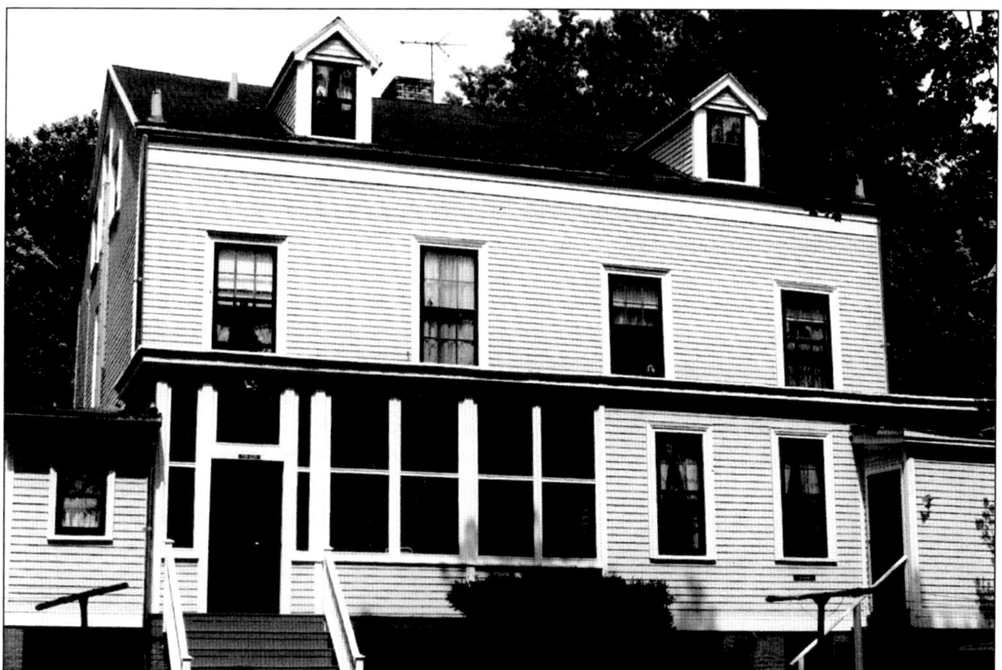

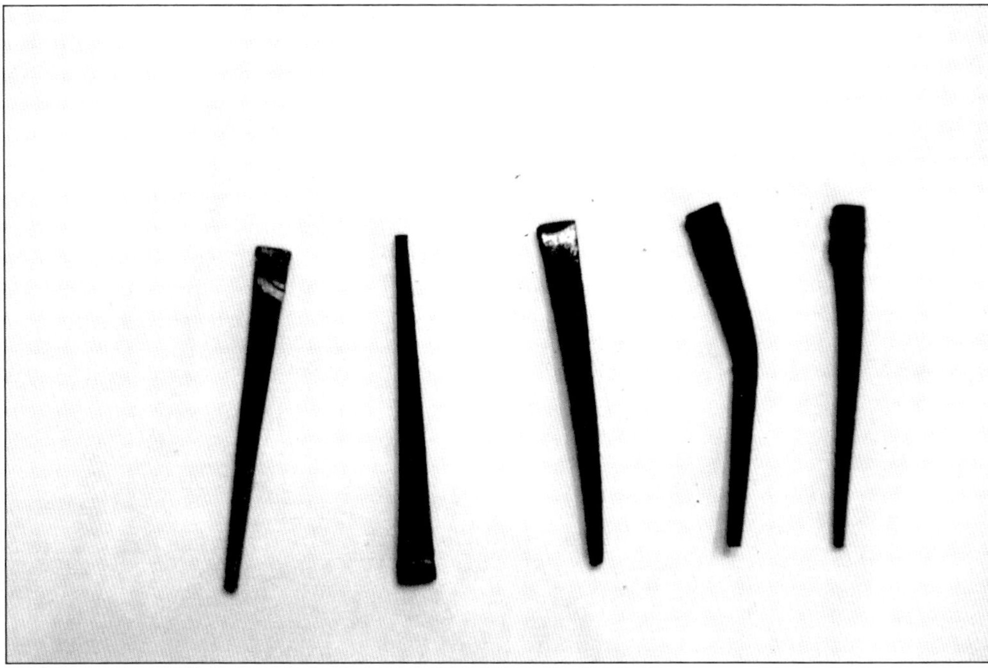

Handmade square nails have been used in many of the original constructions. These are from Quarters 4.

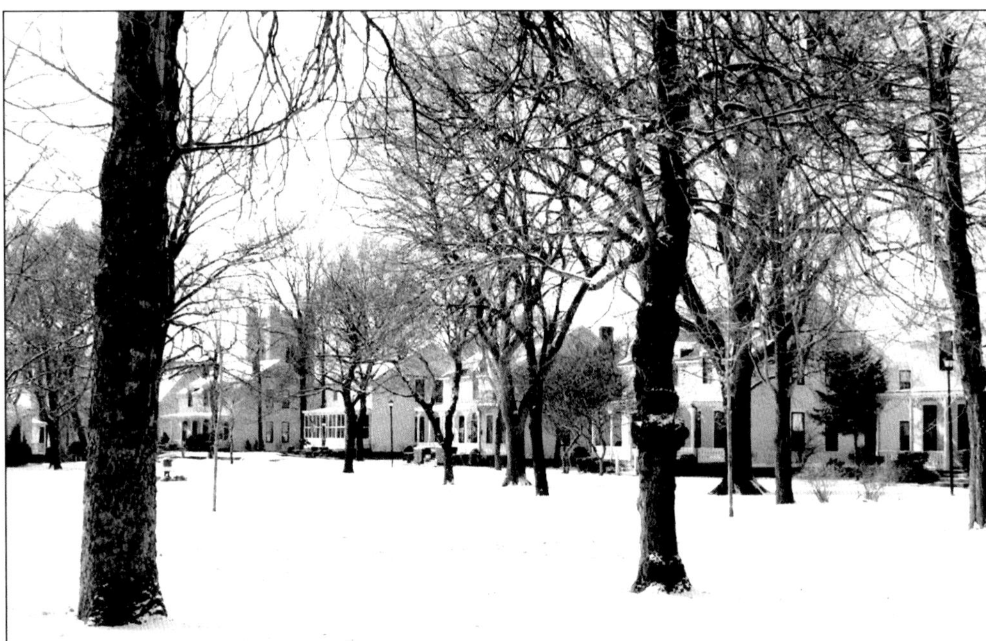

Shown here is the west side of Nolan Park showing houses of the original General's Row after renovation.

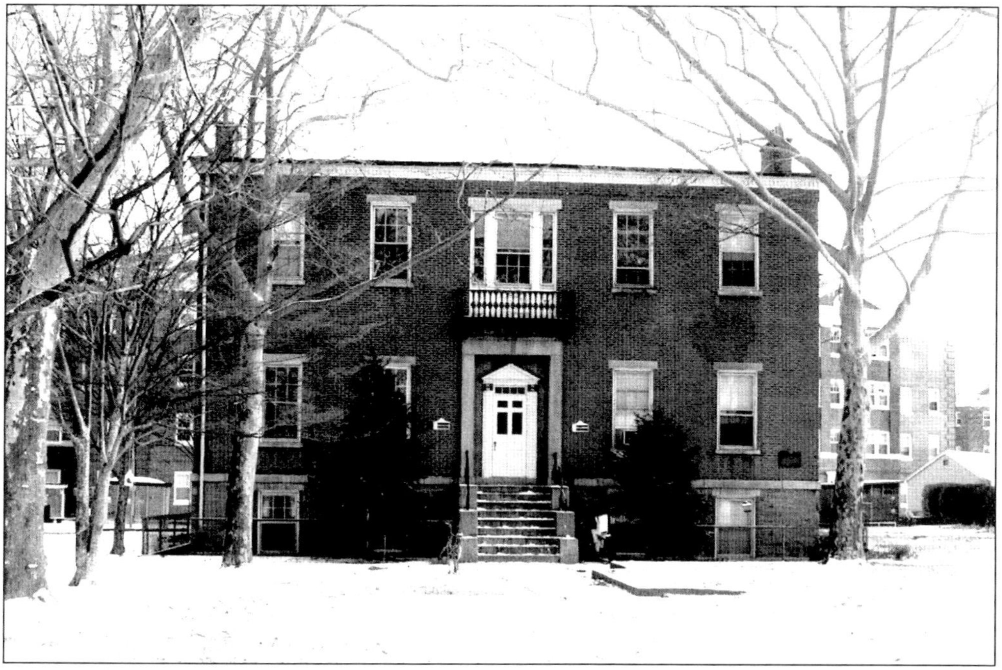

In 1992, the Blockhouse also underwent renovation. Pres. Ulysses S. Grant is believed to have stayed in this building when he was a lieutenant in the U.S. Army.

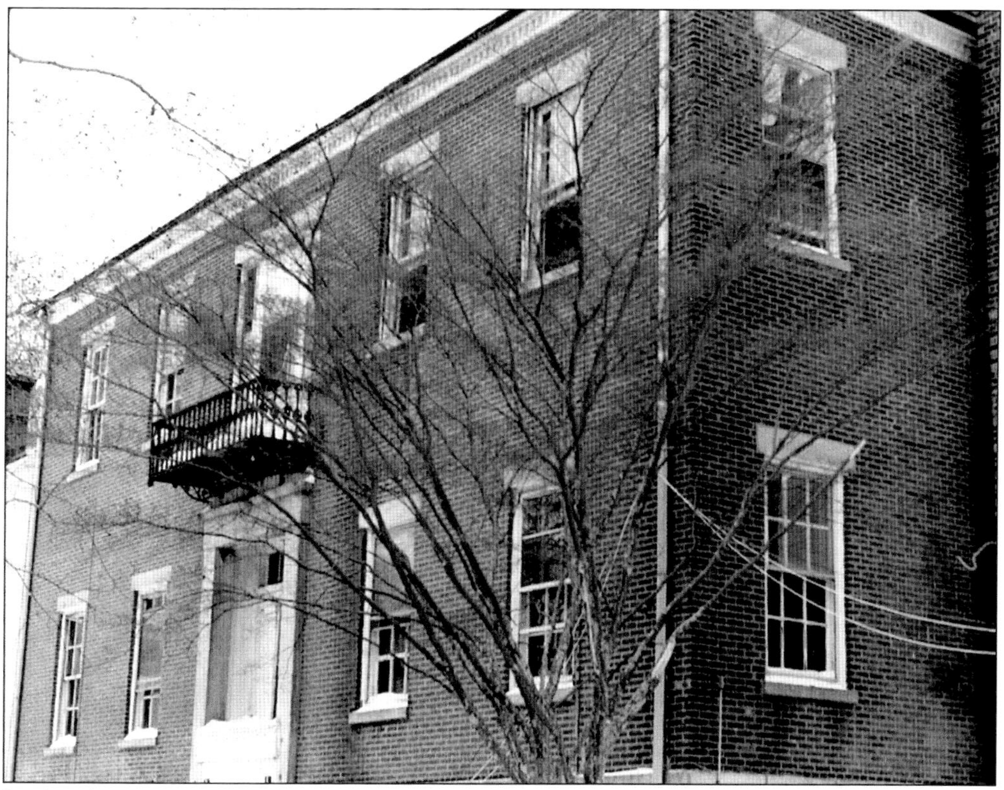

In this close-up, you can observe some of the architectural details of the building.

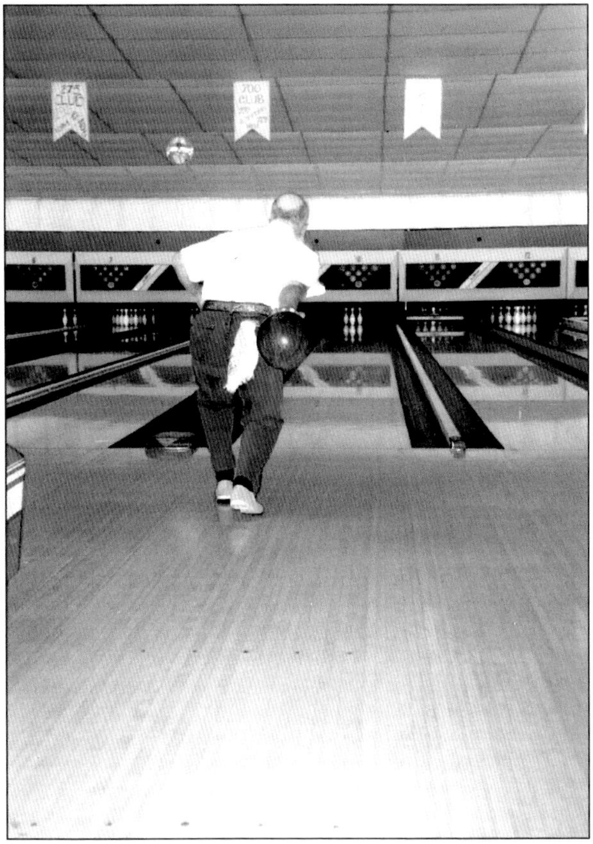

Built in 1968, the island bowling alley provided recreation for all.

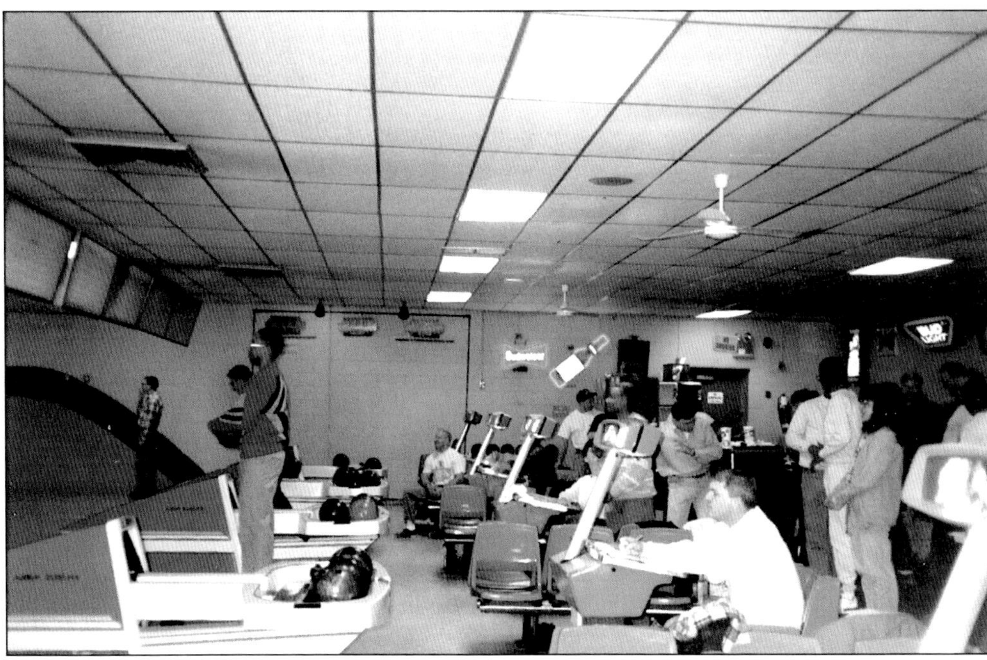

A Burger King attached to the bowling alley served pizza and beer as well as the usual fare.

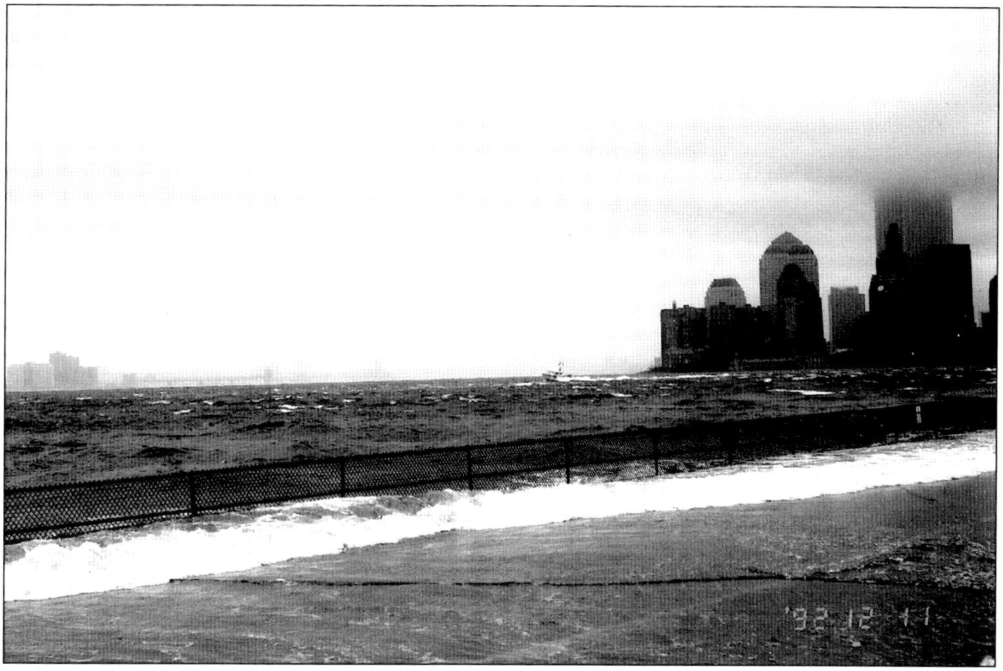

In December 1992, a hurricane came up the Atlantic seaboard causing flooding on the island. New York Harbor breached the seawall around the island.

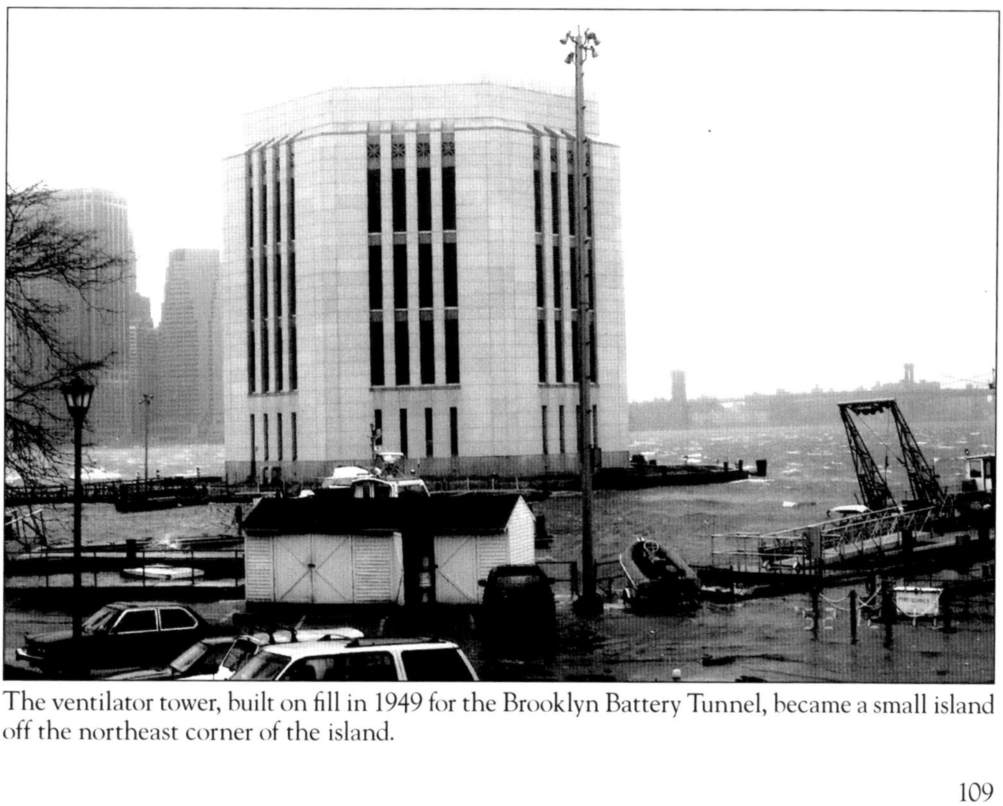

The ventilator tower, built on fill in 1949 for the Brooklyn Battery Tunnel, became a small island off the northeast corner of the island.

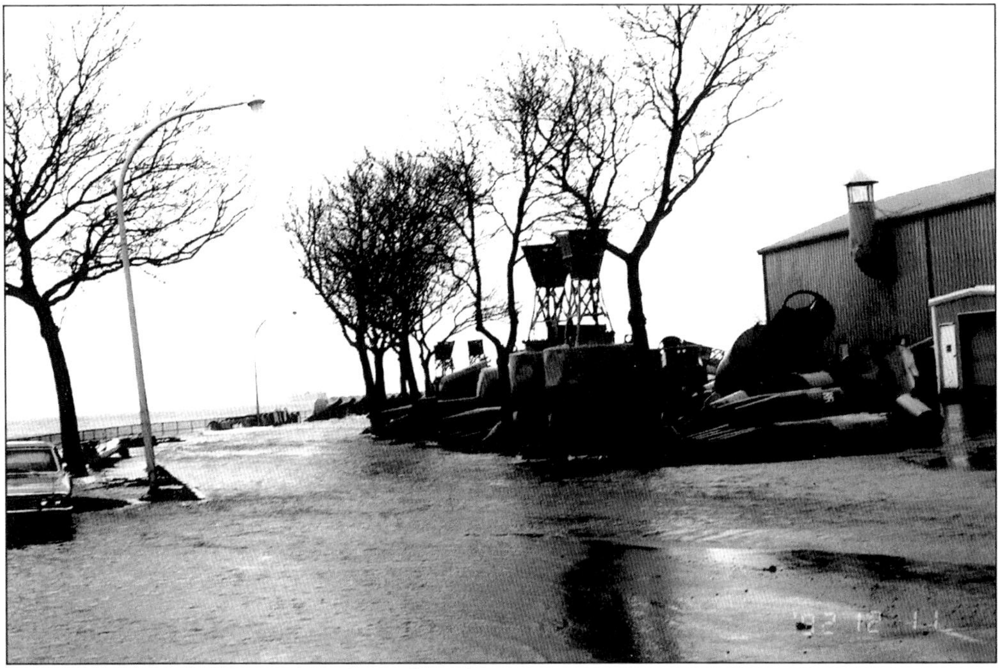

Cars and buoys were floating in the parking lot.

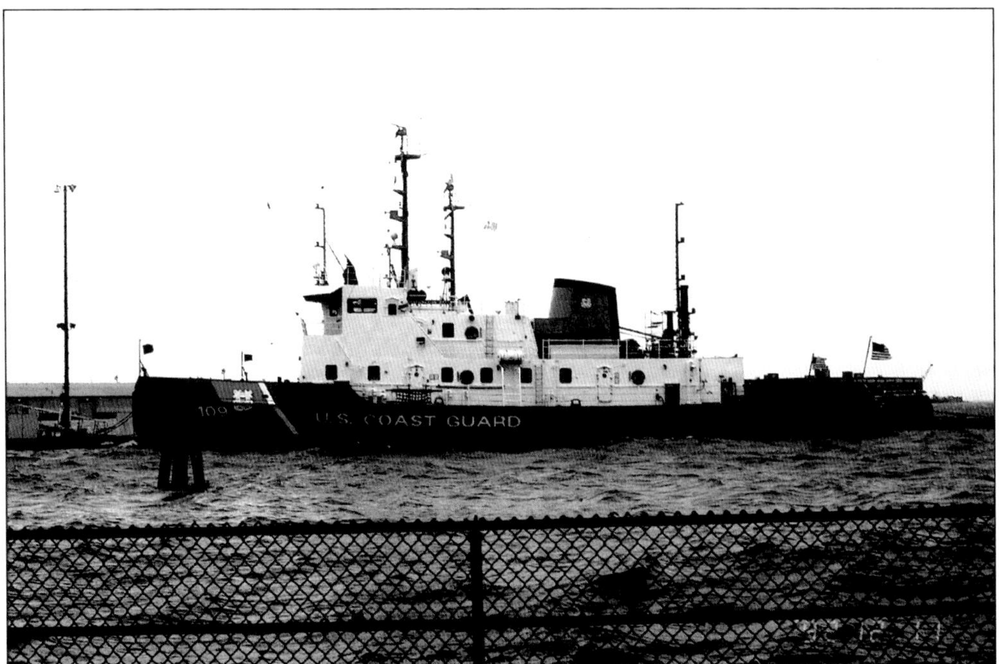

A Coast Guard buoy tender rode the high tide.

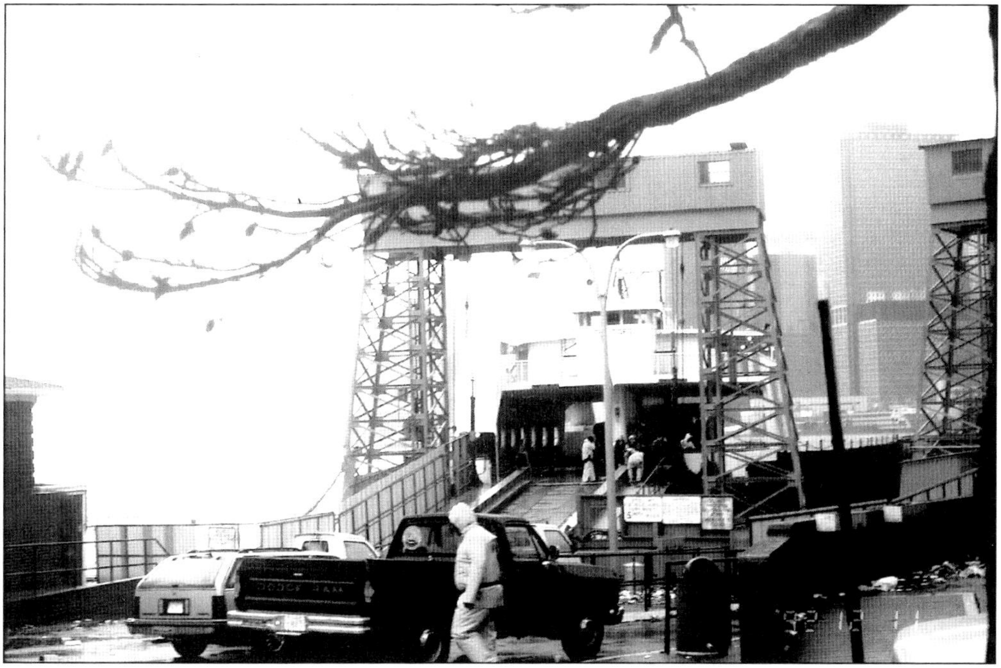

An exceptionally high tide caused the ramp at the dock to rise almost too steep to meet the ferry *Tides*. The *Tides* began service to the island in 1968.

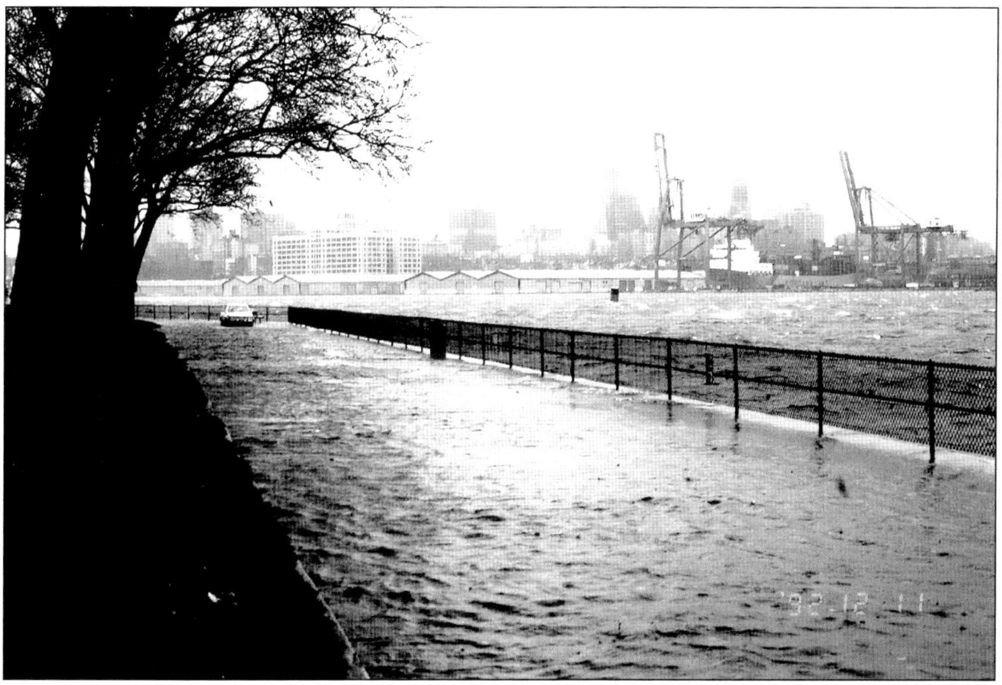

Buttermilk Channel, on the Brooklyn side of the island, ran above the island's seawall.

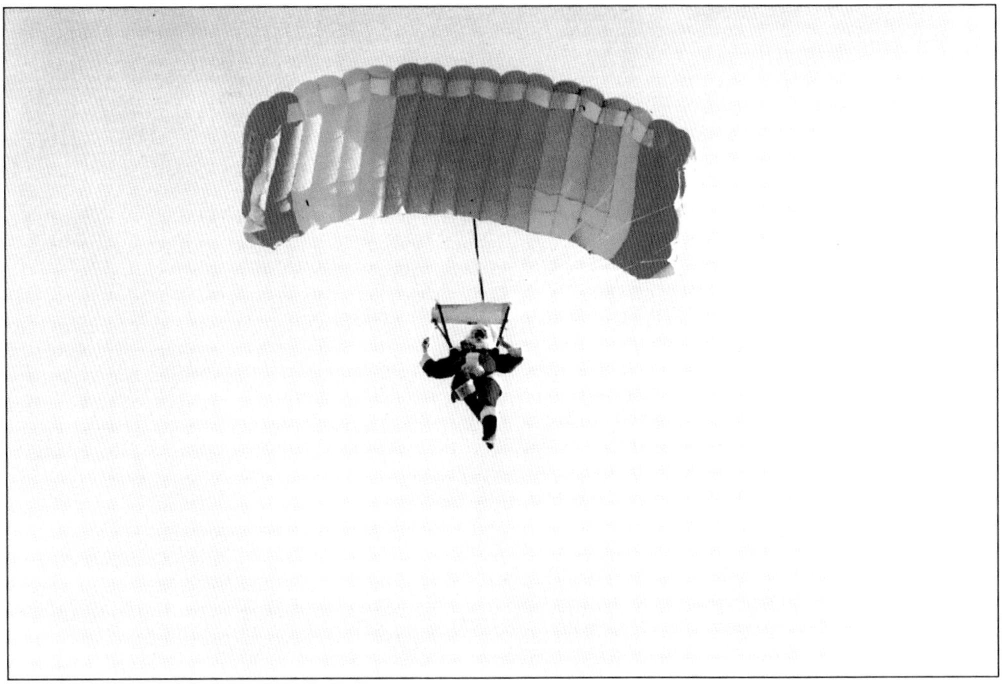

Santa Claus, Michelle Wenk, arrived by air minus her sleigh to the delight of the schoolchildren at Public School 26, Frederick C. Billard School. Built in 1972, it was the island's elementary school. The event was coordinated by Scot Evans with skydivers from Blue Sky Ranch.

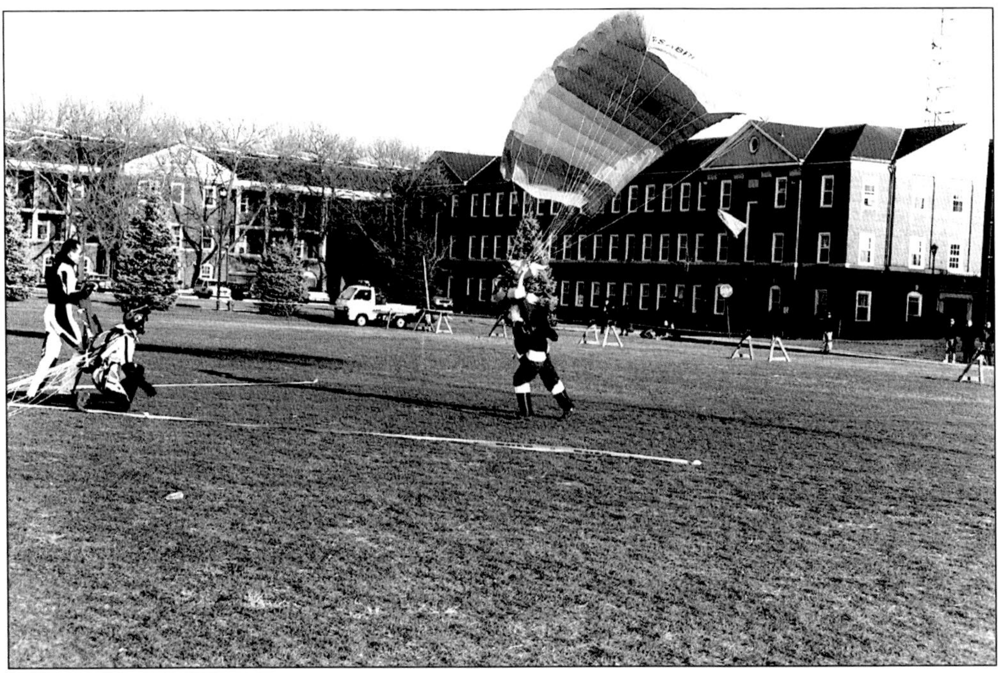

Santa landed on the ground behind building 100. (Courtesy of Willie Botcher.)

Mark Tripari arrived with the American Flag.

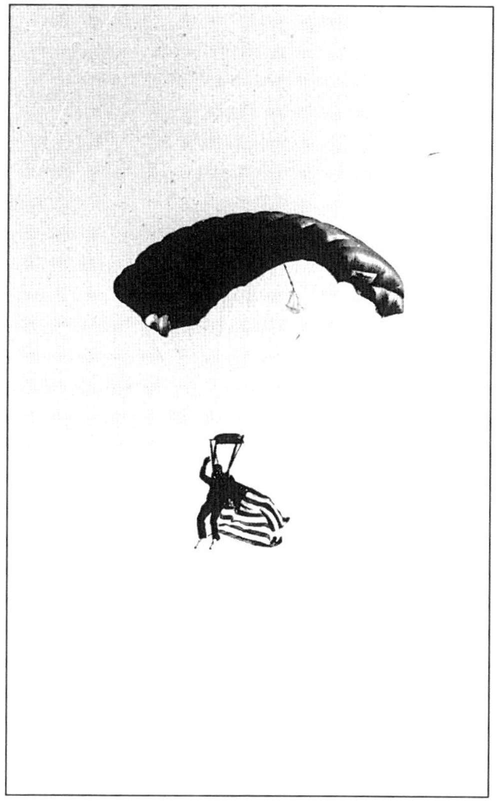

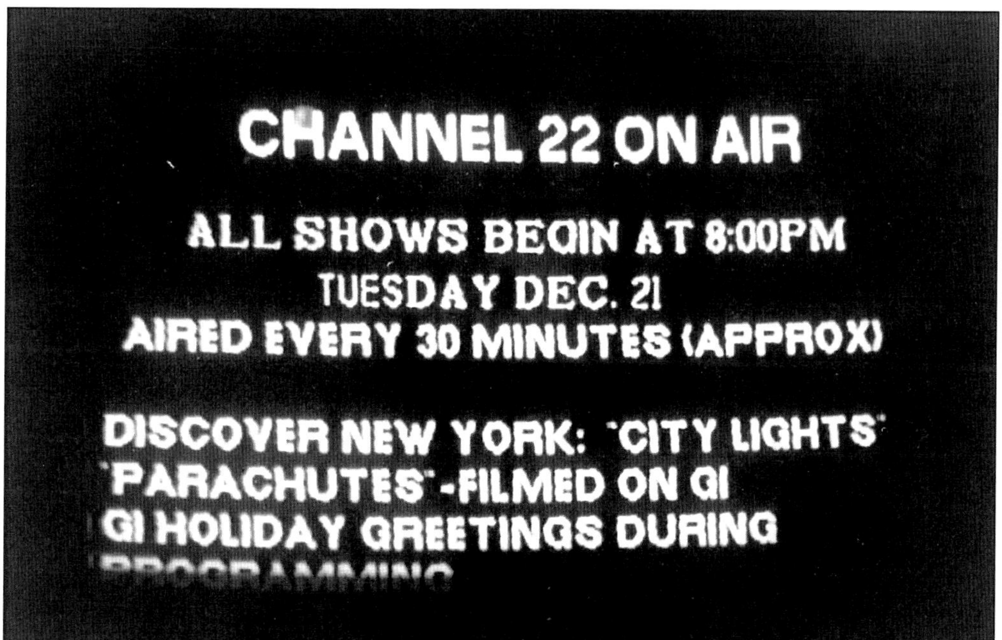

Those unable to witness the arrival of Santa were able to watch a replay on the island's own television station.

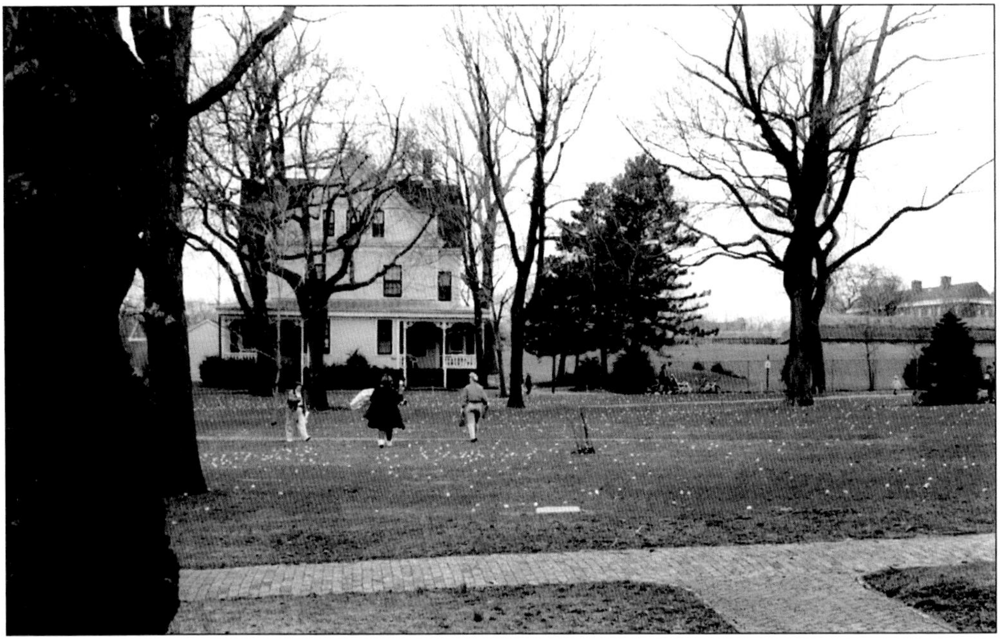

Easter egg hunts were held in Nolan Park for the children living on the island.

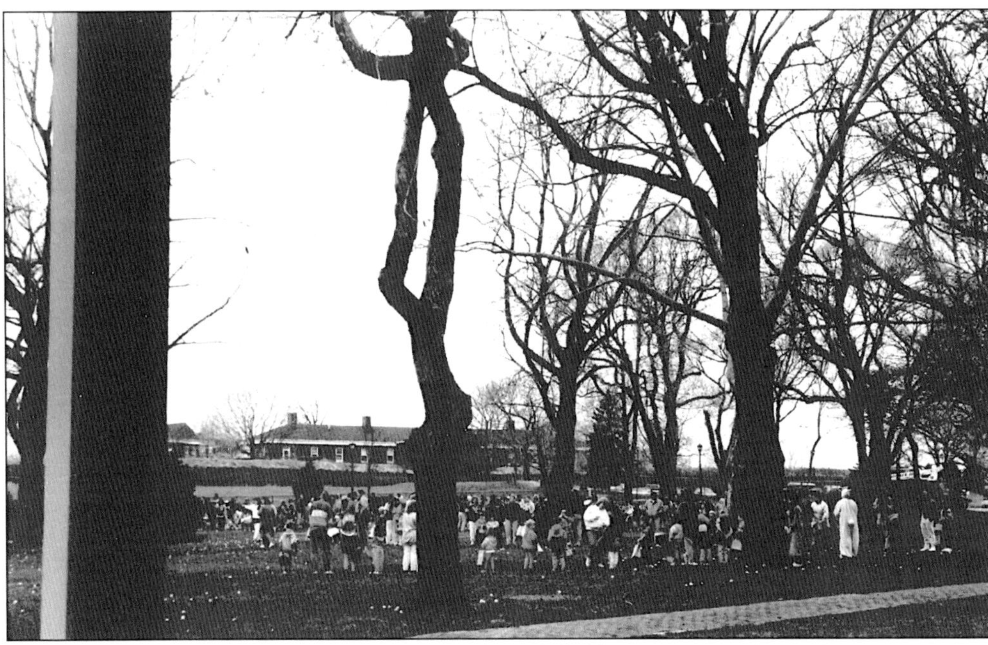

Plastic eggs were scattered throughout the park and children went searching. Sections were set aside for the different age groups.

The snow storm of 1993 piled high drifts blocking many doors. This one led to the Bachelor Officer's Quarters. (Courtesy of Scot Evans.)

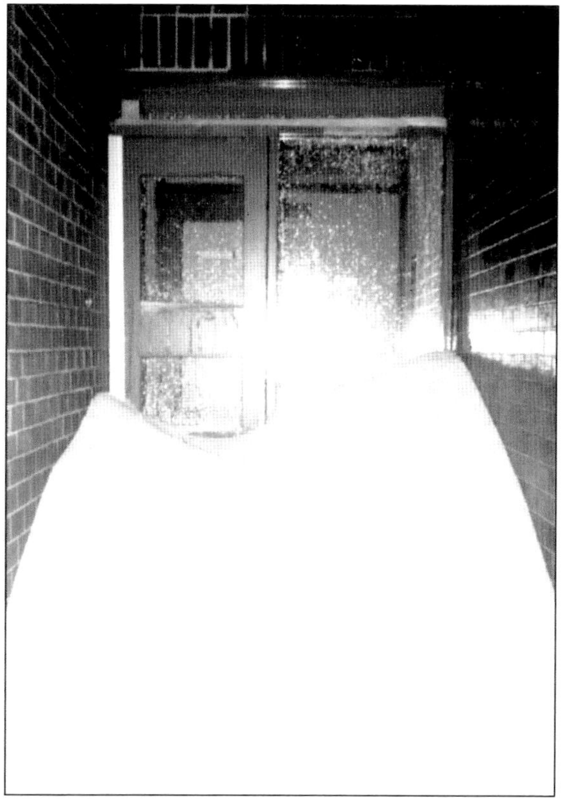

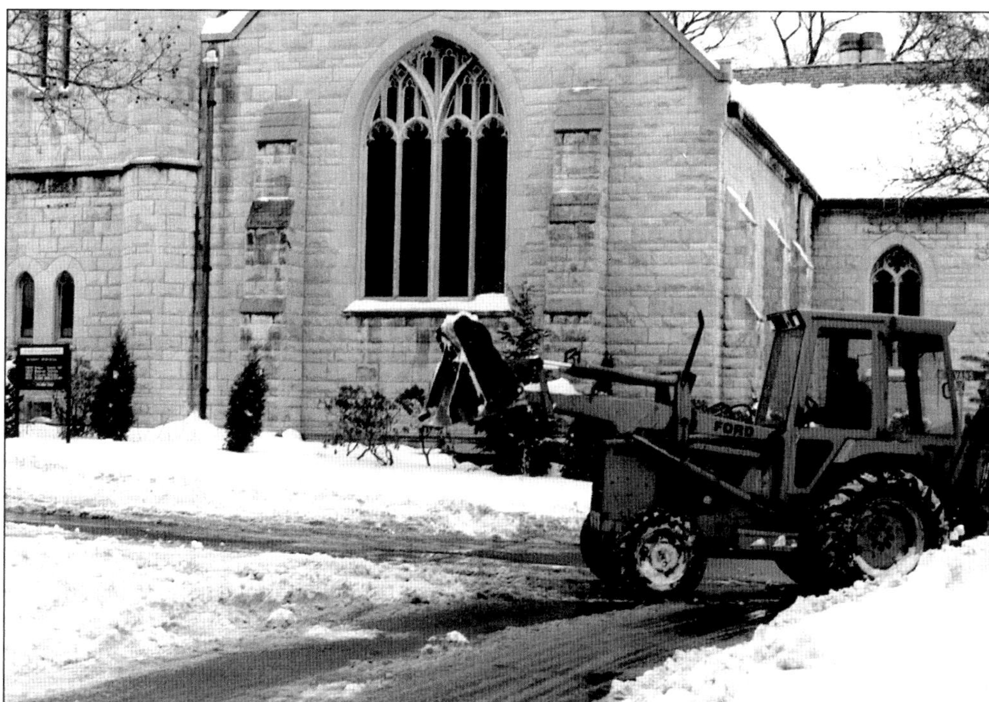

Nolan Park and St. Cornelius chapel were also snowbound.

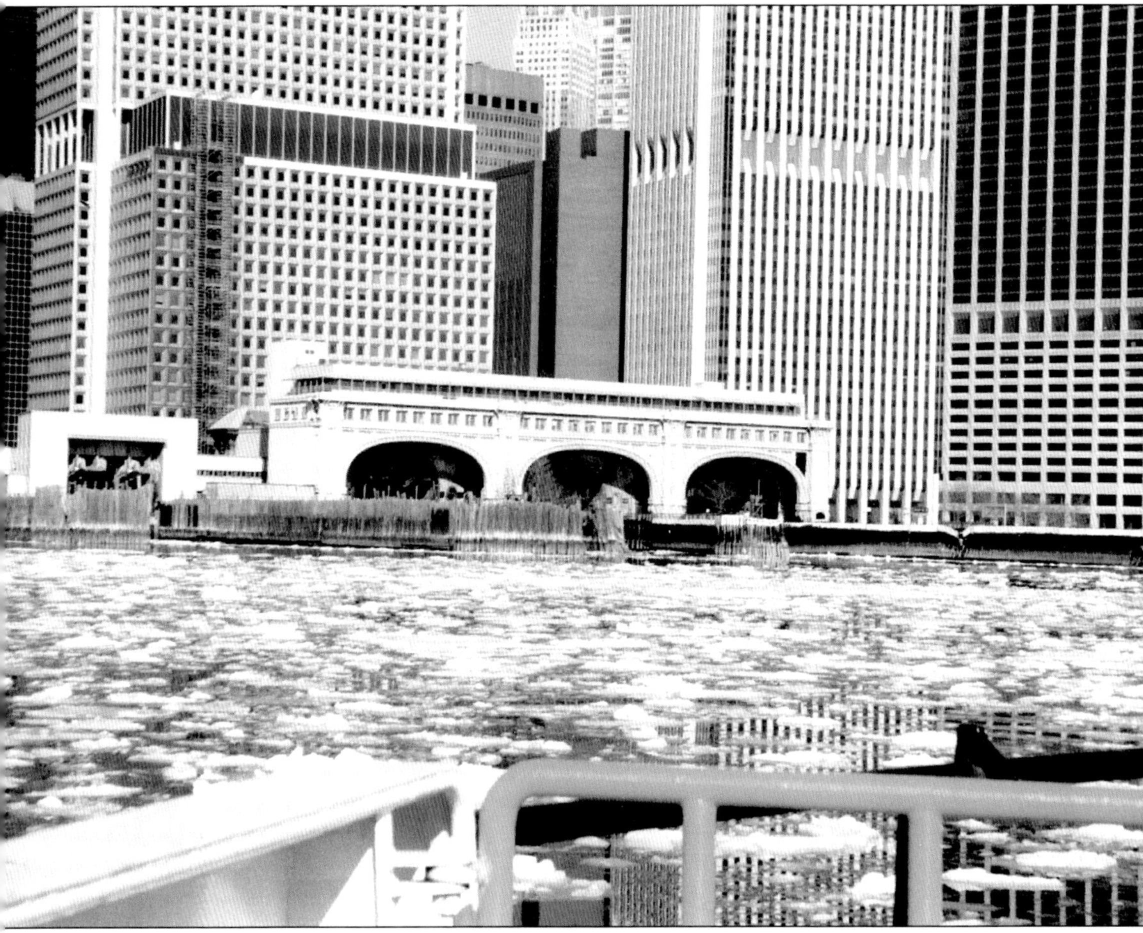

Even the harbor had a layer of ice. The Coast Guard Cutters shown right, and the ferry, on which this picture was taken, had to break through the ice to travel to or leave the island.

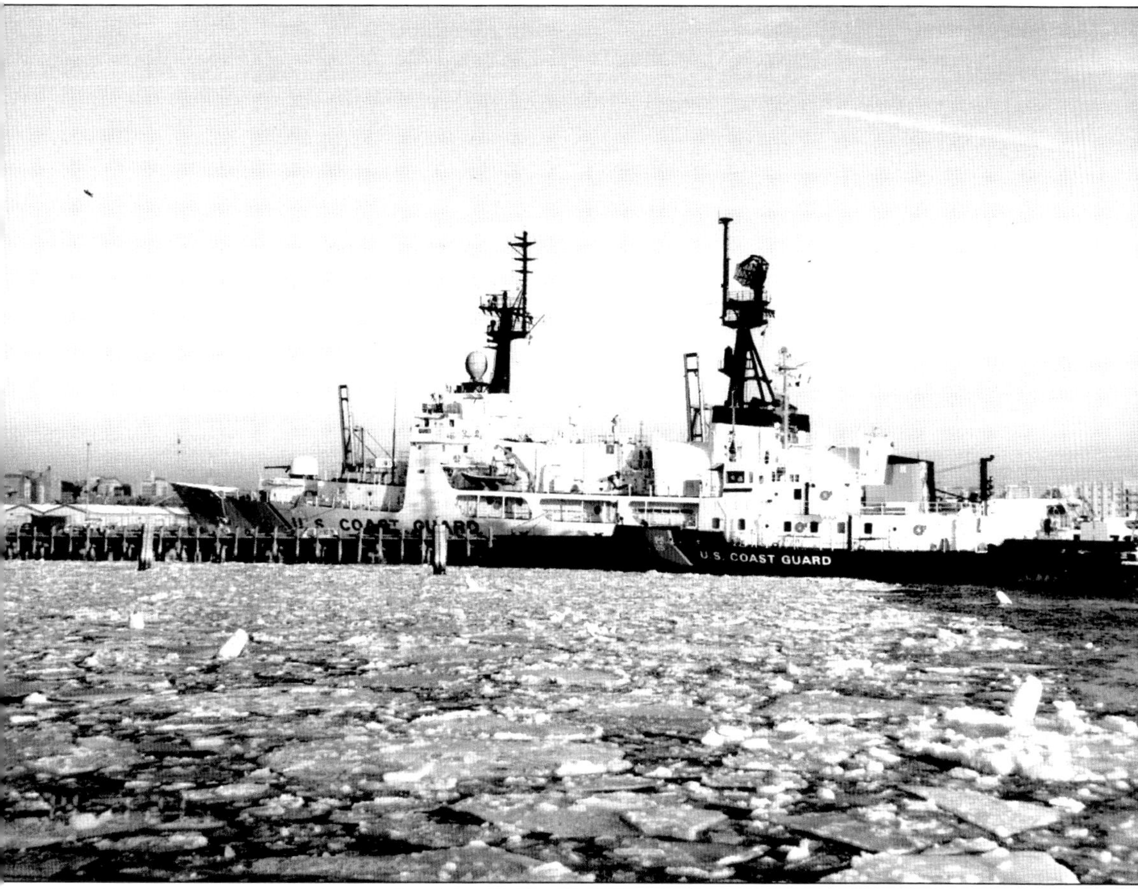

The *Penobscot Bay*, a 140-foot icebreaker tug, broke through the ice in the harbor.

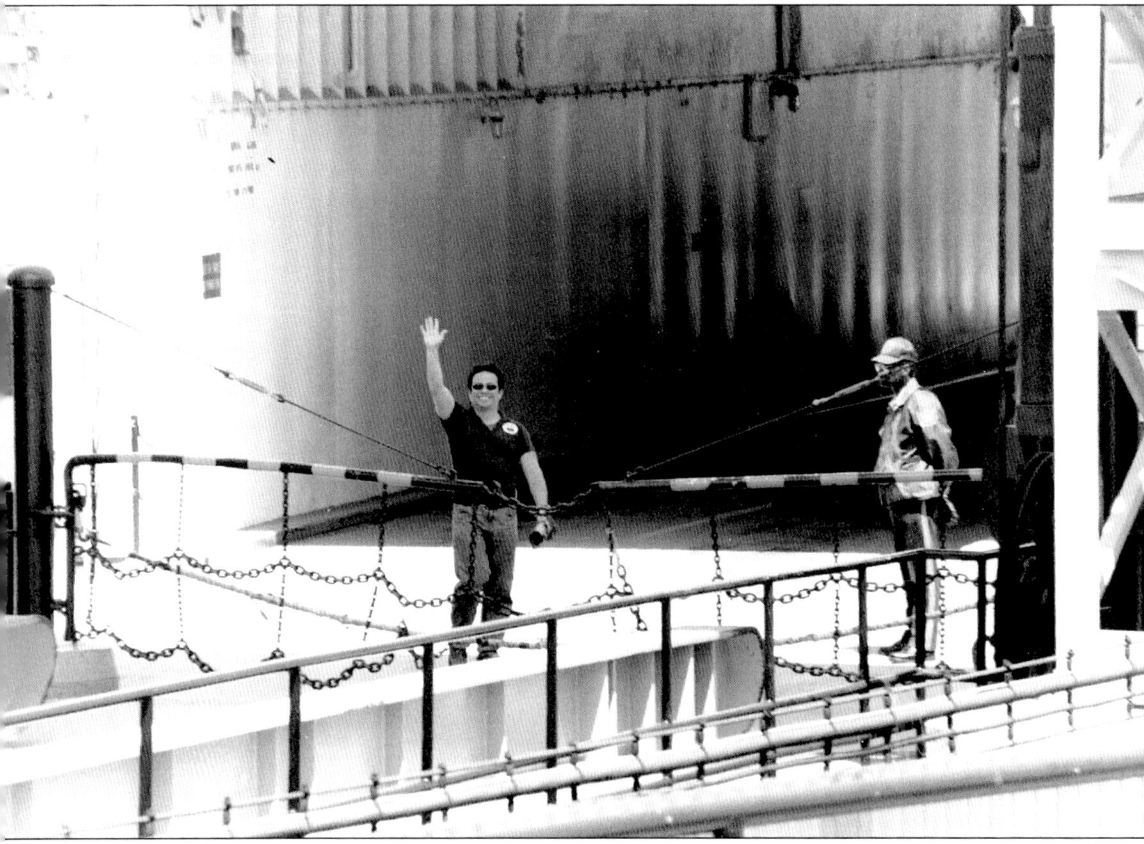

A member of the ferry crew waves as the ferry prepares for its seven-minute ride from the island to Manhattan.

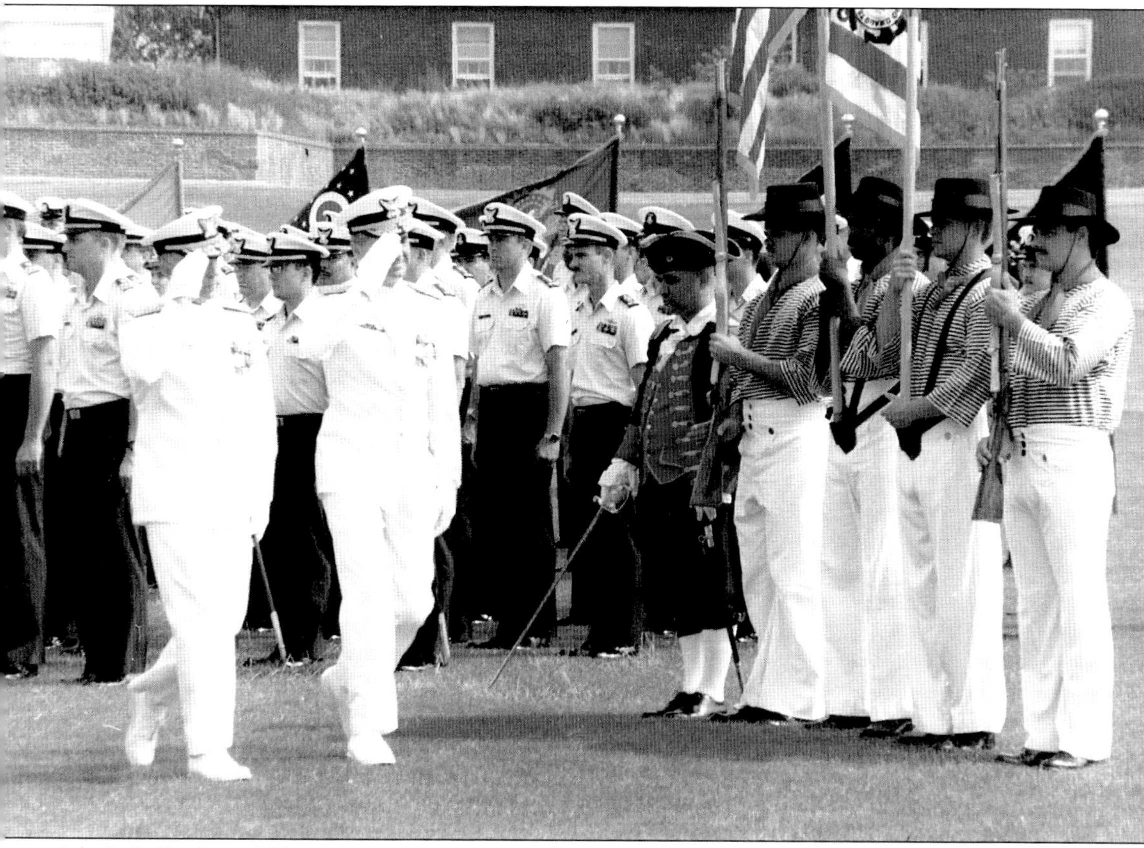

Admirals Faigle and Teeson prepare to inspect the troops on the golf course by Fort Jay.

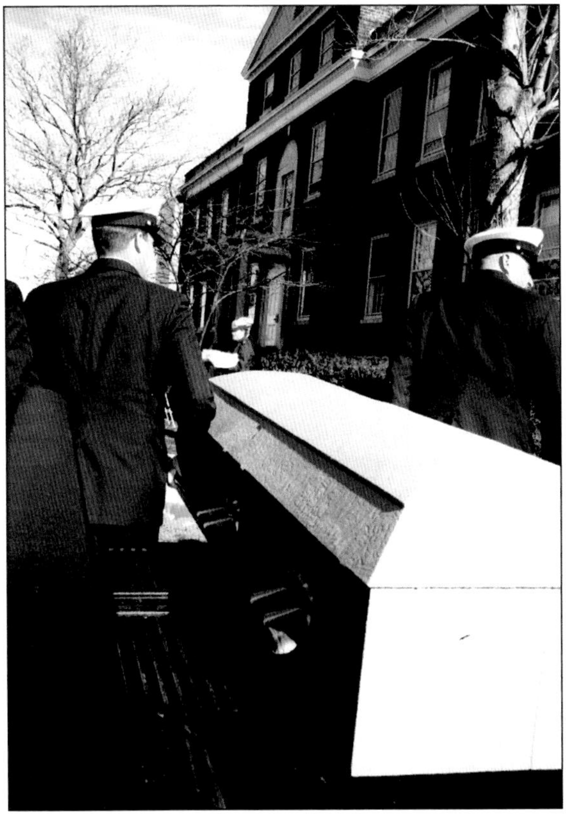

While digging a water line, human remains were discovered in 1994. After forensic investigation they were believed to be those of Revolutionary War seamen and were reinterred in a common grave in 1995.

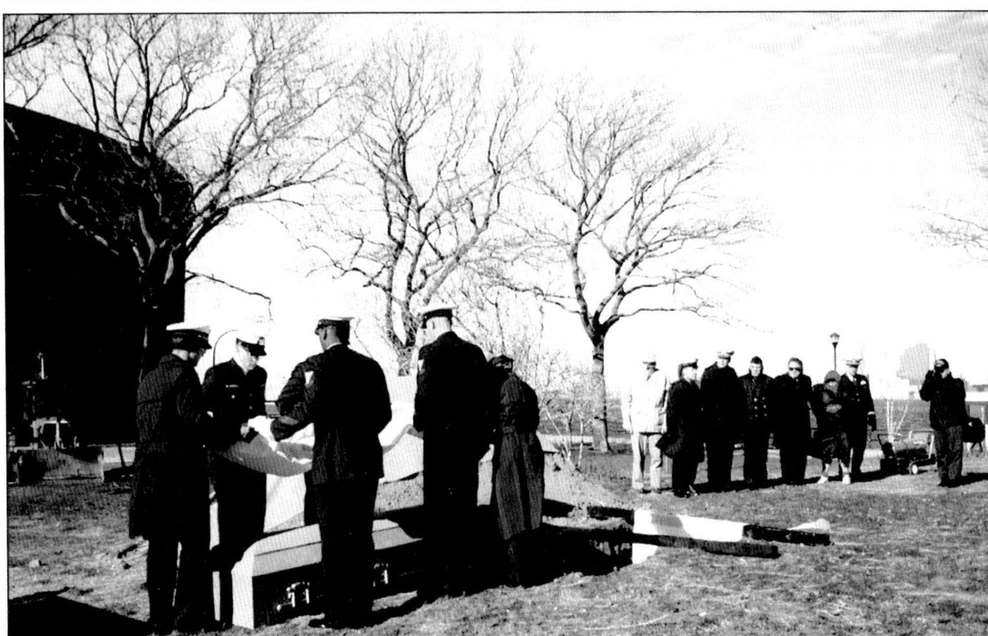

Called the "Andes men" because the remains were found on Andes Road, they were given a burial with full military honors.

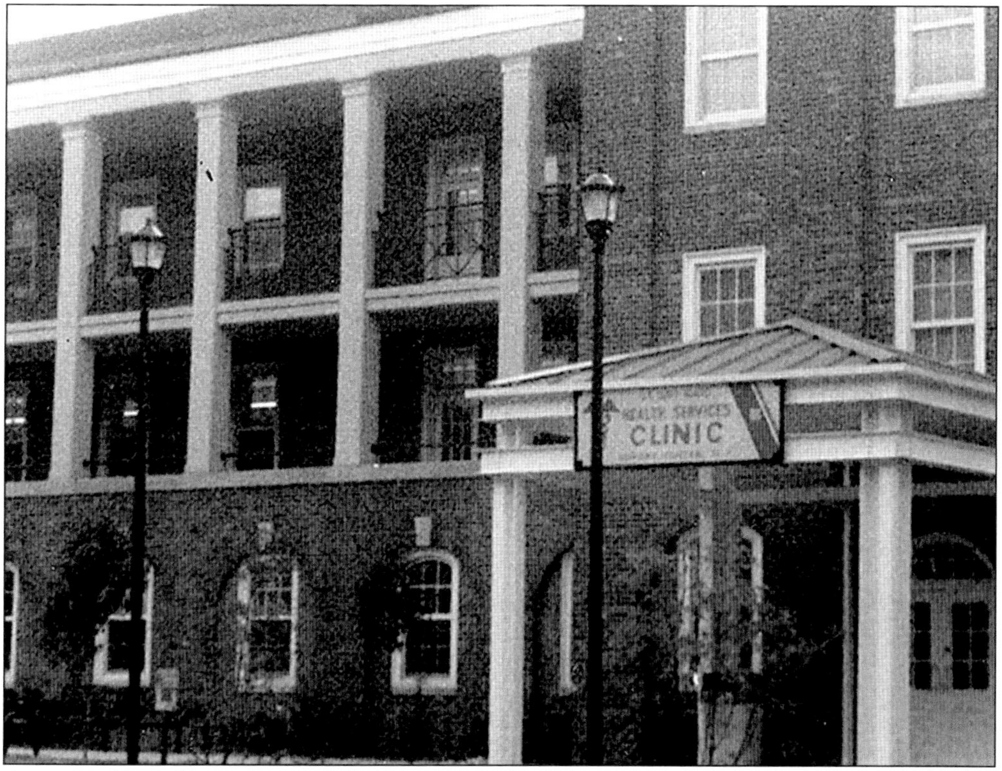

A new medical clinic was opened by the U.S. Coast Guard in 1994.

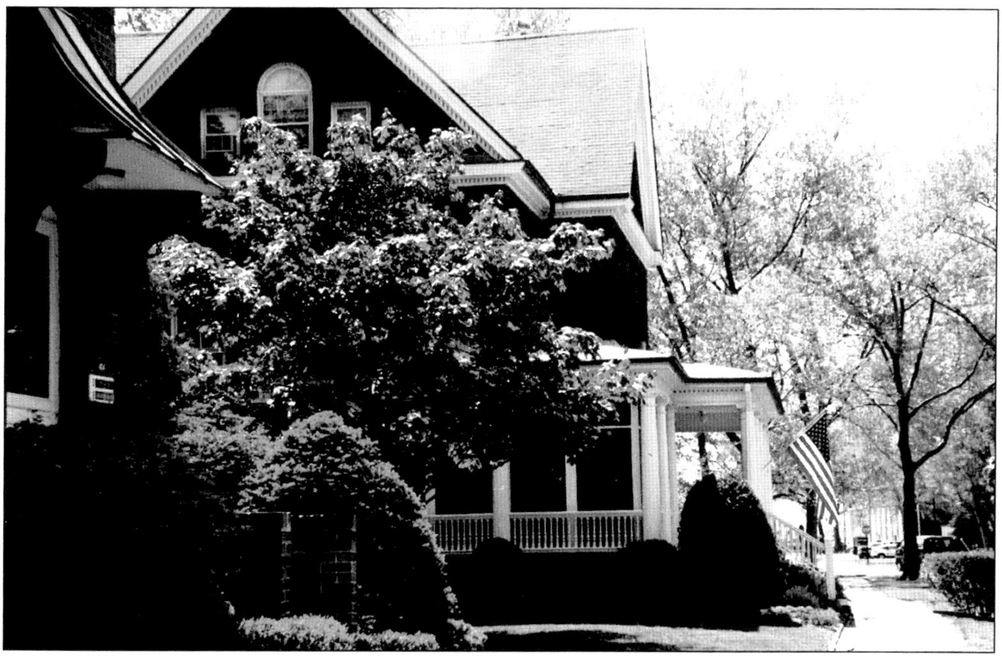

Spring brought life to the numerous varieties of trees on the island as seen here on Colonel's Row. Sycamore, several species of oak, horse chestnut, maple, ginkgo, and elm are a few of the many type of trees on the island.

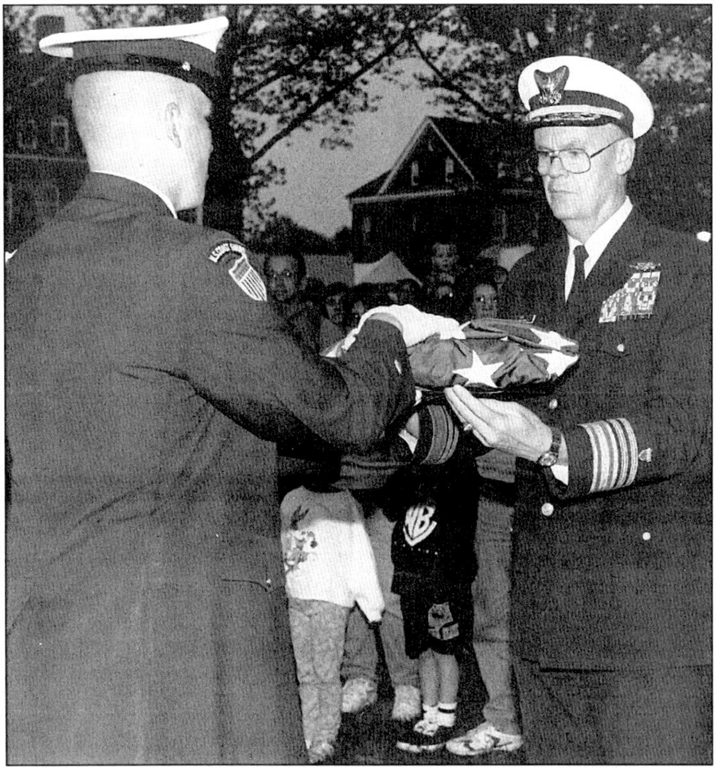

A member of the Coast Guard's Presidential Honor Guard presents Atlantic Area Commander Vice Admiral James Loy with the national ensign after it was taken down for the last time on Governors Island. (Courtesy of *The Governors Island Gazette*.)

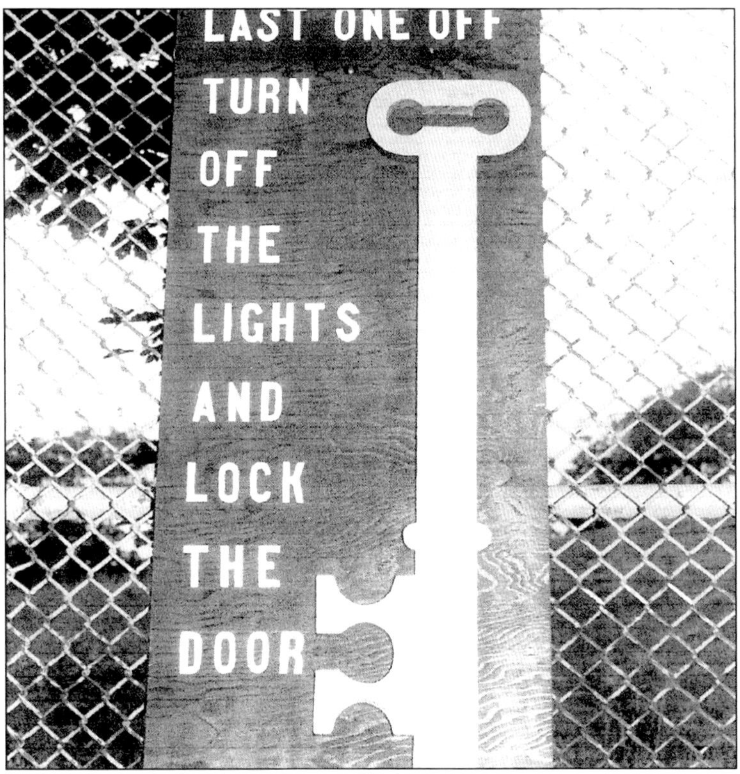

On June 30, 1996, the U.S. Coast Guard left the island. (Courtesy of *The Governors Island Gazette*.)

Four

Today

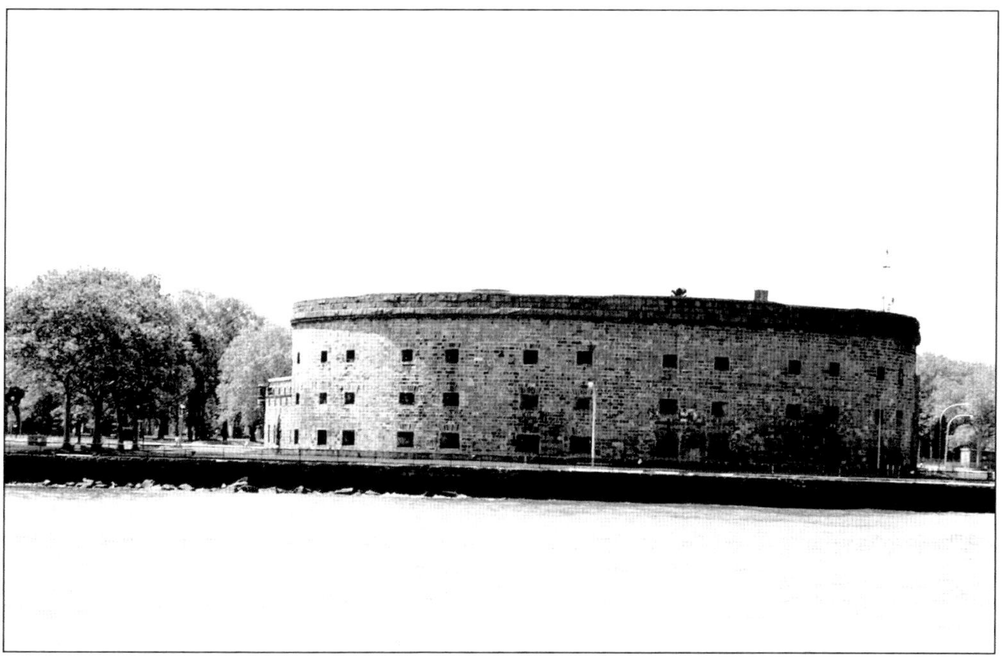

The author returned to the island in the summer of 2005 aboard the ferry *Samual Coursen.*

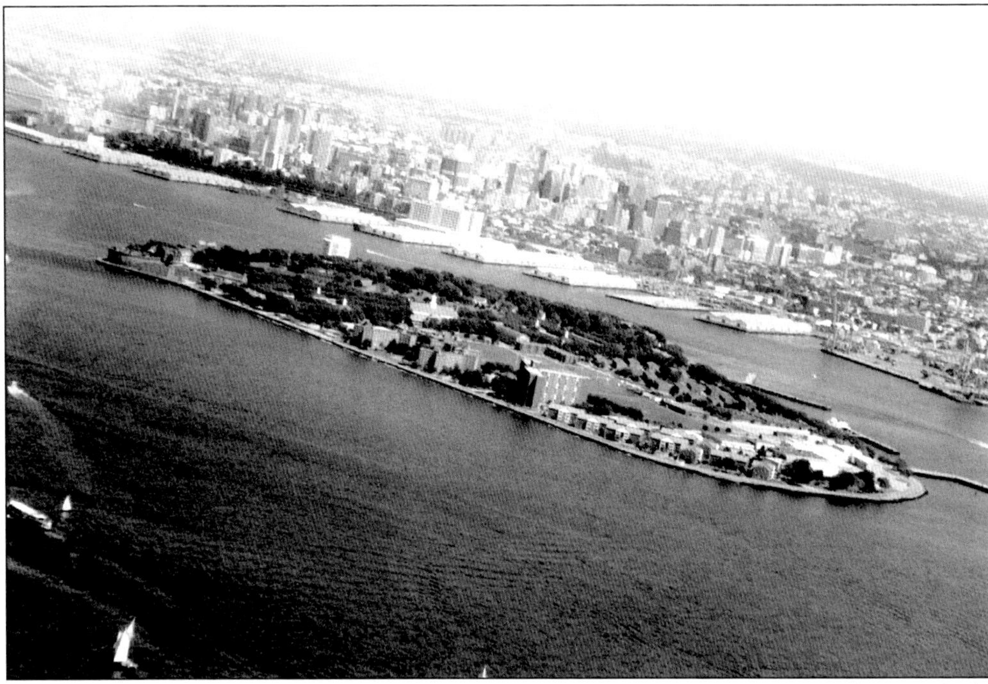

These two aerial views of the island were taken in September 2001. (Courtesy of Rebecca Glen.)

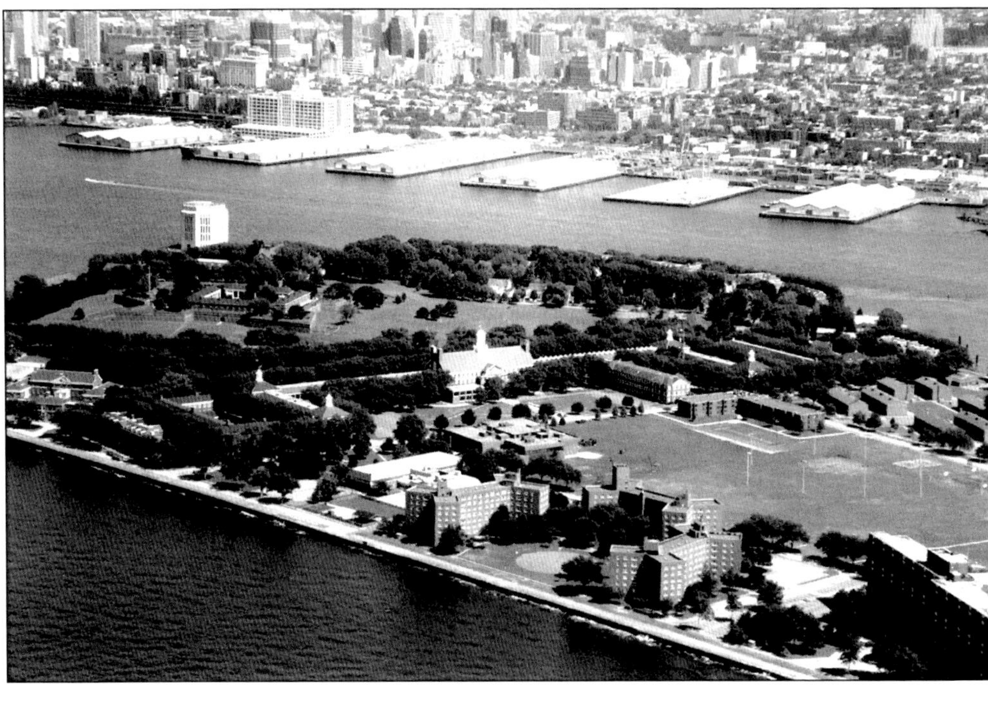

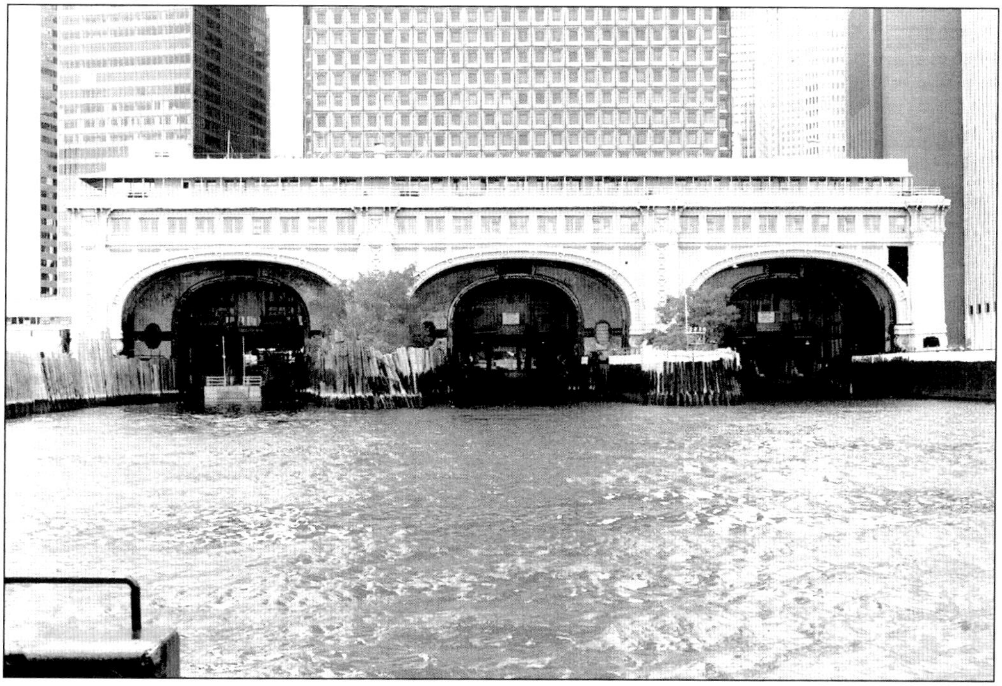

Slip No. 7 at the ferry terminal in 1991 had broken areas on the front, metal fatigue, and was time worn.

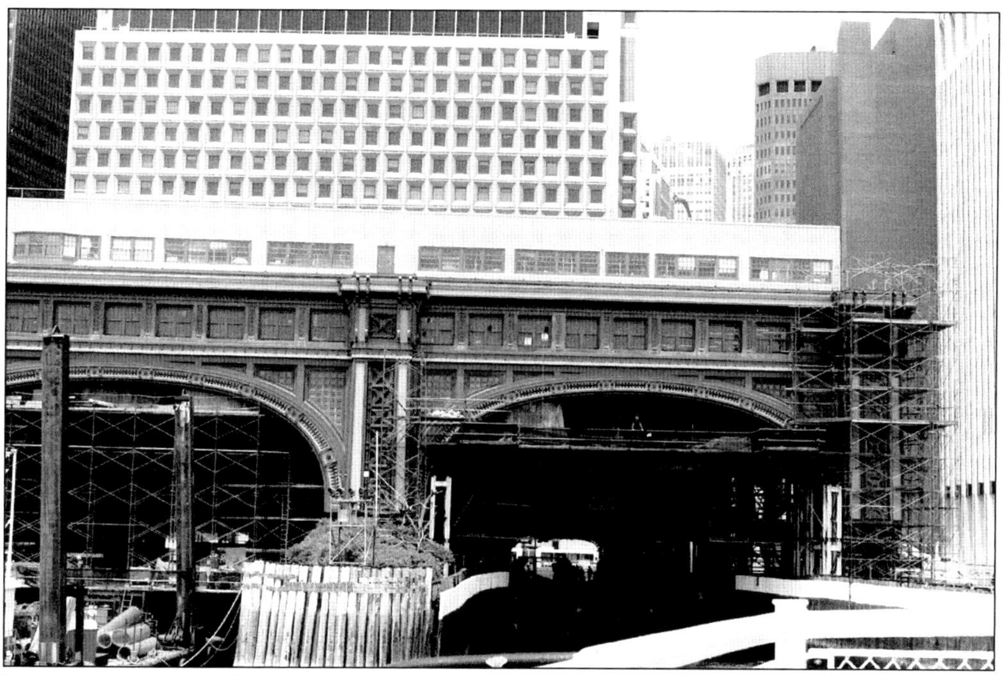

In the summer of 2005, Slip No. 7 was undergoing repair. Metal damage was being restored and surfaces were being painted. The inside the terminal was also undergoing modernization.

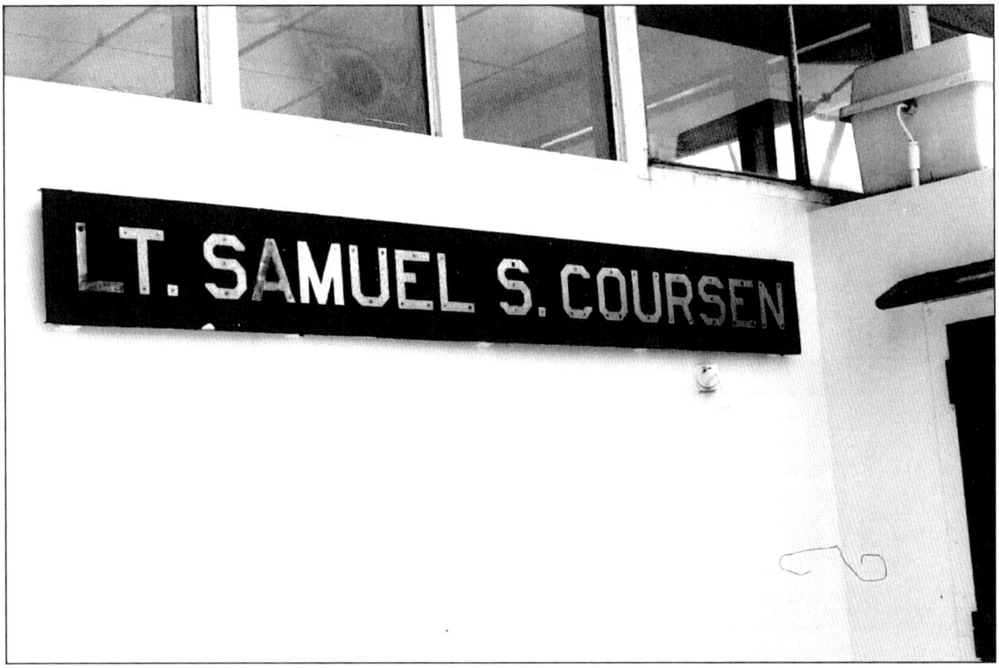

The motor-vessel *Samuel Coursen* is back in service, transporting passengers to the island. The diesel-electric ferry was named for Lt. Samuel S. Coursen, a Medal of Honor recipient. It was first placed in service to the island in 1956, and it was the ferry that brought Queen Elizabeth II to Governors Island in October 1957.

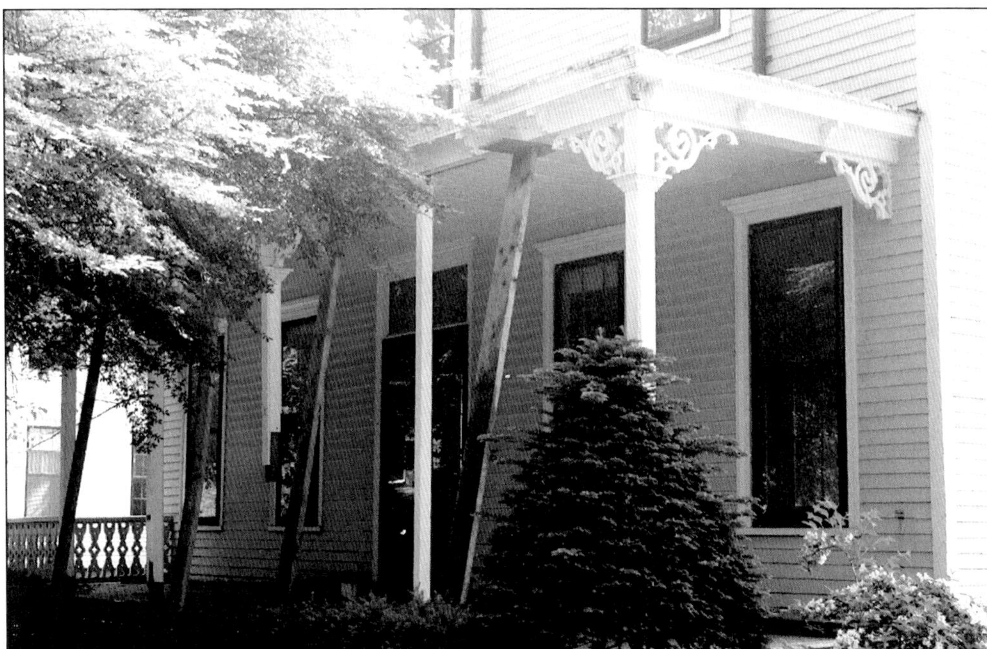

Here, damages to the old buildings are undergoing repair. This house on Nolan Park needed new supports for its porch roof.

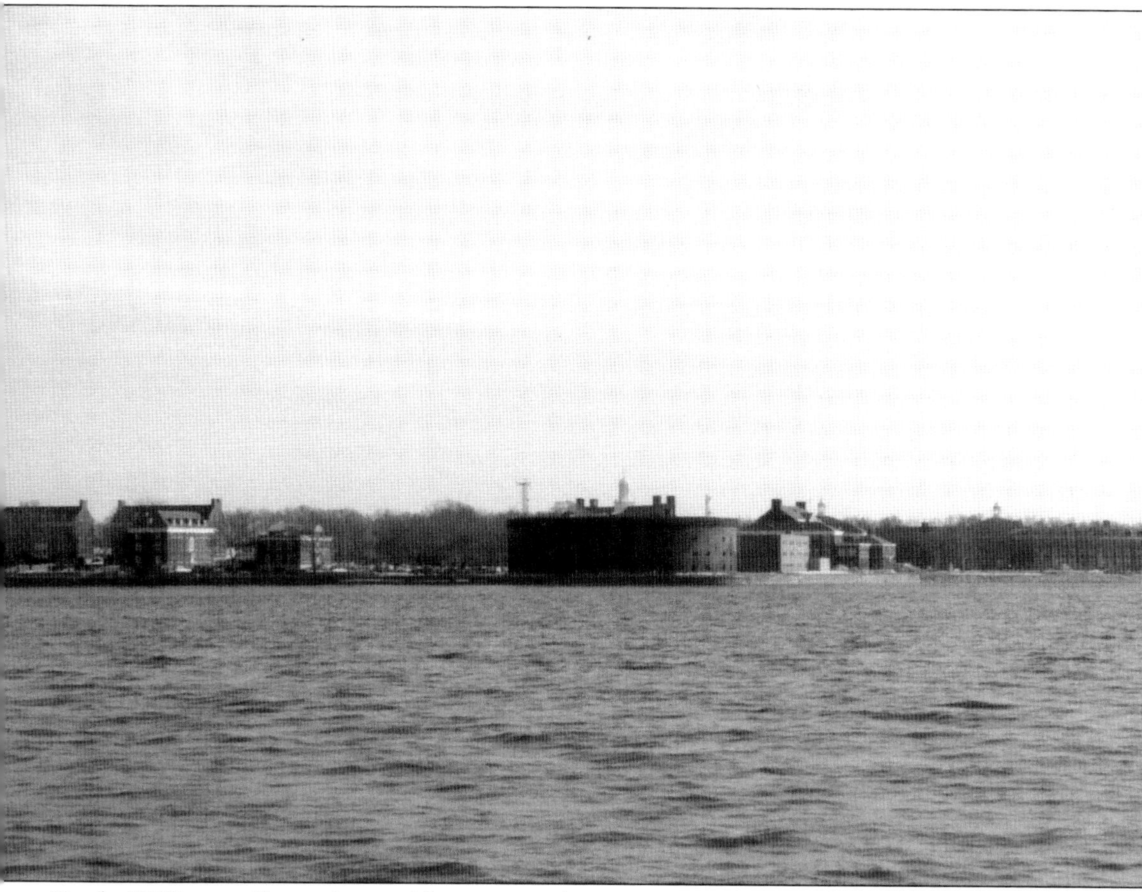

Castle Williams still stands guard but now without its cannon. An aid to navigation light atop the bastions marks the way for ships entering the harbor and a fog horn sounds from the southern part of the island during foggy weather. Seen from the Circle Line, Castle Williams and Governors Island are still guarding New York Harbor. Now a U.S. National Park Monument, the island is open to the public. (Courtesy of Susannah Page.)

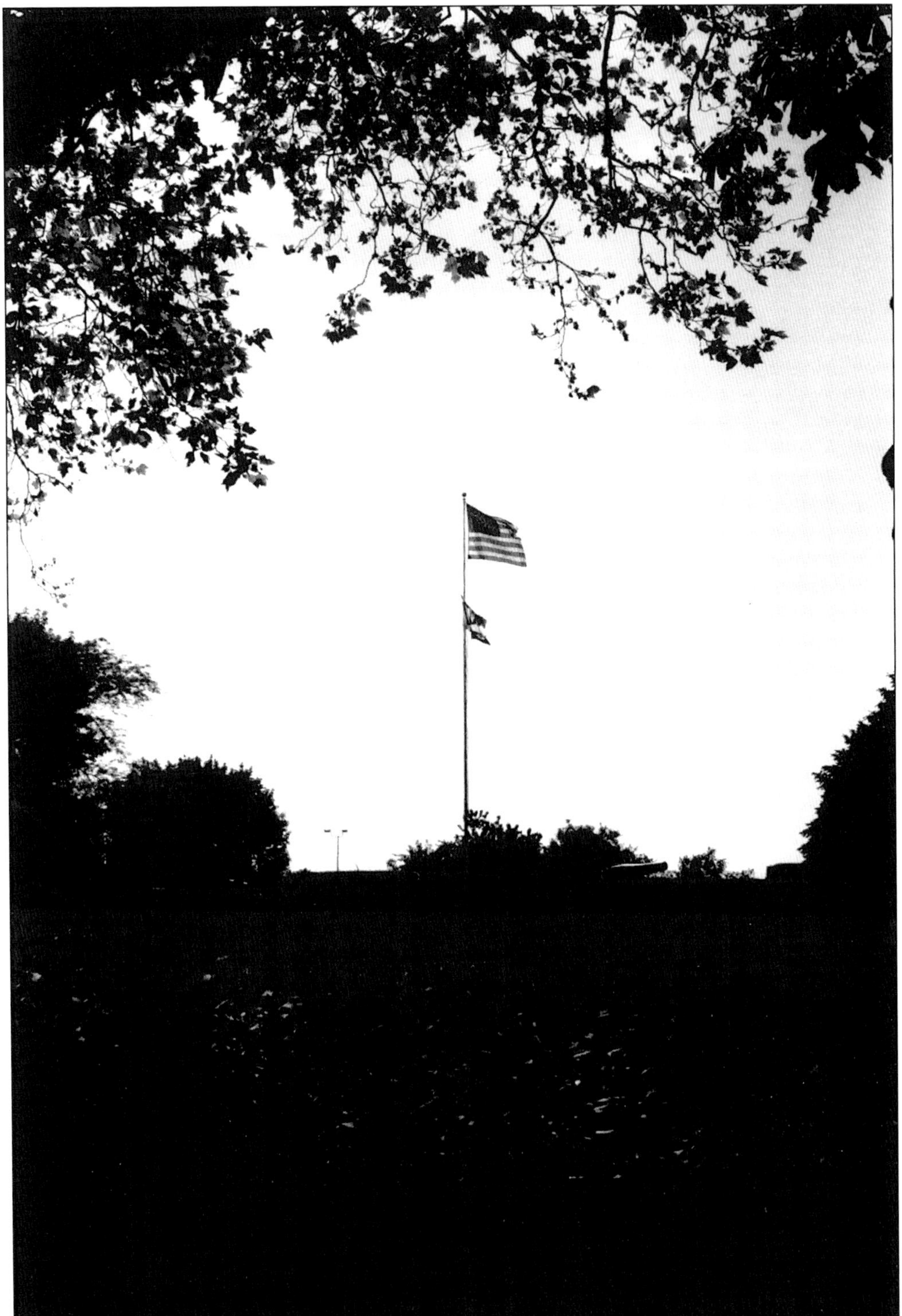
The national ensign flies again over the island.